AMERICA TRANSFORMED

AMERICA TRANSFORMED

Globalization, Inequality, and Power

Gary Hytrek
California State University, Long Beach

Kristine M. Zentgraf
California State University, Long Beach

New York   Oxford
OXFORD UNIVERSITY PRESS
2008

Oxford University Press, Inc., publishes works that further Oxford University's
objective of excellence in research, scholarship, and education.

Oxford   New York
Auckland   Cape Town   Dar es Salaam   Hong Kong   Karachi
Kuala Lumpur   Madrid   Melbourne   Mexico City   Nairobi
New Delhi   Shanghai   Taipei   Toronto

With offices in
Argentina   Austria   Brazil   Chile   Czech Republic   France   Greece
Guatemala   Hungary   Italy   Japan   Poland   Portugal   Singapore
South Korea   Switzerland   Thailand   Turkey   Ukraine   Vietnam

Copyright © 2008 by Oxford University Press, Inc.

Published by Oxford University Press, Inc.
198 Madison Avenue, New York, New York 10016
http://www.oup.com

Oxford is a registered trademark of Oxford University Press

Library of Congress Cataloging-in-Publication Data
Hytrek, Gary J.
    America transformed : globalization, inequality, and power / by Gary Hytrek and
Kristine M. Zentgraf.
        p. cm.
    Includes bibliographical references and index.
    ISBN-13: 978-0-19-517301-7 (cloth)—ISBN-13: 978-0-19-517300-0 (pbk.)
    1. Social stratification—United States.   2. United States—Social conditions—1980–
3. Globalization.   I. Zentgraf, Kristine M.   II. Title.

HN90.S6H96 2007
305.5′120973—dc22

                                                                    2006050311

Printing number: 9 8 7 6 5 4 3 2 1

Printed in the United States of America
on acid-free paper

To Sherry,
Alex, and Jenna

CONTENTS

PREFACE

Globalization has profoundly transformed the United States over the past 30 years. Yet, globalization is often depicted as "something out there," unconnected to societal-level changes, or as a means through which the United States orchestrates global events and dominates the global political–economic system and the internal affairs of other societies. Surprisingly absent from the literature is a focus on globalization's impact in the United States. *America Transformed* is designed to fill this gap.

Our aim is to provide an overview of the debates and controversies surrounding globalization, principally as these relate to the transformation of the United States from a relatively predictable and secure society to a less predictable and less secure one. Readers of *America Transformed* will engage in discussion revolving around three central questions:

1. How is globalization transforming social relations, political organizations, and social and economic structures in the United States?

2. How is globalization affecting the ability (or willingness) of the U.S. government to respond to domestic demands?

3. What are the consequences for the life chances of individuals and the ability of citizens to shape social policy consistent with their needs?

In examining these questions, we draw upon a wide range of scholarship, including theoretical debates and empirical data relating to the nature of global and societal change, class and status inequality, sex trafficking, new destinations of immigration, social capital, civil society, social activism, and public policy. We integrate this literature to achieve four objectives: (1) to provide the reader with the analytical and conceptual tools to define, understand, and critically evaluate the assumptions and various positions within the globalization debate; (2) to show the links between global processes and societal-level patterns of inequality in the United States; (3) to identify some of the key policy challenges of globalization and some of the innovative community-based responses; (4) to demonstrate the utility of the sociological perspective for understanding how global processes impact our lives and how we in turn affect those same processes.

The Argument

Our central focus is on one part of the complex globalization–inequality debate: how the intersection of ascribed and achieved statuses, within the context of globalization, creates specific patterns of inequality and social stratification in the United States. A quick overview of U.S. data on income inequality and poverty rates suggests three trends. First, income inequality and poverty declined significantly from the 1950s to the early 1970s, after which point both worsened (Hytrek and Davis 2002, U.S. Bureau of the Census 2001). Second, the poor today are more likely to be younger than in previous generations and working rather than unemployed. These "new forms" of poverty or inequality—children and working people—contrast with the "older" forms, consisting of the elderly and nonworking adults. Third, rising inequality and poverty has coincided with falling unemployment since the mid-1990s, an outcome once thought unlikely.

Existing explanations for these trends operate under the assumption that a lack of employment opportunities correlates with rising poverty and material inequality. Changes in technology, tax policies, and regulations; falling value of the minimum wage; and immigration have all been cited as contributing causes to this phenomenon (Freeman 1996/1997). Poverty-reduction strategies typically focus on job creation within the context of these issues. Yet, by the late 1990s, the U.S. economy neared full employment,[1] while poverty levels remained stable and real incomes continued to decline for large segments of the U.S. population. Missing from this discussion is the possibility that these outcomes might be rooted in a more fundamental set of conditions: globalization.

We argue that the loss of manufacturing jobs and the growth of service sector jobs are causal agents in the shifting patterns of stratification and inequality in the United States. You will likely recognize these as processes of economic restructuring and deindustrialization that existing explanations identify as contributing factors to inequality and poverty. So what is new in our story? We suggest that these conditions are best understood as *immediate causes* for shifting patterns of inequality and stratification, with globalization as the *primary cause*.

We implicate globalization for several reasons: by compressing time and space, intensifying competition, and converging national economic institutions, globalization is rendering capital more mobile while reducing many of the risks and other obstacles to offshore investment. These objective changes have redistributed power among people, social groups, companies, and communities, as well as between global actors (e.g., corporations, the World Trade Organization) and states. Flexibility, innovation, and risk are at the center of our economy and society, a society that is increasingly polarized by highly paid knowledge workers at one end and low-paid care and informal workers on the other. Who is likely to be located in either category is heavily determined by race, ethnicity, and gender. Subjectively, globalization continually shapes and reshapes our perceptions, values, and needs—examples include an increased emphasis on individualism and an increased need for material goods. Taken together, globalization is forcing us to be more flexible and willing to change where we live and work as demanded by rapidly changing market conditions. Our lives and our friends, like our work, are increasingly temporary.

Although we argue that global forces have had certain effects, this is not the same as arguing that globalization *had to* have those effects; the structural changes resulting from globalization are not inevitably driven by law-like forces in which people have no role or choice. Individuals and groups make choices to liberalize markets and to reduce the role of institutions and of the state in the process of change. Nonetheless, as these choices unleash the market from its social moorings, a new course is charted that may appear as an autonomous process. As market forces unravel the very fabric of society, the disruptions spark a countermovement that attempts to alter the process of change in the form of a "double-movement" that Karl Polanyi identified in his work on an earlier transformation. Thus, our story is about the contested dialectical relationship between global and local forces: how globalization shapes stratification and inequality in the United States and our attempts to mediate those changes.

Finally, our focus on how global processes affect our lives and our communities in the United States is not meant to suggest that we can ignore what happens on the other side of the global connection. Globalization is a concept meant to capture processes and changes that link together heretofore separate areas of the world. These processes facilitate the movement of people, investment capital, and corporations and affect labor markets and growth prospects at multiple ends of transnational connections. One might expect that the United States, an extremely wealthy, powerful, and democratic nation, would be able to control or at least manage the forces of globalization. To a degree, this is true. Certainly, the United States can exert greater control over these processes than can Costa Rica, South Korea, or Brazil. But at the same time, the forces of change are fundamentally altering the structure of global relations and the ability of the United States, or any one society, to control its destiny. As a result, the First World is forced to confront what has long been assumed are "Third World or developing world problems"—governments that are simultaneously ineffectual on the international stage and undemocratic.

Looking Ahead

We have organized the book into three sections. In Part I, we introduce the central issues involved in the globalization debate, the fundamentals of stratification and social mobility, and the conceptual and theoretical links between globalization, inequality, and power. In Chapter 1, we provide an overview of the book and the general process of change in the United States since 1945. Chapter 2 examines the forces and conditions for globalization and the central events and actors in the process leading up to the present period of accelerated globalization. In Chapters 3 and 4, we describe and assess (respectively) the ongoing debate surrounding the links between globalization and economic, social, political, and cultural changes. Chapter 5 returns to the basic issues of globalization and stratification.

In Part II, we address the book's basic empirical question of how globalization has altered stratification patterns in the United States since the 1950s. Chapter 6 analyzes the effects of globalization on the world of work, specifically the blue-collar and white-collar transitions; the distribution of income and wealth; and poverty. In Chapter 7, we focus on the salient issue of globalization and immigration and how the changes discussed in Chapter 6 are reflected in shifting patterns of migration. Chapter 8 examines the distinction between sex and gender as well as the links between global forces and gender-based stratification. Of particular relevance is how class, gender, race, and ethnicity intersect to create patterns of inequality. In each of these three chapters, we refer to global processes but emphasize the United States while weaving in the issues of class and social status.

Part III summarizes the connections between globalization and stratification in the United States, explores some of the policy issues raised by globalization, and discusses innovative community-based responses to problems exacerbated or created by globalization. Chapter 9 examines several local (community-based) and transnational movements that are responding to the dilemmas in the "postwelfare," globalized world. In Chapter 10, we return to our study's central questions by summarizing the transforming effects of global processes on the United States and the connections between globalization, inequality, and power.

ACKNOWLEDGMENTS

In the course of writing this book, Kris Zentgraf and I were fortunate to cross paths with many supportive people; their generosity made this a better book. The idea for this book emerged out of a conversation several years ago with Steve Rutter about a slim volume on globalization and stratification. This is the culmination of that early discussion. I am thankful to Sherith Pankratz for her suggestions in the early stages of this project. My friends and former colleagues at Georgia Southern University, Bill Smith, Peggy Hargis, and Sue Moore, provided great advice and support when this book was merely an image in my mind. Additional thanks go to my past students at Georgia Southern University who helped me sort through many of the complex connections that became part of this book.

A number of individuals at California State University, Long Beach (CSULB), contributed in important ways to the book. In 2003, Kris Zentgraf had the opportunity to explore the complexities of globalization when she co-organized and co-taught the CSULB Odyssey Project's course on globalization with Jim Ellison. Sharon Olson, the project coordinator, and Jim Ellison deserve special thanks: Sharon for her generous support of the project and Jim for his stimulating discussions before, during, and after the Odyssey Project. Thanks also to our colleagues in the department of sociology, Jeff Davis and Walter Nichols, for their comments that gave shape to Chapter 5; to Norma Chinchilla for being what Kris calls her "most honest critic and sounding board;" to the students at CSULB, those in my social change and globalization courses for helping me clarify my ideas and for enduring the early drafts of Part I—especially to Rosina Barrientos, Jesus Campos, and Tim Rose—and those in the Odyssey Project for their questions, challenges, and righteous indignation. Finally, my thanks to the Scholarly and Creative Activities Committee at CSULB for support that allowed me to reduce my teaching load during the fall of 2004 as I pulled together material for Part I.

A great deal of the book came together conceptually while I was on a Fulbright at the National University in Costa Rica during part of 2004. Long conversations with my friend and fellow sociologist Miguel Sobrado crystallized my thoughts about community development and political participation in the age of globalization. His tireless work on the part of those most marginalized by social change is a constant inspiration. I am also grateful to the staff and those connected to la Escuela Planificación y Promoción Social at the National University; I hope their influence on me and the optimism that is Costa Rica come through in the following pages. I graciously acknowledge the support of the Council for International Exchange of Scholars for making this opportunity possible.

Oxford University Press has been extremely supportive of this project since the beginning. Thanks to our editor Peter Labella for his tolerance and guidance through the various twists and turns in the road from proposal to book. Our thanks to Chelsea Gilmore, Josh Hawkins, John Carey, Andrew Pachuta and others at Oxford for their expert hands in helping us finalize the manuscript and navigate the process leading to publication. Kris and I also thank three anonymous Oxford reviewers who provided comments on the manuscript as a whole. It was a pleasure working with Oxford.

I am extremely grateful to Genoa Shipley who meticulously read the unfolding manuscript; it was a privilege to work with someone so gifted. Genoa contributed enormously to this book with her incisive comments that forced me to resolve my often convoluted thinking and writing. She will see a great deal of herself in the following pages.

To Kris Zentgraf, my friend, colleague, and coauthor, I cannot offer thanks enough. Kris agreed to come onto the project after my original coauthor had to resign. Jumping into an ongoing project was not easy, yet she rearranged her life and gave generously of her time to offer invaluable comments on ideas, arguments, and style. Most important, she took the lead in pulling together the material in Chapters 6, 7, and 8. Her expertise on gender and immigration issues added important dimensions that took the book in a much more satisfying direction. Collaborating with Kris was an immensely rewarding collegial experience.

I am indebted to a number of individuals who have implicitly and explicitly influenced my views on the book's central questions. Among these is Ray Geigle at California State University, Bakersfield, who first showed me the importance of measuring change in terms of its effects on the human condition. The work of David Held has been tremendously influential to my thinking about globalization and social change. David Lopez and Maurice Zeitlin at the University of California, Los Angeles; Gi-Wook Shin at Stanford; and Jeff Frieden at Harvard all contributed in important ways to my understanding of social change. I apologize to others I may have missed; the omission was not intentional.

Last, but certainly not least, thanks to my parents Jim and Marilyn Hytrek for reminding me that rural America has always been a product of global forces, from land grant–driven immigration to the power of export markets to the growing dominance of agribusinesses. Small farmers, like small business people and workers everywhere, need not be—nor should be—the casualties of globalization.

Finally, to my *compañera* Sherry, whose enduring love and support contributed more to this work than can be put into words.

G.H.
Long Beach, Calif.
July 2006

PART I

Theoretical and Conceptual Considerations

CHAPTER 1

Globalization and Change in America

Overview

- Today's two-income family earns 75 percent *more* than the single-income family a generation ago but actually has *less* disposable income.
- Having a child is now the single best predictor that a woman will end up in financial collapse.
- The average middle-class family can no longer buy a home without two incomes.
- In 1981, about 69,000 women had filed for bankruptcy; by 1999 that figure had jumped to 500,000.
- An estimated one in seven families with children will declare bankruptcy in the first decade of the twenty-first century.

So began the twenty-first century, according to Elizabeth Warren and Amelia Warren Tyagi in their book *The Two-Income Trap* (2003). These examples are illustrative of the profound transition in U.S. society over the past 30 years: a society that has evolved from a predictable world with the opportunity for upward **social mobility*** to a less predictable and less secure one. From roughly 1945 until the 1970s, workers married, had children, bought homes, enjoyed a balanced work and home life, and enjoyed a range of financial and social benefits provided by their employers and the **state** (Rubin 1996, 8; Fraser 2001, 10).

The idea that hard work should be and would be rewarded dominated not only the cultural values and social norms of the United States but also the actions of its employees and employers. An optimistic spirit meant that social problems were not intractable but resolvable through individual *and* **government** efforts. **Social movements** organized in response to society's most pressing problems and forced the local, state, and federal governments to create social programs that would increase civil and political rights and

---

* All boldface terms are defined in the glossary at the end of the book.

3

opportunities (Rubin 1996). Many will recognize these as the basic elements of the American Dream. While we do not want to romanticize the period—which was also characterized by entrenched gender, racial, ethnic, and class inequalities—the changes depicted in *The Two-Income Trap* provide a revealing contrast to the 1950–1980 period (Rubin 1996, Munck 2002).

In this chapter, we summarize these basic patterns of change. In so doing, we introduce the essential connections between globalization and the transformation of the United States and identify the concepts used in our analysis. We begin by clarifying our frame of reference: globalization.

Globalization Defined

As you may have already gathered, defining *globalization* is no easy task. Let's begin with the word *global*. Although over 400 years old, the term *globalization* seems to have emerged in the 1960s (Waters 1995, 2). According to Waters (1995, 1), by the 1990s globalization eclipsed "postmodernism" as *the concept*, becoming the "key idea by which we understand the transition of human society into the third millennium." Social, political, and economic trends are increasingly discussed in terms of global processes and connections, from global production to global politics to global culture. In short, we are said to be experiencing "globalization," to be living in a "global era."[1]

Does this mean that globalization is new? As we discuss in later chapters, one of the more contentious issues in the globalization debate is over its novelty. For many, globalization reflects a significant historical development, differentiating the present period from earlier ones. Consider the following examples that bring to life some of the cultural and technical transformations of the last third of the twentieth century. Today, major banks store money not in vaults but in cyberspace; fast-food lovers consume McArabia sandwiches in the Middle East and Teriyaki McBurgers in Japan; and millions of children in the United States have been mesmerized by the Japanese produced Pokémon game and television program *Dragon Ball Z*. Costa Ricans listen to Mexican music on stereos manufactured in China, while in Iran the popularity of Valentine's Day continues to rise, despite attempts by authorities to halt the spread of the celebration.

Others are not so convinced that globalization reflects a dramatic break with past patterns. For instance, as early as AD 1000, the global reach of science, technology, and mathematics was changing the nature of the world, with innovations typically moving from the East to the West and later from the South to the North. While we are all familiar with the global contributions of the Chinese (the technologies of printing, of gunpowder, and of the magnetic compass, to name only a few), how many know that the word *algebra* comes from the title of a book by the Arab mathematician Musa al-Khwarizmi? How many of us are aware that Chinese technology produced the world's first printed book? Or that the book, an India Sanskrit treatise on

Buddhism, was translated into Chinese in the fifth century by a half-Indian and half-Turkish scholar who had migrated to China from a part of eastern Turkistan, called Kucha (Sen 2000)?

So what does all this mean for our definition of *globalization*? Our point of departure is that globalization is a multifaceted *set of processes* involving objective and subjective dimensions, a long uneven course that is linking together the people of the world. Globalization is not a *thing*; it is not reducible to economics and free markets; and it is not a new phenomenon. The unfolding of globalization can be distinguished by various phases, the most recent dating from the 1970s. In this book, we take a particularly close look at this current phase of accelerated globalization to examine the factors that distinguish it from earlier ones.

The characteristics of contemporary globalization include fewer barriers and risks to trade and financial and investment capital flows and, thus, greater global economic integration, greater flexibility in labor markets, a compression of time and space, universally recognized cultural symbols, the growth of new global actors and declining state power, and finally **deterritorialization** or supraterritoriality. Subjectively, individuals experience these conditions through an increasing recognition that they belong to something larger than the more immediate **nation-state** (e.g., a "world society"). In other words, globalization is a process of growing transborder connectedness representing significant changes at both the objective-structural and subjective-individual levels. We return to these issues in Chapters 3 and 4.

Globalization: From Fordism to Flexibility

Although the influence of global processes is not new, until quite recently the United States enjoyed the luxury of a relatively self-contained and isolated economy because of its extensive resource base, large domestic market, and the natural insulation provided by the Pacific and Atlantic Oceans. After the 1960s, increasing global integration engendered a transition in the United States (and most advanced capitalist societies) from a "fixed" (highly regulated) development model centered on mass production, mass consumption, and social welfare to a "flexible" (unregulated), individualized, and market-based neoliberal one. The shift not only marked a reversal in economic philosophy and strategy, as well as cultural values and social norms, but also initiated a process of change that altered the institutional structures of society and the lives of the individuals embedded within those institutions.

The fixed model of development, dubbed **Fordism**, is an idea and a strategy of production, technology, and distribution. The model originated in the early decades of the twentieth century when Henry Ford used F. W. Taylor's time-and-motion methods to increase the efficiency of his technologically driven factory assembly line.[2] Ford's ideas revolutionized production and dramatically increased the output of consumer goods; the time needed to build an automobile, for instance, declined from 12.5 hours to 1.5 hours. Lurking in the background, however, was a fundamental question: Who would buy all these new goods produced by Ford's innovative and machine-driven process? Clearly, increased production would require an equal increase in consumers. As John Maynard Keynes would later argue in his *General Theory of Employment, Interest and Money* (published in 1936), too few consumers able to buy the goods produced would result in layoffs, which would produce still fewer consumers, causing more layoffs in an ever downward cycle. Aware of this possibility, Ford introduce the idea of the "daily wage," not only to attract workers to his automobile factories but also to ensure that employees could afford the goods they produced. When President Franklin D. Roosevelt responded to the Great Depression by introducing the New Deal regulatory and social welfare policies in the 1930s (theoretically legitimized by Keynes's *General Theory*), the package was complete and "Fordism" was born.[3] The Fordist model was considered rigid or fixed because it involved social welfare policies and high levels of state regulation—or, in some cases, state ownership of industries—that constrained the economic behavior of the business sector.

After the Second World War, the Fordist mass-production/Keynesian regulation strategy increasingly dominated Western Europe, Mexico, Brazil, parts of South Asia, Japan, and South Africa (Tichell and Peck 1995). Particularly in the United States, Britain, and most of Western Europe, the approach culminated in the 1950s with a **social compact**, or a set of formal rules and regulations and informal social norms, that institutionalized class conflict, stabilized the social system (Munck 2002), and created the predictable and secure world of the 1945–1970 period.[4]

The global corollary to local Fordism was the Bretton Woods system. Designed to stabilize the global system, the Bretton Woods system consisted of the World Bank, the International Monetary Fund, and the General Agreement on Trade and Tariffs/World Trade Organization. As we discuss in Chapter 2, a series of events occurred in the 1970s to bring about the end of the Fordist era, which also included fundamental shifts in the Bretton Woods system. One crucial and immediate cause for the collapse of the Fordist strategy and the Bretton Woods system was the onset of **stagflation**, or the simultaneous occurrence of stagnant economic growth and inflation with high unemployment.

Stagflation was particularly troubling. According to Keynesian theory, stagflation was impossible. Yet, during the 1970s, the United States was experiencing falling productivity, declining profits and investment, increasing interest on consumer loans, and growing unemployment. Economic anxieties deepened as imports increasingly competed with U.S.-produced goods and the Arab oil embargoes pushed the price of gasoline to record highs. The volatile decade culminated in 1979 with the Iranian Revolution and the taking of U.S. hostages, which convinced many in the United States that the country was dangerously vulnerable and unable to control events at home or abroad. By the end of the 1970s, there was a growing consensus that the United States was in the midst of no ordinary cyclical economic downturn.

Conservative analysts blamed the crisis on labor unions that had become too powerful in conjuncture with a tax-and-spend government that over-regulated capital and labor markets and monopolized activities that were traditionally the function of markets. Thus, a new consensus emerged among many economists and politicians that state intervention *was not* essential to the operation of the market economy, as Keynes thought, but *the* cause of economic contraction.

In response to the chaos, despair, and uncertainty of the 1970s, U.S. voters elected Ronald Reagan as president to restore order, hope, and respect—order and hope at home and respect abroad. Reacting to a similar set of economic and social problems and with the hope of restoring domestic order and growth, English voters elected Margaret Thatcher as prime minister. Within the changing global context, domestic social coalitions in both countries shifted away from largely a labor-based one to a more middle- and upper-class one. The transforming social coalitions empowered the Reagan and Thatcher administrations to fundamentally alter the existing economic philosophy and strategy that had dominated government policy since the Great Depression. Beginning in the early 1980s, Fordism and the interventionist theory of Keynes were replaced by the **flexible market strategy** of Friedrich von Hayek, known as neoliberalism (see Table 1.1).

In contrast to the earlier Fordist strategy that involved state regulation of the economy and social welfare, neoliberal policies called for tighter global economic links through privatization and market (deregulation) reforms as a means to generate competition, efficiency, and ultimately growth (Hytrek 2001). Likewise, corporate taxes (and taxes on the wealthy) and social welfare spending should be decreased as a means to lower the cost of production and stimulate further economic growth and job creation. Based on these ideas, politicians weakened or outright destroyed unions, deregulated and privatized the economy, and reduced social spending and corporate taxes in order to free markets from rigidities thought to hinder innovation and risk taking. Now, markets, not governments, would "efficiently" guide investment decisions and open up opportunities for generating wealth. Governments would continue to support the business sector but would no longer regulate it. As these policies shifted power away from the state to **capital**, corporations became more flexible, mobile, and global. Between 1970 and 1998, for instance, the number of **transnational corporations** (TNCs), or corporations headquartered in one country with design, production, marketing, and service divisions in many other countries, grew from 7,000 to an estimated 53,600. Today, there are over 65,000 TNCs with some 850,000 foreign affiliates coordinating global supply chains which link firms across countries, including local subcontractors who work outside the formal factory system and outsource to home workers (ILO 2004, 33).

Table 1.1 Neoliberalism

Neo means something new, a "new" kind of liberalism. Neoliberalism is rooted in the classical or "old" liberal ideals of Adam Smith (1723–1790), who wrote *The Wealth of Nations* (1776), and David Ricardo (1772–1823), who published the *Principles of Political Economy* (1817). The economic strategy of the day, called "mercantilism," was based on state control and promotion of economic activity. Smith instead advocated the abolition of state intervention in economic matters, asserting that markets self-regulate and the natural balancing forces of the marketplace tend toward equilibrium, stability, and efficient utilization of resources. Forty years later, Ricardo developed the theory of comparative advantage that established the basis for international trade and an international division of labor. He suggested that the optimum use of worldwide resources would be best achieved if countries specialized in and exported products that were the least expensive for that country to produce and imported products that were the most expensive to produce. Together these two basic ideas formed the theoretical basis for laissez-faire (literally, "to leave alone" or "noninterference") capitalism. This system permitted no restriction on ownership, production, or trade. Such ideas were considered "liberal" in the sense that they ran counter to the prevailing orthodoxy of state control. Thus, the principal actors in this theory are competing individuals. Individualism is believed to encourage "free" enterprise, "free" competition, and the survival of the fittest; it spurs innovation and wastes fewer resources. Classical economic liberalism ended with the market crash in 1929, while the economic crisis of the 1970s revived this theory; hence, the term *neoliberalism*.

Philosophical Tenets of Neoliberalism
In the United States, neoliberalism began around 1980 with the election of Ronald Reagan. If you have not heard the term *neoliberalism*, it is because in the United States we tend to use such expressions as "Reaganomics," "trickle-down economics," or more recently the "**Washington Consensus**." The latter also reflects a shift to a more global application of the tenets of neoliberalism.

1. *Rule of the market*. The markets and private sector are the primary engines of economic growth; growth is promoted by liberating private—individual—enterprise and markets from any bonds imposed by the federal government—the state—unions, or public ownership. Note that the strengthening of the market does not mean that the state no longer supports capital, only that state control of capital through regulation and taxation declines.

2. *Emphasis on individual responsibility*: The concept of the public good is replaced with "individual responsibility." The value of competitive individualism in the United States is the hallmark of individual responsibility, meaning that individual success or failure is based on individual effort. Therefore, the solutions to poverty are to be found at the individual level; the poor themselves are supposed to find solutions to their lack of health care, education, and employment.

Basic Policies
1. Privatization of public enterprises
2. Deregulation of the economy
3. Liberalization of trade and capital markets
4. Tax cuts (for corporations and the wealthy)
5. Strict control of interest rates
6. Reducing the power of organized labor
7. Cutting social-service expenditures
8. Reducing the size of the government

These policies roll back the welfare state and create the neoliberal state.

Source: Adapted from Martinez and Garcia n.d.

The shift in economic philosophy and strategy engendered two structural changes:

Nationally, the Keynesian–Fordist regulation model was replaced by the **neoliberal state**, a new flexible strategy based on the deregulation of labor and capital markets and a shrinking of the social-welfare system. The key change is a shift in government priorities; social welfare spending was deprioritized in favor of continued and even increasing support for capital (i.e., the business sector). These policies restructured state–society relations and changed the way people worked, governed themselves, related to each other, and understood their world and their place in it.

Globally, the strategy accelerated transnational interactions among people, knitting an ever-tighter weave of globally crosscutting relations: for the first time in human history, anything could be made anywhere and sold everywhere (Thurow 1996, 114). As these processes eroded the territoriality of social geography, national borders were becoming, if not obsolete, at least less meaningful in the new globalized world order.

Globalization and Power

Ultimately, globalization invokes issues of power and the changing distribution of power between the global and the local and among the (local) society, social movements, **nation-states**, and (global) transnational organizations and institutions. This raises several questions: Is globalization inevitable? Is globalization concentrating power into the hands of global actors at the expense of local ones? How is globalization transforming economic structures, and what are the political and economic effects? How is globalization shaping individual- and group-level responses to these political and economic changes?

Structures, Agency, and Power

If you think about the shift to neoliberalism in the United States and England and the effects of these strategic and ideological shifts, it becomes clear that globalization did not simply happen out of necessity or law-like forces (see also Chapter 2). Nonetheless, as Roberto Mangabeira Unger (1998) points out, the globalization debate often suffers from "necessitarianism," or the notion that we are simply "puppets" in a social world created by objective forces. To ignore the role of agency, however, is to miss the way in which globalization has been, and *is being*, designed. As we suggest in Chapter 3, globalization is a deeply political and contested process that empowers and strengthens some actors and institutions while disempowering and weakening others. How globalization is altering U.S. institutions that shape patterns of inequality and how people embedded within these structures respond to these challenges are central concerns of our analysis. We take up these issues in later chapters by examining the connections among globalization, institutional changes, and patterns of inequality with a specific focus on class, gender, race, and ethnicity.

Understanding the local (societal and societal sublevel) effects of globalization is impossible without examining how the evolving relationship between the state and transnational organizations shapes state–society relations. Fundamental to this relationship is the degree to which globalization has shifted power away from the state and nationally based social actors toward global organizations. As global actors, such as TNCs or the World Trade Organization (WTO), gain power relative to the state, they can undermine the state's ability to define and pursue national economic development.

First, evidence suggests that with the greater integration of financial markets and increased financial and investment capital mobility, transnational organizations and financial class actors gain advantage. A corporation's ability to produce anything anywhere in turn weakens nationally based social movements, including labor unions, which have typically provided a social basis for the **welfare state**. How, for example, can labor unions that are organized nationally combat falling incomes and disappearing benefits when a corporation can hire computer programmers in India under prevailing Indian wages and conditions to work on computers located in the United States? How can unions enforce overtime regulations when corporations can hire across time zones to "staff" 24-hour customer-service centers? The next time you have a product-related problem and call the customer-service line, ask the company representative where he or she lives—you may be surprised. With globalization, corporations can more easily move jobs to workers (Firebaugh 2003, 198–201), effectively eliminating problems of labor immobility for many jobs.

Second, the mobility of corporations affects taxation and the fiscal health of the state. Corporations and jobs that have moved **offshore** reduce the amount of tax revenue owed local and national governments. Today, for instance, a U.S. corporation can move its headquarters to the Bahamas and declare that the company has no U.S. profits and therefore owes the U.S. government no taxes. As Clawson (2003, 136) points out, "not so long ago this would have been illegal; today it is an increasingly common corporate practice." This can exacerbate the federal government's budget deficits. Equally disastrous has been the general withdrawal from progressive taxation, a shift in the tax burden away from capital to labor as a means to enhance the attractiveness of the United States (or an individual state) as a site for investment.

Third, as TNCs disinvest in the industrial sectors of societies such as the United States, millions of workers are displaced from their manufacturing and ancillary jobs in a process of deindustrialization whereby regions, societies, or cities lose entire subsectors of the manufacturing sector.[5] This shifting of investment restructures the economy away from industrial to service occupations. Today in the United States, for instance, more than eight out of every ten jobs are in the service sector. Is this necessarily problematic? No. However, those moving out of the industrial sector and into the service sector enter a highly diverse world that ranges from accountants and attorneys to street sweepers and street vendors. Inequality is worsened by the shift to service sector jobs as factory workers untrained and "uncertified" in law or accounting end up in the low-wage service sector. What we find is a service sector characterized by wage polarization as the growth in low-paying service sector jobs outpaces the growth in well-paying ones, meaning the $20 per hour factory job is often replaced with a $7 or $8 per hour service one.

Finally, with the erosion of the social and fiscal bases of the state, the state is less able to respond to economic dislocations through classic social welfare policies. The inability to resolve basic social problems weakens the responsiveness of democratic institutions, creating what has been labeled the **"democratic deficit"**—or the inability of citizens to shape public policy consistent with their needs. Thus, the potential for globalization to shift power to the global level raises the fundamental issue of efficacy: if the structural changes accompanying globalization are reducing the power of states and undermining democratic institutions, you may well respond: "How can I possibly affect processes beyond the reach of my government?" "Why should I bother to try and make a difference in the world if my government is incapable of challenging global actors?"

Such reactions reflect a process in which power is being redefined and the limits of politics and state power are being exposed. With globalization, power is less something to "seize" than a "diffused and plural element woven into the fabric of society" (Munck 2002, 20). As a result, there is a trend for social movements to emphasize autonomy from party politics and to prioritize horizontal organizing around issues of social justice within **civil society** to pressure government officials. For some scholars, local nongovernmentally developed and implemented programs and projects are emerging in the political vacuum—i.e., democratic deficit—created by the withdrawal of the federal government from the lives of ordinary people and the shrinking of the welfare state (see McGrew 1997; Brecher, Costello, and Smith 2002).

A widespread set of issues, from increasing **poverty** and crumbling social infrastructure to the environment to classic labor issues of wages and jobs, are potentially creating the objective basis for a "globalization from below" movement to emerge and respond to the challenges of globalization. As people increasingly inhabit transnational spaces and begin to connect their struggles with similar struggles in other parts of the world, localized forms of resistance may evolve into a global countermovement (Brecher, Costello, and Smith 2002, 10). This is what Munck (2002) and others (e.g., McGrew 1997) seem to suggest when they argue that globalization is increasingly integrating the world and simultaneously creating the possibility for transnational processes of empowerment. In other words, the conditions allowing "corporate and political elites to reach across national borders to further their agendas" (Brecher, Costello, and Smith 2002) are the same conditions allowing social movements (e.g., environmental, human rights) and labor activists to create a countermovement capable of confronting the corporate agenda.

As globalization diffuses power *downward*, the emerging movement may offer a resolution to the democratic deficit by engendering a process of democratization (globalization) from below. Central to this process is the emergence of opportunities for new actions and strategies that may interface with old ones to directly pressure governments, to bypass governments and act directly on corporations, and to forge meaning in a more and more complex and less intelligible world. As this happens, globalization is altered in small and big ways. To be sure, we do not wish to suggest that globalization can be easily or quickly changed or that most people can easily or quickly become social activists; globalization is too powerful and many people too powerless. In Chapter 9, we return to this issue of how local efforts are responding to globalization and attempting to redefine the relationships between civil society and the state as they forge new connections with *various levels* of government.

Globalization and Stratification

At the beginning of the twenty-first century,

- Fifty-four of the world's largest "economies" are corporations.
- General Motors is larger than the combined **gross domestic products** **(GDP)** of sub-Saharan Africa (Newman 2002).
- The world's richest three individuals have assets greater than the GDPs of the 48 least developed countries (Crossette 1998).
- Wal-Mart surpassed General Motors to become the largest employer in the United States in 1997 (*Forbes* 1996, 1997).
- Seventy-one percent of white children in the United States are covered by health insurance compared to 44 percent of black children (Lusane 1997, 18).
- The unemployment rate for black workers in the United States is twice that of white workers (U.S. Department of Labor 2002).
- The infant mortality rate is 13.5/1,000 for black children and 6.8/1,000 for white children (Mathews and MacDorman 2006).
- The term *jobless economic recovery* emerges as economic growth coincides with low job creation.

What springs to mind when you read this list? At some point we hope that you think inequality; these are all illustrations of different forms of inequality or a condition in which groups of individuals have unequal access to goods, services, resources, and opportunities. These examples further illustrate that inequality can be based on a number of characteristics from class to race to gender to geographical location. You may also recognize that these are not new problems but reflect traditional social problems of poverty—unequal access to health and education, a lack of available well-paying jobs or of affordable housing.

So what are the connections to globalization? Our point is that globalization is not necessarily creating new problems; rather, globalization is redistributing power and exacerbating and sharpening existing contradictions manifested in patterns of inequality. In some cases, global processes are creating new forms of inequality, as we mentioned in the Preface, by changing who joins the ranks of the poor, unemployed, underemployed, homeless, or hungry; in other instances, globalization is exacerbating existing patterns of inequality. Yes, inequality and poverty remain entrenched social problems, but what do we mean by *inequality*?

Inequality and Stratification

We all use the terms **inequality** and **social stratification** to refer to unequal distribution of *things*, such as material possessions, abilities, or technology. Social scientists make an important distinction between the two terms: *inequality* is the unequal distribution of things, while *stratification* refers to a hardening or institutionalizing of inequality. Stratification, then, is an institutionalized hierarchical ranking of groups of individuals based on such variables as class and social status.

Historically, different forms of stratification have dominated the social relations of societies, such as slavery, caste, and estate; some of these forms continue to exist today, and even class inequality has evolved over time. A major form of stratification is **class**, understood as an **achieved status**, meaning that we have some control over our class position. *Class* is defined as a group of individuals with similar political and economic interests who share similar **life chances**[6] and possess similar resources (including power). Measures of class typically include such variables as **income, wealth**, and occupations. As we discuss in Chapter 5, class is closely connected to other inequalities, such as health, education, and political power.

Class is also related in complex ways to **ascribed status** dimensions of stratification, such as race, ethnicity, and gender. These are attributes given (ascribed) to us at birth and over which we have little or no control, one's **sex** for instance. *Status*, as Kerbo (2003, 14) points out, is often used in two different ways: to indicate a position within the social structure, such as student, mother, or child, with certain rights and duties attached to such positions, or to indicate a noneconomic position in a hierarchy. In this book, we use this latter notion of status as a form of "popularity" or respect accorded groups based on certain social criteria (e.g., education) that can vary independently of class. Following Weber (1978, 305–307), we understand status as involving a specific *style of life*, with expectations and restrictions on social interaction imposed on all those who "wish to belong to the circle." **Race, ethnicity**, and **gender** are unequal statuses that, in many instances, reflect restrictions (social and legal) on social interaction, occupational position, and control of and access to power.

Our discussion would be incomplete without reference to **power**. What is power? For Weber (1978), power is the ability to accomplish one's goals despite resistance from others. Power is a generalized commodity—expressed as economic, military, and political, among others—that can serve a variety of goals and interests; power is central to any stratification system that fundamentally depends on some group dominating other groups.

Finally, stratification functions as both a distributional and a legitimizing mechanism through which goods, services, and resources are dispersed and outcomes are justified. These goods, services, and resources include the obvious, such as money and wealth, but also occupations, health, life expectancy, literacy, and power. Unequal distribution of these goods is also *explained* by the system as equitable; those who contribute more to a society or hold more important positions within a society deserve greater rewards, for instance. Within any stratification system, people come to expect that individuals and groups with certain positions will be able to demand more influence and respect and accumulate a greater share of goods and services. Although such inequality may or may not be accepted equally by a majority in the society, it is recognized as the way things are (Kerbo 2003, 11). Therefore, any discussion of social stratification implies reference to the economic system, but most social scientists agree that stratification is closely linked to other institutions, such as politics and culture.

Social Mobility

The effects of politics and culture are clearly evident in different systems of stratification. In **closed stratification systems**, such as slave or caste systems, the primary means of legitimizing the social location of groups are legal (political) and ideological (cultural practices) and often a combination of the two. Importantly, in these systems there is little or no possibility of moving from one social location to another. A second system, called an **open stratification system,** is represented by the class system and differs from the above examples in several ways. First, class systems are based on an industrial (as opposed to an agrarian) economic base. Second, there is the possibility of social mobility, upward or downward, in the system. Positions in the hierarchy are based to a greater degree on merit—or achievement—rather than on qualities ascribed to an individual or those beyond an individual's control, which we find in caste or slave systems.

Nonetheless, legitimization of inequality also relies on the political and cultural systems in class societies. Let's look at health care, for instance, where 64 percent of the over 41 million people in the United States under age 65 with no health coverage have incomes below 150 percent of the **poverty line**—the poor and near poor (National Center for Health Statistics 2004, Table 131). The fact that individuals with higher incomes are more likely to have health-care coverage in industrial societies makes sense. After all, in open stratification systems, as the argument goes, social mobility is possible as individuals with different abilities and motivations compete for scarce resources (e.g., education or high-paying jobs), which then translates into access to other goods, such as health care. The system simply rewards and punishes individual efforts accordingly. In the United States, the idea of competitive individualism holds that those who work the hardest and have the greatest abilities will be rewarded with upward mobility and greater resources; less successful individuals will remain in the same social location or experience downward mobility.

You may ask if such outcomes are *unfair*. Is inequality inevitable, or even desirable, as a mechanism to motivate the "best" and the "brightest" to excel? Can inequality be lessened? Should individuals be blamed for their lack of upward mobility? Should social structures and institutions that affect available opportunities be blamed? Or should both individual efforts and social structures factor into the analysis? Has inequality increased or decrease over time? What have been the effects of globalization on patterns of inequality? These are some of the central debates within the globalization and stratification literature, which we focus on in this book.

Global–Local Class Inequality Patterns

Within the context of globalization, patterns of inequality reflected in the distributional data on income, wealth, poverty, and employment reveal geographically new and complex forms. One manifestation is the blurring of the global geographical division between the wealthy "northern core" (e.g., the United States, Western Europe) and the poor "southern periphery" (e.g., Africa, Latin America, South Asia). As the traditional forms of vertical stratification erode between wealthy industrialized societies and poor developing ones, new horizontal patterns that crisscross national boundaries emerge. One can take Sunset Boulevard in Los Angeles, for instance, and travel west to east passing through wealthy "First World" affluence to "Third World" poverty in less than an hour; or Rio de Janeiro, where neighborhoods with open sewers abut those whose residents drive Range Rovers and vacation in the Mediterranean. Throughout the world, contemporary forms of stratification often retain patterns that were shaped by conquest and racial, ethnic, and gender attributes, yet these patterns increasingly show little regard for national borders as globalization renders geographical location less meaningful. Let's take a brief look at some of these patterns in the United States and the world.

Local Class Inequality in the United States

Between 1979 and 2001, the top 5 percent of the total population in the United States increased their average income from $68,360 to $280,312 (U.S. Bureau of the Census 2001), while the number of children in poverty increased from

3.4 million to 12.2 million, or from 14.9 percent to 16.9 percent of the population (Eitzen and Baca Zinn 2003, 182–183). Today in the United States, there are over 7.5 million millionaires (Christie 2005), over 400 billionaires (Forbes 2006), and 37 million officially defined as poor.

Often, however, we forget that real people exist behind these statistics. We hear about individuals like Bill Gates who can lose $30 billion in one year and still remain the richest individual in the world worth $60 billion (*Forbes* 1999, 2000). A second is Jeffrey Bezos, the force behind Amazon.com, who at the age of 35 was worth an estimated $10 billion (*Forbes* 2003). On the other hand, we seldom hear about people such as Amanda Tomberlin, who worked for Pillowtex. Formerly the largest employer in Kannapolis, North Carolina, Pillowtex made sheets and towels before declaring bankruptcy in August 2003. For these workers, the area's best options for employment after Pillowtex required a high school degree, which excludes almost half of the Pillowtex workers. Low levels of education combined with an average age of 46 years means the future prospects for former Pillowtex employees are few. J. C. Ward, a former Pillowtex employee, perhaps summarizes the feelings of millions of former factory workers across the United States: "I'm 57 years old and feel trapped; too young to retire, but too old to start a new career" (Hochberg 2003).

While the closing of Pillowtex made for a brief story on National Public Radio, other stories seldom make the news. The Hobbs family, from Beattyville, Kentucky, has lived for years in a house without indoor plumbing, insulation, or a safe foundation. "We could feel the air coming through the cracks in the walls, [and] hear animals in the walls" (cited in Hurst 2004, 2). Or Russell Tanner, who in his mid-40s had 21 years of seniority with General Motors when the plant at which he worked closed. Russell represented the third generation of Tanners who had worked in this plant. As his wife began working two jobs, the sudden role reversal placed a great deal of strain on their marriage and on his relationship with his children. He began to withdraw and drink more and more, which put even greater strain on the family (Bradshaw and Wallace 1996).

Global Class Inequality

So what about the rest of the world? The kinds of patterns depicted above in the United States are replicated throughout the world, although with sharper distinctions between the impoverished and the new globalized super wealthy elites in countries such as Mexico, Thailand, India, Chile, China, and the Philippines. According to the United Nations Development Program (UNDP 1999), the income gap between the fifth of the world's people living in the richest countries and the fifth in the poorest was 74 to 1 in 1997, up from 60 to 1 in 1990 and 30 to 1 in 1960. In 1999, the number of people worldwide living below $1 a day, considered the benchmark for abject poverty, was estimated at 1.3 billion—up 200 million from 1993.[7]

Who are the rich and famous? Consider, for instance, Mexican billionaire Carlos Slim Helú who purchased CompUSA in 2000 and has other holdings in telecom, retailing (e.g., OfficeMax, Circuit City, and Borders), and financial services. Carlos Slim Helú lost $3.4 billion in a 2-year period and was still worth $7.4 billion in 2003; in 2006, *Forbes* listed him as the third richest individual in the world at $30 billion (*Forbes* 2006). Or the Indonesian Rachman Halim family who is worth $1.9 billion (2006) and own and run the publicly traded PT Gudang Garam Company, Indonesia's largest producer of clove cigarettes (*Forbes* 2006). Compare these two examples to Maria Guadalupe, who started working in a Mexican *maquiladora* (or assembly factory) at the age of 16 earning $27 for a 48-hour workweek (Guadalupe 1999). Or the Indonesian Sadisah (the only name on her pay stub), who worked 10.5 hours a day, 6 days a week for 14 cents an hour for Nike in the early 1990s (Bradshaw and Wallace 1996).

Global–Local Connections

In thinking about these data, reflect on how the lives and fortunes of producers and consumers are increasingly linked and shaped by decisions made far from the point of impact. Globalization means that corporations, now more agile than ever, can more easily take advantage of sharp disparities between production costs in the United States and other parts of the globe. As U.S. capital moves offshore or companies **subcontract** jobs to lower their production costs, low-income nations become more industrialized, thereby employing Sadisah or Maria, and the United States becomes more service-oriented, causing Russell Tanner or Amanda Tomberlin to take service sector jobs. While the movement of investment capital may industrialize low-income countries and actually *decrease* economic inequality between countries, the process potentially *increases* inequality within high-income countries as these societies become more service-oriented (Firebaugh 2003). At the same time, if consumers in the United States boycott Nike because of its labor practices, Sadisah may lose her job because of weakening market demand. Similarly, if labor costs in Indonesia increase relative to Vietnam or labor costs in Mexico increase relative to Haiti, Sadisah and Maria's jobs will be jeopardized as corporations relocate to areas with lower labor costs. With accelerated globalization, the notion that production and consumption are social processes has taken on new and more complex dimensions.

Sociology has a long history of examining these kinds of changes, emerging as a discipline within the context of an earlier transformation—the industrial revolution—which restructured societies that had been relatively stable for generations. Then, as now, some of the most profound changes are reflected in new productive systems that are undermining existing occupations and expanding or creating others as well as technological advances that are altering the physical and social environment and affecting the way people raise families, educate their children, govern themselves, and live their lives. Thus, the forces underlying the industrial revolution continue to induce change as manifested in the introduction of new concepts such as globalization, downsizing, **economic restructuring,** and **deindustrialization.** How these forces (and conditions for globalization), which we examine in the next chapter, are transforming the nature of social relations, political organizations, and social and economic structures in the United States is the focus of this book.

Conclusion

With the emergence of neoliberalism in the 1970s, the pace and nature of change reflecting the greater importance of global processes allow us to talk of a different—though not necessarily new—period in human history. The scope of these changes is vividly manifested in the reorientation and restructuring of U.S. society. As Peter Drucker points out, the United States is no longer the single most powerful global actor but one of several "centers" in the global economy. This transformation is further reflected in strategic and ideological shifts responsible for changes in the quality and quantity of jobs in the United States Thus, an understanding of contemporary U.S. society is impossible without reference to globalization.

Globalization is a multifaceted and *abstract* process, which leads many to conclude that it is a product of powerful unseen forces far removed from their daily lives. Yet, this is only partly true. Globalization is indeed a complex *set* of processes, but the danger is in ignoring the consequences of our actions *and* inactions and believing that globalization is inevitably unfolding along a path predetermined by the world's most powerful individuals. To be sure, globalization has evolved along the lines determined by powerful forces—as we note in a later chapter—but millions of women, men, and children have begun to challenge the existing course of globalization through their struggles to make their communities safer, cleaner, and healthier. We focus on some of these efforts in later chapters, motivated by a belief in the potential for social activism to transform ordinary people into the architects of their own destinies. By calling attention to the impact of these global forces in our private lives and our reactions to these changes, we can more clearly understand the meaning of these larger forces in our lives and the lives of others around the world.

CHAPTER 2

Globalization

The Context

- In 1935, President Franklin D. Roosevelt charted a new activist role for the U.S. federal government with the passage of the Social Security Act.
- In 1944 at Bretton Woods, New Hampshire, leaders from 44 nations designed a new global institutional framework to stabilize and manage international economic relations based on John Maynard Keynes's idea that markets often fail to resolve problems of unemployment and poverty.
- In 1946, the U.S. Congress passed the Employment Act, committing the government to full employment and reflecting Keynes's idea that the state has a role to play in stimulating economic demand and maintaining full employment.
- In 1978, President Jimmy Carter signaled the onset of a new era of less government control in the United States with the passage of the Airline Deregulation Act.
- In the 1980 campaign, candidate Ronald Reagan defined a new strategy by invoking Friedrich von Hayek's idea that governments were not part of the solution to unemployment and poverty but the causes of such problems.
- In the early 1980s, David Stockman, President Ronald Reagan's budget director, argued that the vision of the good society rested on the strength and productive potential of free persons in free societies, reflecting the idea that unfettered corporations and individuals would solve the most pressing social problems.
- In the 1980s, leaders of the International Monetary Fund and World Bank, founded at Bretton Woods, no longer saw markets as fallible and began to champion market supremacy by forcing countries to privatize and deregulate their economies as solutions to the problems of unemployment and poverty.

These examples illustrate two ideas that have long shaped debates over how best to resolve unemployment, inequality, and poverty. The debate pivots on the fundamental question of what should be the proper role of the state and markets in society: should governments or markets organize society and resolve social problems? Understanding why one idea gains primacy over another requires an examination of the sociopolitical context. For instance, in the aftermath of the Great Depression and the Second World War, the world adopted a new approach to these old problems. As we discussed in the previous chapter, John Maynard Keynes argued that, in contrast to the idea of classical economic liberalism, markets do fail and produce such catastrophes as the Great Depression. To avoid inevitable recessions and depressions, governments should actively intervene to control markets and manage economic change. A new consensus took root—based on Keynes's theory—and informed the policies of Franklin Roosevelt in the 1930s and the Bretton Woods convention in the 1940s. Keynes's ideas guided government policy for almost 30 years. Beginning in the late 1960s, however, a shifting sociopolitical context created the possibility for an alternative set of ideas. The unraveling of the Keynesian strategy in the 1970s is illustrated by President Carter's deregulation of the airline industry and by Ronald Reagan's popularizing the idea that state intervention was the *cause* of economic and social problems. Reagan's approach to poverty and inequality reflected the neoliberal ideas of Friedrich von Hayek, who argued that any state control of markets would be disastrous for economic stability and growth. The crisis of the 1970s provided an opportunity to put Hayek's theory into practice.

Initiated in the United States and England during the late 1970s and 1980s, policies of deregulation and privatization replaced Keynesian intervention. As Hayek's neoliberal market ideas spread throughout the world, the accompanying policies triggered the contemporary—or "accelerated"—phase of globalization. For students of Hayek, the demise of Keynesianism was inevitable. In their view, attempting to control markets, which are natural forces like the "waves of the ocean," is something that can be done only "at one's peril." From this perspective, globalization is also an inevitable and natural process. The story is more complex, however. The problems of the 1970s created an opportunity for the shift to neoliberalism and thus neoliberal globalization, but how globalization evolved must be seen within the context of the economic, political, institutional, and technological changes that occurred after the Second World War. In this chapter, we examine these changes in order to better comprehend how politics and political policies created the current form of globalization.

Strategic Shifts

Struggling with the combined effects of the Great Depression and later World War II, many scholars, activists, and politicians came to believe that capitalism had an inherent tendency toward self-destruction. Unregulated markets, they believed, would create ever deeper crises that would devastate democratic societies. Economists such as Keynes and the social historian Karl Polanyi argued that the Great Depression was a normal by-product of a system that prioritized profits above the well-being of people.[1] Profits, Keynes argued in his *General Theory of Employment, Interest and Money*, depend on lowering wages and production costs by substituting machines for labor. You might recall from the last chapter that Keynes's theory suggested that by lowering wages and laying off workers employers could increase profits but only at the expense of reducing the number of consumers able to buy the goods produced. Decreased sales lead to additional layoffs in an ever downward cycle. Keynes's solution proposed that governments manage economic development and ensure full employment by actively regulating the business sector and by acting as an investor to stimulate the economy when private capital was either unwilling or unable to provide needed investment.

Keynes's ideas that societies could manage and control economic forces were revolutionary and led many to believe that he had discovered the solution to such problems as poverty and unemployment. His ideas spread quickly and legitimized interventionist "Fordist" legislation in the United States, Western Europe, Canada, Australia, and elsewhere. As a principal participant in the Bretton Woods Conference, Keynes also provided the theoretical basis for a new global institutional structure. Yet, by the 1970s, Keynesianism came under increasing criticism as domestic instabilities, particularly stagflation, challenged the viability of the strategy. What happened? Why did the Keynesian *solution* for economic stagnation become viewed as the *cause* of the economic malaise that materialized in the 1970s? To answer these questions, we need a historical vantage point; our answer begins with a discussion of the changing conditions through which the basic economic forces operate.

Forces and Conditions for Globalization

Capitalism is the economic system of our age. The key forces of capitalism—profits and competition—are central to creating what we call today "globalization." Yet, profits and competition have been around a long time and cannot *explain* the current manifestation of globalization. To understand globalization in its present form, we must study the *conditions* through which these basic forces operate. Specifically, we need to examine the composition of the global information infrastructure and recent advances in communication technologies, improvements in transportation, and finally politics and political ideology.

Information Infrastructure

Transformations in the information infrastructure contribute immensely to the compression of time and space to which Anthony Giddens (2003) and others refer when discussing globalization. By the *information infrastructure*, we mean networks of communication technology, including communication satellites, fiber-optic lines, digital information formats, and the Internet (see, e.g., Castells 2000). The information infrastructure affects globalization by

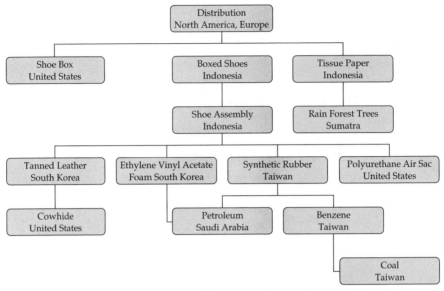

Figure 2.1 Global production of an athletic shoe. *Sources*: Ryan and Durning (1998), McMichael (2000).

facilitating or constraining the intensity and extensity of global connectedness and interaction. Likewise, the potential scale of interaction among the world's people is determined primarily by technological capacity and communications technology. Radical innovation in these technologies and the emergence of instant and almost real-time communication have significantly altered the nature of global interaction. We all talk about the "global assembly line," for instance (see Fig. 2.1). Changes in the information infrastructure have allowed corporate and individual capital to create such processes by coordinating production across national boundaries. This ability also means that companies can take advantage of differences in resources and regulations between nation-states or regions by switching activities between them in the competitive pursuit of profits (Dicken 1998).

Two points are significant:

1. *Intensity*: Changes in the information infrastructure precipitated a dramatic increase in the speed and volume (or intensity) of goods and services circulating in global markets—though we cannot neglect how the movement of goods and services is also linked to advances in transportation and decreasing costs of moving goods (see Held et al. 1999, 168–175). The intensity is illustrated by declining transportation costs, unprecedented flows of capital, and the increase in the volume of communication. For instance, between 1960 and the late 1990s, airline transportation costs fell by more than 60 percent; between the early 1970s and 1997, the balances on transborder bank

loans increased from $200 billion to $10.383 trillion (Scholte 2000b, 86); in 1999, $1.5 *trillion* moved across international borders *daily*, up from "mere" billions in the 1980s; between 1985 and 1998, Internet users increased from 0 to 180 million (Scholte 2000b, 86); between 1990 and 1998, transborder telephone traffic increased from 33 billion minutes to 70 billion minutes (UNDP 1999, 25); between 1965 and 1995, trade between developing and industrialized countries increased from 32.5 percent of total world trade to 38 percent, while trade between developing countries increased from 3.8 percent to 14 percent during the same period (Held et al. 1999, 172).

2. *Extensity*: As we already mentioned, the information infrastructure creates the possibility for global factories to produce goods in decentralized global assembly lines. The advent of global assembly lines illustrates the extensity—or expansion—of the global system. The European version of the Ford Escort offers a useful example. In the early 1990s, the Escort was assembled in the United Kingdom and Germany from components produced in 15 different countries, including the United States, Italy, Switzerland, Japan, Canada, The Netherlands, Spain, and others. Another example is the Toyota Motor Company, which is headquartered in Japan and produces and markets products using 56 manufacturing plants in 25 countries, including the United States, Brazil, and Thailand (Gabel and Bruner 2003, 40–41). An even more dramatic example is Nike, which is headquartered in the United States and subcontracts 100 percent of its production to 75,000 workers in China, South Korea, Malaysia, Taiwan, and Thailand (Steger 2003, 49).

Computer-based technological advances make possible global factories by facilitating the coordination of activities across geographical space and the **outsourcing** of jobs previously confined to local areas (see Gwynne, Klak, and Shaw 2003, Chapter 11). The informational infrastructure *institutionalizes* these underlying global networks and patterns of interaction (movement of car components, e.g.) across time and space. As these interactions are institutionalized or regularized, new possibilities are opened up for the geographical (re)configuration of activity through the inclusion of different countries or regions into the global productive system. Thus, as corporations confront the competitive pressures of global markets, they often create sophisticated global factories that expand the system—and intensify global competition. Figure 2.1 illustrates the global production system.

At this point, you may be wondering if transnational corporations, or for that matter foreign investment, are really recent inventions? The answer is no; both have a long history. We can think of the East India Company, formed in 1600, or U.S. Singer Sewing Machines, which opened a factory in Scotland in 1867 as examples (Gabel and Bruner 2003, part III). Beginning in the 1980s, however, the nature of global interaction changed: competition intensified, the number of transnational corporations increased dramatically, while foreign investment soared and diversified beyond the traditional European and U.S. sources. Today, almost every country is connected through transnational production and investment, and these connections are far stronger than portfolio investment (the buying of stocks of foreign companies) that dominated earlier forms of globalization (see Gabel and Bruner 2003). The process of global intensification and extensification cannot be understood, however, without reference to the shift in political ideology that we touched on in the previous chapter.

Political Policies and Ideology

After 1980, two intertwined political processes emerged. First, regional projects that subordinate national governments to supranational institutions were negotiated. Examples of these include the Maastricht treaty, creating the European Union; the North American Free Trade Agreement (NAFTA) between Canada, the United States, and Mexico; and the Asia-Pacific Economic Cooperation (APEC), designed to enhance intergovernmental cooperation among Pacific Rim–Asian countries. A more dramatic example is the incorporation of the former Soviet Union countries and China into one (or more) global organization such as the **G-7 group**, the **North Atlantic Treaty Organization** (NATO), and the World Trade Organization (WTO).

Second, the shift in political philosophy reflected in the rejection of Keynesianism and the reversal of state intervention deepened the intensity and extensity of global interconnections. Policies deregulating and privatizing economies transformed nationally (publicly) owned industries into private (often foreign) ones and accelerated the mobility of goods and services by opening up societies and freeing markets. Even in the United States, where deregulation has been the hallmark of the neoliberal strategy, "no part of the public sphere has been immune to the infiltration of for-profit corporations" (Bakan 2004, 113). Bakan notes that political debates surrounding the attempt to partially or fully privatize public utilities, such as water,[2] as well as Social Security, prisons, and highways are all part of the vision of a "new society." In effect, the idea is to reduce the function of the state to perhaps no more than maintaining a military (Bakan 2004, 113–114), but even here outsourcing and privatization are creating a new privatized military industry (Singer 2003). In cases where deregulation or privatization has not been politically feasible, such as eliminating the Environmental Protection Agency, the Occupational Safety and Health Administration, or the Securities and Exchange Commission, the strategy in the United States has been to reduce funding for these agencies. As budgets shrink, regulatory agencies find they lack the resources necessary to enforce existing laws. In these cases, big business can ignore regulations and laws, such as those governing child labor, minimum wages, working conditions, accounting practices, stock trading, and others, with little fear of being held accountable.

Thus, the goal of domestic policies is to minimize state interference in markets and maximize the freedom of capital either by eliminating national-level institutions or by reducing the resources necessary for remaining institutions to control the behavior of private economic actors. As societies become more open to the global system and capital becomes more mobile, the competitive struggle for profits accelerates.

Proponents of neoliberalism often neglect what these political shifts mean: the way globalization has unfolded was by no means inevitable or apolitical, as they assume. Policies of deregulation and privatization initiated in the United States and England shaped this process; yet globalization implies that other nations also reduce barriers to interaction. Had the shift to neoliberalism stopped in the United States and England, the current globalization trajectory would have failed to materialize. Thus, some mechanism was necessary to globalize the neoliberal strategy, to reduce barriers to interaction *throughout* the global system. This mechanism was the global institutions founded at Bretton Woods after the Second World War.

Global Institutions

In the aftermath of the Second World War and with the Great Depression fresh in mind, leaders from 44 nations converged in Bretton Woods, New Hampshire, to decide the future of the global system.[3] Led by England and the United States,[4] negotiations produced three major agreements intended to achieve global and national financial and economic stability. First, participants established a set of rules of international activities, such as the removal of restrictions to the flow of goods. Second, they created a stable monetary exchange by establishing a "flexible" **gold standard**, through which the currencies of other countries were pegged to a fixed gold value of the U.S. dollar (Steger 2003, 38). This meant that the dollar could be exchanged for gold or, in other words, the U.S. dollar "was as good as gold." Third, the group created an institutional framework, the "**Bretton Woods Trio**," designed to govern the economic and monetary activities of the international economy. The Trio consisted of the International Monetary Fund (IMF), the World Bank (WB), and the General Agreement on Trade and Tariffs (GATT); over time, these three institutions became the world's most powerful forces for globalization. As we summarize below, the Trio's original division of labor began to break down after 1980.

International Monetary Fund

The IMF began operations in 1947 with 29 member nations; today, there are 182. The original mission of the IMF was to administer the international monetary system: to oversee a system of fixed exchange rates, to ease the exchange of one currency for another, and to act as a "lender of last resort," meaning it would be the world's banker in emergencies. The overall intent of the IMF was to act as a mechanism to stabilize the international monetary system by providing funds to maintain adequate global demand, employment, and hence global economic stability. A driving force behind the creation of the IMF was Keynes, who was convinced that inadequate global demand was largely responsible for the Great Depression of the 1930s. To prevent future global depressions, Keynes wanted to create an institution that would provide funding when necessary to maintain global demand. You may be surprised, but in Keynes's initial design the institution had no control over a government's economic decisions, nor could it intervene in national policy.

The IMF was intended to function like a credit union. In the case of the IMF, member-nations contribute funds that can be lent to other member-nations experiencing temporary shortages of resources needed to stimulate domestic economic growth. Funds provided to the IMF are based on a quota determined by the size of the member-nation's economy: the larger the economy, the larger the quota. The size of the quota in turn determines how much foreign exchange member-nations have access to in emergencies and, more importantly, how many votes member-nations have in deliberations over which country will get a loan and under what conditions.[5]

Over time, the conditions under which the IMF provides funds have changed. Increasingly after the 1980s, the IMF provided funds *only* if countries agreed to adopt what have become know as **structural adjustment programs** (SAPs). Essentially, SAPs require governments to deregulate the economy, privatize the public sector or state-owned enterprises, reduce barriers to trade, cut government spending on social programs and social services, raise (usually noncorporate) taxes, and raise interest rates (see Stiglitz 2002; Gwynne, Klak, and Shaw 2003, 111–112). The SAPs not only represent the very opposite of what Keynes had in mind but are precisely the kinds of policies that open societies to the global system and deepen the intensity and extensity of global interactions.

International Bank for Reconstruction and Development (World Bank)

Keynes's other innovation was the WB, founded in 1946. As with the IMF, the WB was designed to prevent global depressions—and future conflicts—by lending reconstruction and infrastructure projects necessary for economic growth. Initially focused on rebuilding Europe after the devastation of the Second World War, the WB's focus expanded in the 1950s to include funding for projects to further industrialization throughout the world. Since its inception, the WB has created several additional departments to support private-sector investment and to provide insurance to foreign corporations investing in member countries.

As was the case with the IMF, the WB's mission shifted dramatically in the 1980s to focus more narrowly on making certain kinds of loans: structural adjustment loans (Stiglitz 2002, 13–15). Increasingly, both institutions concentrated on furthering the neoliberal policies of deregulation and global market integration by forcing countries to participate in the world economy under their rules. Today, the WB will provide funding *only* if a country commits to an IMF SAP.

General Agreement on Tariffs and Trade/ World Trade Organization

The third pillar of the Bretton Woods Trio was GATT. Created as a forum for negotiations on trade liberalization, its mandate was to provide a means to lower trade barriers through the establishment of multilateral trade agreements. The idea was to avoid the competitive trade policies that had hobbled the global economy before the Second World War (Ellwood 2002, 32). Always intended as a temporary agreement that would be replaced by a permanent trade organization, GATT was succeeded by the WTO in January 1995. Currently, there are 137 member-nations and 30 "observers" that participate in the WTO.

The WTO continues to function much as GATT did, as a means to lower trade barriers, with several significant differences (NAFTA can be understood as a smaller version of the WTO). First, the WTO has the official status of an international organization, rather than a loosely structured treaty. Second, the WTO's mandate has been vastly expanded beyond traditional commercial matters of **tariffs** and import **quotas** to include telecommunications, banking and investment, transport, education, health, and the environment (Ellwood 2002, 32). Third, the WTO is much more powerful than GATT. Armed with a **dispute settlement body** (DSB), the WTO has the authority to make binding judgments in cases where trade rules are subject to dispute (Held et al. 1999, 165).

Under current WTO rules, any form of regulation or standard can be challenged as an unfair impediment to free trade. General issues, including local content laws, direct and indirect government subsidies, and product labeling policies, as well as specific issues, such as regulation of chemicals in children's toys, can all be viewed as "unfair" trade policies. In contrast to GATT rules that required every member to agree on decisions concerning free trade, the WTO's DSB panel of corporate experts hears and decides cases behind closed doors. Once the DSB hands down a decision, it is final; the only way to nullify the decision is if *all* WTO members oppose the decision—a virtual impossibility, according to Ellwood (2002, 34).

Post-1945: Crisis and Change

Initially, the Bretton Woods agreements created a tripartite system of supranational institutions that allowed nation-states to set their own political and economic agendas. In Western Europe, Australia, New Zealand, and the United States, the interventionist Keynesian–Fordist strategy evolved within this global "macromanagement" framework to create what is often called the "**Thirty Glorious Years**." Between the 1940s and the 1970s, the strategy produced that stable and predictable world of near full employment and the expanding welfare system we mentioned in the last chapter. In the United States, this was a period of unprecedented upward social mobility for blue- and white-collar workers alike. Thus, individuals without high school diplomas, like those with high school diplomas and college degrees, could expect to step into jobs promising long-term security, jobs that would enable them to buy homes and cars, send their children to college, and retire comfortably.

All of this changed in the 1970s with the end of the Keynesian era. For Hayek, the demise of Keynesianism was an inevitable result; it is simply impossible to control markets without stifling individual initiative and economic growth. As we have suggested, however, the situation was more complex. Yes, Hayek and his students identified serious problems in the economy, but the problems they focused on were *symptoms* of the crisis, not the primary cause—globalization. As a result, the global economic integrationist tendencies and the dispersion of economic and political power were ignored. So, what were these twin processes of integration and dispersion?

Beginning in the 1950s and continuing through the 1960s, there was a dramatic expansion of private investment money, called "**Eurocurrency**." **Eurocurrency markets** developed out of money deposited in Western European banks by the Soviet Union,[6] and transnational corporations that did not want to send profits back home where they would be taxed. Eurocurrency markets grew as European banks lent out dollars they received rather than converting them into national currencies; in other words, a *parallel* source of funding emerged outside the control of national governments. Thus, investors could raise funds on the Eurocurrency markets that were not subject to national banking regulations. Eurocurrency markets expanded because they were a convenient and largely unregulated source for raising huge sums of money for large public corporations, private global corporations, and public authorities. With the growth of the unregulated Eurocurrency markets, there was increasing strain on the Bretton Woods system, which worked because it could control the international credit system. As the supply of "private" and "unregulated" dollars in the international system increased, the political institutional regulation of the Bretton Woods system eroded.

With the world's economies increasingly open and globally connected, inflation could no longer be controlled at the national level. Recall that one of the goals of the Bretton Woods system was to reduce international barriers to exchange. By the 1970s, these efforts had produced a much more integrated set of commodity, product, and capital markets. As a result, inflation could more easily flow throughout the system (see Gilpin 1987). As the United States tried to fund both the war in Vietnam and its Great Society social programs, its excessive monetary creation spread inflation throughout the global system. This, in turn, eroded global confidence in the U.S. dollar, which served as the basic currency for international exchange.

Finally, by the 1970s the U.S. economy was no longer the single most dominant economy in the global system. From 1960 to 1973, for instance, Japan's annual production of per capita goods and services increased four times faster than that of the United States and West Germany's grew more than twice as fast; between 1973 and 1988, Japan's level of production expanded five times and West Germany's four times faster than the U.S. economy (Craypo and Nissen 1993, 231, note 2). As the Japanese and West German economies grew, so too did imports into the United States, producing the first **balance-of-trade** deficit since 1893 (Cohn 2003, 167). By the mid-1980s, the United States was importing 26 percent of its cars; 25 percent of its steel; 60 percent of its televisions, radios, and tape recorders; and 53 percent of its numerically controlled machine tools. Twenty-two years earlier, imports had accounted for less than 10 percent of the U.S. market for each of these products. Overall, foreign-made products were competing with more than 70 percent of goods produced in the United States (Fraser 2001, 115).

Thus, by the 1970s Western Europe and Japan were challenging the dominance and ultimately the autonomy of the United States in the global system: (1) European and Japanese exports were successfully competing with U.S. products; (2) the vast amount of dollars held by Europeans (due to the Eurocurrency markets and the growing trade deficit) meant that European countries could use these holdings to control the value of the U.S. dollar.[7] These factors not only conspired to create the domestic problem of stagflation but reflected a diffusion of power in the global system. Finally, declining international barriers to exchange created a more integrated global system sensitive to national-level phenomena such as inflation.

Responding to these global changes, the Nixon administration suspended the official convertibility of the dollar into gold. The dollar quickly lost value vis-à-vis other major currencies, making U.S. exports cheaper and imports more expensive. It was hoped that this would improve the deteriorating U.S. trade position. Additionally, Nixon imposed a 10 percent surcharge on all dutiable imports, promising to remove it when other countries, such as West Germany and Japan, altered the "unfair" exchange rates that made U.S. exports expensive and Japanese and German exports cheap (Cohn 2003, 127–128). The immediate result of suspending the convertibility of the dollar into gold on August 15, 1971, was to shatter the Bretton Woods system (Gilpin 1987, 139–141).

The world of the 1970s was a changed one. The ability of the United States to control global economic and political events had declined, as evidenced by the taking of U.S. hostages in Iran, mentioned in the previous chapter; by the Organization of Petroleum Exporting Countries (OPEC) quadrupling the price of oil; and by the inability of the United States to win the war in Vietnam. At the end of the 1970s, the stock market was in a prolonged slump, the worst the nation had seen since the 1930s, interest rates were approaching 20 percent, inflation was close to 15 percent, unemployment was over 8.5 percent, and productivity continued to decline (Fraser 2001, 114). David Rockefeller, then chair of Chase Manhattan Bank, appears to have recognized the profound nature of these changes when he wrote in the bank's 1971 annual report: "It is clear to me that the entire structure of our society is being challenged" (quoted in Clawson 2003, 38).

With the crisis spreading throughout the increasingly integrated global system, politicians and political parties associated with Keynesianism suffered electoral defeats at the hands of market-oriented (neoliberal) politicians. Although Nixon formally ended the Bretton Woods era, the Bretton Woods Trio still existed and the rise to power of neoliberal politicians in the United States and England after 1980 allowed neoliberal politicians to place like-minded economists in charge of the IMF and WB. Recent WB Chief Economist Joseph Stiglitz (2002, 13–14) argues that the activities of the two institutions became increasingly intertwined in the 1980s and demonstrated a more ideological approach to global and domestic political policy than they had in previous decades. In contrast to the Keynesian idea that markets were a means to an end, the strategies of both organizations began to emphasize free markets as an end in themselves. The WB began to provide countries with funds for infrastructural projects *only* when the IMF gave its approval, and with that approval came IMF-imposed SAP conditions. As the global crisis of the 1970s deepened and spilled over into the 1980s, developing countries were even more in need of financial help and that financing came from the IMF and WB. Based on the new market ideology, the growing involvement of the IMF and WB in the financial affairs of countries extended and reinforced global integration and, thus, globalization.

The WTO and NAFTA

As we have discussed, the IMF and WB performed a central role in accelerating globalization, but what about the third leg of the triad: the WTO? We mentioned earlier that the WTO—and its regional counterpart NAFTA—continues to operate in much the same way as the GATT. Unlike the GATT, however, the rules of the WTO—and NAFTA—cover a vast array of issues previously the purview of the nation-state, including food safety, the environment, social-service policies, intellectual property standards, government procurement rules, and more.

For instance, the Chapter 11 provision of NAFTA states that no government may directly or indirectly nationalize or expropriate an investment or take a measure tantamount to nationalization or expropriation (Mooney 2001, Moyers 2002). Cases of nationalization or expropriation are heard in NAFTA's investor-to-state system. To date, however, the majority of cases have not challenged policies of nationalization or expropriation but have focused on environmental laws, regulations, and other government decisions at the national, state, and local levels:

- Foreign corporations have taken two lawsuits they lost in U.S. domestic courts to be "reheard" in the NAFTA investor-to-state system, one challenging the concept of sovereign immunity regarding a contract dispute with the city of Boston and one challenging the rules of civil procedure, the jury system, and a damage award in a Mississippi state court contract case.

- The U.S. company United Parcel Service (UPS) filed a suit challenging the governmental provision of parcel and courier services by the Canadian postal service.

- A Canadian steel fabrication company challenged a federal "Buy America" law for construction projects in the United States.

Similarly, the WTO enforces "fair" trade throughout the global system with its general rules on trade or more specific rules, such as the Trade-Related Aspects of Intellectual Property (TRIP) agreements, which set enforceable global rules on patents, copyrights, and trademarks. Often, these rules are used to circumvent or obstruct the enforcement of local regulations or laws:

- Switzerland and the European Union challenged U.S. steel import duties that were introduced in March 2002 to protect the struggling U.S. steel industry. In fall 2003, the WTO ruled that the duties were "inconsistent" with trading regulations, requiring the George W. Bush administration to remove the tariffs.

- The U.S. Gerber Products Company refused to comply with Guatemalan infant formula labeling laws based on the World Health Organization/United Nations Children's Fund (UNICEF) "Nestlé's Code" on the grounds that the laws violated trademark protections provided in the WTO's TRIP agreement. While the local law may have withstood the challenge, the prohibitive cost of mounting an uncertain defense forced Guatemalan authorities to exempt imported formula from the law.[8]

Placed within the earlier discussion, these examples reveal something quite important about the present world; yes, globalization is increasingly interconnecting the globe, but the *way* in which the process has unfolded has been determined by specific rules and regulations. In contrast to what is often portrayed, globalization has been a politically constructed process dependent upon the opening of societies throughout the world, with the shift in ideology key to understanding the nature of globalization. Specific ideas emphasizing the centrality of markets to development and as solutions to unemployment and poverty underlie these policies and strategies. As the United States and England deregulated and privatized the labor and capital sectors, like-minded neoliberal technocrats placed in charge of the IMF and

WB globalized the strategy by requiring other societies to adopt similar policies. The results were to intensify and extensify global connectivity.

Conclusion

The often-used quotation from Thomas Friedman is a fruitful way to conclude this chapter. In his book *The Lexus and the Olive Tree* (2000, xxi–xxii), Freidman argues, "I feel about globalization a lot like I feel about the dawn. Generally speaking, I think that it's a good thing that the sun comes up every morning. . . . But even if I didn't much care for the dawn there isn't much I could do about it." Yet, is this an accurate description of globalization? As we have argued in this chapter, the current globalization trajectory, based on maximal market freedom and minimal state intervention, was neither inevitable nor apolitical; rather, it evolved within the context of changing technical, economic, and political conditions after the Second World War.

Changes in the role of the Bretton Woods Trio have been central to this process. None of these conditions alone would have produced the present globalization trajectory. In combination, however, they created what many still see as an inevitable and natural process of change that is much like the "dawn." The intertwining of these factors is evident on two levels:

The societal level: Governments seeking international loans were compelled to adopt neoliberal policies of financial and market deregulation and privatization. These reforms created neoliberal states by opening often closed or heavily state-directed societies to global pressures.

The global level: Neoliberal states pursuing neoliberal policies accelerated global capital mobility, global integration, and hence globalization.

Thus, as the basic forces of profit and competition operated under the emergent conditions of the post-1970s period, the present globalization trajectory took shape. Yet, even among those who agree that these dramatic changes have been a political construction, there is disagreement over whether these processes of change constitute globalization. As we discuss in the next chapter, the fundamental point of debate is whether *globalization* is an accurate term to capture these changes evident in the past 30 years.

CHAPTER 3

The Globalization Debate

In 1997 Max Perelman, a young U.S. college student, was traveling through remote regions of China. While stranded by winter weather in west Sichuan, fifteen hundred miles from Beijing, he encountered a group of Tibetans bound for Lhasa, their capital. Perelman recalled that these young Tibetans had never strayed far from their native village, and apparently had never seen anything like his camera. As they shared with him bites of meat from an unspecified animal retrieved from their rucksacks, the group began to discuss things American. Just how, one of the Tibetans asked Perelman, was Michael Jordan doing (LaFeber 2002, 14)?

Such vignettes are suggestive of the world in which we live. As Anthony Giddens (2003, 7) writes, "We are being propelled into a global order that no one fully understands, but which is making its effects felt upon all of us." Attempting to capture the nature of these effects, globalization has emerged as *the* concept by which we are to understand the transition of human society into the third millennium (Waters 1995, 1).

Intense disagreements over the meaning and usefulness of globalization have spawned a tremendously rich and often contradictory body of literature that does not neatly fit into existing categories, such as conservative, liberal, or socialist. Equally discomforting, no one account has achieved the status of orthodoxy (Held and McGrew 2000, 2–3). In this chapter, we sort through these inconsistencies and contradictions by focusing on how writers conceptualize and explain the economic, political, cultural, and inequality outcomes. Taking the lead from David Held and Anthony McGrew (2000), we categorize the authors into two general groups, distinguished by their assumptions and understandings of the processes of change: the **globalists** and the **skeptics** (see also Sklair 2000, Michalak 1994).[1] We begin by describing the positions of the skeptics and globalists and follow with an assessment of these arguments in the next chapter.

Table 3.1 Perspectives: Skeptics and Globalists[a]

	ACTORS	PROCESS	GOALS
Globalists			
Liberalists[b] (neoliberalists)	Individuals are the dominant actors.	Individuals strive to maximize individual utility, free markets create options for individuals to make choices which lead to the highest level of subjective satisfaction.	To maximize happiness. Individuals are rational utility maximizers, making trade-offs among various goods and services to maximize happiness.[c]
Social democrats	Classes are the dominant actors.	Classes strive to maximize their economic interests. Global structures and rules favor the most powerful classes, but the system can be reformed to produce more equitable outcomes.	To equalize social, political, and economic outcomes. To reform the system so that a more equitable distribution of costs and benefits of change is achieved.
Skeptics			
Marxists	Classes are the dominant actors.	Classes strive to maximize their economic interests. Structures and rules of the global system favor the most powerful classes. Globally a capitalist–labor split crosscuts political boundaries, where a global capitalist class strives to maximize extraction of surplus value (i.e., profits) and the working class, to minimize exploitation.[d]	To create a new sociopolitical–economic system. System cannot be reformed and must be replaced.
Realists	Sovereign nation-states are the dominant actors. There is no higher authority than the nation-state.	States exist within a geopolitical international system that is anarchical and arranged in a hierarchy with the most powerful state(s) on top. Each state is solely dependent upon its own resources for survival; no state is obligated to help another. International order is based on a state hegemony or balance of power.	To maximize power[e] and independence. Power is a zero-sum game. Failure to maximize power increases the threat from competing states. States are rational actors and use cost–benefit analyses to determine which policies will maximize power.

[a] Social democracy is similar to the Marxist perspective; the social democrats, however, believe that capitalism can be reformed. Markets are an important source of innovation and wealth. It is not necessary to nationalize the basic industries of society under true social democracy. Regulatory and institutional control over capital, however, is essential to minimizing the negative externalities of markets and to reducing poverty and inequality created by the operation of the capitalist system.

[b] See Chapter 1.

[c] In the classic liberal scenario, there is no basis for conflict. Under conditions of free markets, everyone will have the opportunity to be as well off as possible, supply always equals demand, and a harmony of interests will prevail. Therefore, the need for state intervention in the economy and society is limited (see Hayek 1944).

[d] The wealthy, powerful classes in the advanced industrialized societies ally with wealthy, powerful classes in the less industrialized societies.

[e] Power is not just economic but also political and military.

Perspectives on Globalization

Following Held and McGrew (2000), we define *globalists* as those who consider contemporary globalization a real and significant historical development, while the *skeptics* are those who understand "globalization" as primarily an ideological or mythical construction that has marginal explanatory value. The level of analysis for the globalists is the transnational (global) processes, with the nation-state existing within a global web of supranational actors and institutions. Among these are the World Trade Organization (WTO) and North American Free Trade Agreement (NAFTA), as well as transnational economic and financial corporations such as General Motors, Deutsche Bank, and Bank of Tokyo-Mitsubishi. In comparison, the skeptics emphasize the national level, with the nation-state understood as the major actor within an interstate system.

Three points are important. First, although there is disagreement over the specifics of change, both the skeptics and globalists agree that capitalism has radically transformed in the last 25 years. Second, depending on the particular political, economic, or cultural issue, the skeptic and globalist categories further break down into skeptics who are either Marxists or realists and globalists who are either neoliberals or social democrats. For instance, skeptics reject the notion of globalization; rather, they understand the root of current changes to be either internationalization (in the case of realist skeptics) or **imperialism** (in the case of Marxist skeptics). In a similar fashion, globalists disagree about whether globalization is increasing inequality, which is the opinion of the social democrats, or decreasing it, which is the position held by the neoliberals. Third, these categories are ideal-type constructs[2] and, as such, do not exhaust the complexities or subtleties in the literature (Held and McGrew 2000, 2). Table 3.1 provides an overview of these four perspectives.

Conceptual Issues

Conceptually, both skeptics and globalists agree that we are living in a world that is more intensively and extensively "global." There is, however, no agreement between them as to whether the concept "globalization" is a useful construct for understanding the processes. The basic positions are summarized in Table 3.2.

Skeptics: Conceptual Issues

Skeptics generally understand globalization as primarily an economic or geopolitical process, viewing change as internationalization, regionalization, or a new form of imperialism (see Gilpin 1987; Gwynne, Klak, and Shaw 2003; Hirst and Thompson 1999; Krasner 1993; Vilas 2002). For the realist, the central actors are sovereign competing nation-states embedded in an

Table 3.2   Conceptualization of Globalization

	NATURE OF CHANGE	LEVEL OF ANALYSIS	FUNDAMENTAL PROCESS
Globalists			
Neoliberals	Globalization, a global age. A positive process in which all will benefit equally.	Transnational processes.	Global economic processes.
Social democrats	Globalization processes and an emerging global age. A contradictory and uneven process, not all benefit equally.	Transnational processes, classes, and institutions.	Numerous multilayered global through the local links among economic, cultural, and political interests.
Skeptics			
Marxists	Imperialism. Continued process of exploitation of the peripheral ("Third World" or "South") by the core ("First World" or "North").[a]	Capitalist system; classes and institutions at the national and international levels.	Exploitative class system: the haves versus the have-nots.
Realists	Internationalization or regionalization. An internationalization process created and maintained by the most powerful state(s).	International relations between nation-states.	Interstate (geopolitical) system.

[a] From the 1950s to the 1990s, the terms *Third World* and *First World* were commonly used when discussing countries within the rich, industrialized regions—the First World—and those outside the rich industrialized regions. Today, the more common term is *emerging markets* to describe the former Third World countries.

interstate system characterized by anarchy insofar as the sovereignty of the nation-state rules out the possibility of any overarching (global) authority (Waltz 1979). The goal of any nation-state is to maximize military, economic, and political power, which will increase its autonomy within this system of competing nation-states. The basic relation is a horizontal one between sovereign nation-states with growing cross-border flows of trade, investment, and financial capital that are increasing international economic integration (*Economist* 1997, 4; Keohane and Nye 2001). Integration, however, is not occurring along the lines that would suggest globalization.

First, integration is limited to the major industrialized countries that make up the **Organization for Economic Cooperation and Development** (OECD),[3] to the exclusion of the rest of the world (Jones 1995). Second, exchange is increasingly organized within three core blocs, comprising Europe, the Pacific Rim, and the Americas; obstacles to exchange are decreased *within* these blocs and increased *between* them. Thus, integration within these blocs is at the expense of integration between them (Hirst and Thompson 1999; Held and McGrew 2000, 20). Both trends point to the continued importance of geography. Third, there remains a great deal of diversity in terms of economic and political institutions among societies. State–society relations in Sweden remain very different from those in the United States, for example, indicating that states retain autonomy within the international system. This continued diversity runs counter to the globalists' argument that globalization is creating policy and institutional convergence across nation-states. Thus, it is not globalization we are witnessing but something different and best conceptualized as *internationalization*—or a deepening of interstate relations and international economic integration—or *regionalization* in blocs.

Marxists, as you might expect, understand the existing order as driven by the most powerful economic interests, specifically by the financial capitalists within the most powerful states (the OECD countries, e.g.). For Marxists, globalization is a myth or an ideological justification for renewed imperialism. Illustrating this perspective, Carlos Vilas (2002) begins an essay by stating that globalization has been "invented" as a way to conceal U.S. attempts to increase economic penetration into other nations (see also Tabb 2001, 2002; Yates 2003). For the Marxists, globalization is used to maintain the old division of labor, whereby the world's poorest societies continue to export primary products in exchange for manufactured goods from the wealthy ones. Thus, it is the continual expansion of capitalism that "compels all nations, on the pain of extinction, to adapt" (Marx [1848] 1955). Globalization, then, is nothing more than the most recent manifestation of capitalism and imperialism (Vilas 2002).

Globalists: Conceptual Issues

Globalists respond that current changes reflect something more than internationalization or imperialism. As Scholte (2000b) argues, social space is reconfigured and no longer wholly mapped in terms of territorial places, distances, and/or borders; it is a process of deterritorialization that reflects supraterritoriality (e.g., global flow of ideas). Time and space are being compressed as space is dislocated from place and time is separated from space (Giddens 1990, 18–19). A convergence of political (neoliberal) policies among nation-states is redistributing power and reducing the autonomy of national governments. These changes embody a transformation in the spatial organization of the social relations and transactions that generate transcontinental flows and networks of activity, interactions, and the exercise of power (Held et al. 1999, 16). In other words, these are distinct transformations accurately captured by the concept of "globalization."

Within this general conception, neoliberal globalists understand these changes as inevitably driven by uncontrollable but progressive market forces that will ultimately bring wealth and democracy to all. For the social democrats, however, this is an unequal and indeterminate "yet to be written" process. Thus, the neoliberals see globalization in uncritical and positive terms, while the social democrats remain unconvinced that globalization is necessarily benign.

Two points underlie the conceptual disputes that structure the larger debate in the literature. First, for the globalists, we are in the midst of a process—consisting of a series of phases—that appears to be leading to some form of political, economic, and cultural convergence. In contrast, the skeptics assess change in relation to how it conforms to the ideal-type of "globalization" and respond that the evidence does not support the conclusion that a global socio-economic system exists. Moreover, these conceptual differences reflect profound disagreements over the economic, political, cultural, and distributional outcomes. Let's begin with the economic and political issues.

Economic–Political Issues

Recall our discussion of the basic forces of, and conditions for, globalization in the previous chapter. Clearly, profits and competition are central to these changes; yet, as we have argued, shifting conditions are responsible for shaping the present trajectory. But do these changes truly identify the onset of a new phase of global change—or globalization—or are these changes better conceptualized as an intensification of internationalization or imperialism? The answer hinges on two related questions:

Economic: Is a global economy emerging, and is it subsuming national economies?
Political: Is globalization eroding democracy? How autonomous is the nation-state?

These questions are interrelated: if a global economy is emerging, by definition the nation-state is losing its autonomy to determine the course and pace of change. If the nation-state is losing its autonomy, then the democratically determined process that vests it with control of the economic sphere is undermined. A summary of the economic and political positions of the skeptics and globalists appears in Table 3.3.

Skeptics: Economics

Note from Table 3.3 that, according to the skeptics, there has been little change regarding the basic political and economic relationships. Skeptics base their conclusions on a comparison with the 1870–1913 period, the so-called **belle époque** of globalization or the most recent era of rapid global integration. In terms of the openness and the magnitude and geographical scale of the flows of trade and capital, the international economy is not as globalized today as it was toward the end of the gold standard in 1913 (Thompson 1996, 123; Hirst and Thompson 1999, Chapter 2; Held and McGrew 2000, 19–23). Flows of

Table 3.3   Economic and Political Processes

	ECONOMIC	POLITICAL	POWER
Globalists			
Neoliberals	Fully developed borderless global economy. National economies are redundant, and all economic actors are driven by the need to be globally competitive.	Dissolved national borders. Nation-state in the process of disappearing.	Posthegemonic order with growing integration between major world centers: United States, Europe, Japan. Diffusion of power is mainly upward toward transnational economic actors.
Social democrats	Intense interdependent, integrated, and restructured global informational economy. New global division of labor: industrialization of the "Third World."	Erosion of state sovereignty, autonomy, and legitimacy. National policy making is constrained, welfare state in decline. Hollowed-out state (democratic) institutions. Emergence of a democratic deficit.	Diffusion of power upward (to transnational capital), outward (privatization), downward (transnational groups in civil society). Emergence of global civil society and multilayered institutional structure of global governance.
Skeptics			
Marxists	New imperialism and continuation of the old division of labor between core (First World) and periphery (Third World).	Capitalist system with politics driven by class struggles at the national and international levels.	Class system dominated by global capitalists allied with local capitalists.
Realists	Separate national economies exist but with a trend toward regional blocs.	International relations between nation-states. Continuation of unitary nation-states protecting the interests of citizens. National-level policies determined by citizens.	Continuance of a hegemonic world order based on a hierarchy of nation-states. The politically, economically, and militarily most powerful state enforces order throughout the system.

investment capital continue to be concentrated within the advanced capitalist states, meaning the persistence of the old core–periphery inequalities (and international division of labor). Moreover, the popular portrayal of capital as "footloose" is false. The world's major corporations remain confined to the major world powers, with their fate heavily determined by local and national laws and conditions. This reflects the persistence of a hegemonic world order where the most powerful national governments govern and enforce order in the world economy since they alone wield sufficient power to control and regulate economic activity (Held and McGrew 2002). While there may be an intensification of internationalization for realists or a deepening of imperialism for Marxists, national economies remain viable and nation-states control national, regional, and international economic and financial activity.

Globalists: Economics

Conversely, globalists insist that global market conditions and forces have dramatically altered the autonomy of nation-states and national economies. They point out that in comparison with the 1870–1913 period the daily turnover of the world's foreign exchange markets exceeds some 60 times the annual level of world exports (Held and McGrew 2000, 23). Daily foreign exchange transactions now amount to $1.2 trillion per day—some 65 times more than the value of international trade, a staggering amount of money shifted around the globe at the click of a button (Williamson 2002). Financial integration has produced a convergence in interest rates among the major economies, and global integration means local crises spread rapidly: witness the Mexican peso crisis of the early 1990s and the Asian crash in the late 1990s (Held and McGrew 2000, 23–24). Changes in the past 25 years mean that outsourcing and capital mobility have significantly reduced the ability of the democratic state to control capital movements. Moreover, any policy initiative that might affect the rate of return on investment—interest rate policy, taxation, social and ecological regulation—has to be considered carefully in light of the risk of capital flight or reduced inward investment (Koenig-Archibugi 2003, 4).

Globalists conclude that we live in a posthegemonic order of diffused power. States may still be the "gatekeepers" to the territory over which other states recognize their authority, but "if no foreign firms want to go through their gate," there is little chance of keeping up with more welcoming governments for world shares of investment (Strange 1997, 368). The result is to increase the leverage of corporations, enabling them to effectively subordinate the national economy to global exigencies.

Local Politics: The Democratic Deficit

So what does all this mean politically? Is globalization eroding democracy? What are the national/local effects on political participation and ultimately on democracy? Are global processes reducing the ability of citizens to influence public policy? Not all scholars see globalization as a challenge to democracy.

Skeptics: Politics

For skeptics, the process of change is being driven by choices made at the level of the nation-state. Although they admit there may be a loss of control, they claim that "bargains" are still struck between governments and electorates and policies are still articulated at the national level. For instance, political leaders of individual OECD states decided to pursue Keynesian policies in the 1950s to the 1970s, and the same states engineered the transition to neoliberalism in the 1980s and 1990s.

Realists argue that governments retain the legitimate right to rule in the international system. States are not passive victims of "global" changes; rather, they are the primary architects of the present world system. The national-level political system determines policies, and governments enforce them as a means to maximize state power within the international system. Marxists also see the state as central to the creation of the present system, although the goal is to further the interest of the capitalist class. In fact, the policies of privatization and deregulation have been pursued in the interest of big business, meaning that the state remains a primary site of struggle over political policies. Thus, both the realists and the Marxists understand the state as a principal actor in setting policy and furthering "globalization." In the capitalist's quest for international "competitiveness" (Marxists) or in the state's quest for power (realists), production costs, social conflict, and disorder must be kept at a minimum. A principal point of contention between the two positions is that Marxists believe democracy in capitalist societies is a privilege of the rich.

Globalists: Politics

Globalists respond that the nation-state is less and less a unitary autonomous actor; rather, it is one fragmented and permeated by transnational networks. As proof, the globalists point to the growth of global and regional institutions (e.g., WTO, NAFTA, **nongovernmental organizations**) that have decreased the state's autonomy and ability to control the movement of goods, services, and money. For instance, the number of international nongovernmental organizations (INGOs) increased from under 20 in the 1940s to over 120 by the 1970s (cited in Boli and Thomas 1997, 176) to nearly 5,500 in the mid-1990s (Held and McGrew 2000, 11). Another example of the erosion of state power is the proliferation of offshore banks and corporate subsidiaries. Locating the headquarters of a firm offshore or using offshore banking facilities allows corporations (and individuals) to hide their assets, which in turn creates strong tax competition in the private sector of the world's major economies. A way to entice big business (and individuals) to stay "onshore" is to reduce the tax rates for corporations and high-income individuals.

Globalists see these developments as evidence of the growing inability of national and state/provincial governments to control global economic and political forces. In both views, transnational forces are eroding the sovereignty, autonomy, and legitimacy of the nation-state and diminishing the state's role as a central entity in people's lives. Neoliberals dismiss this issue based on their belief that globalization *spreads* democratic cultural values to nondemocratic societies (note here the argument that political freedom is predicated upon economic freedom). In fact, they argue that globalization has been responsible for the "third wave" of democracy that has recently swept across the globe. Social democrats counter that privatization and deregulation reduce local democratic control, shifting power *upward* to transnational economic actors and *outward* to private actors as public services—water, education, health care, fire protection—are outsourced to private capital.

A second difference between neoliberals and social democrats is the role of agents in the globalization process. Neoliberals think of globalization as an inevitable process with many players and no dominant actor(s), a process in which states react to pressure in much the same way as billiard balls. The social democrats place more emphasis on the constructed nature of these processes and on the central importance of political policies. On this point, the social democrats and the Marxists agree; both perspectives understand globalization as being driven by the world's most powerful economic and political actors, where the most powerful global actors write the rules of the game to further their (geo)political and economic interests with little or no regard for local interests. They disagree, however, over whether the system can be reformed (Marxists, no; social democrats, yes) and over terminology— the *Washington Consensus*, a *global elite*, or a *global class* (see Gailbraith 1999, Naím 2000, Robinson and Harris 2000, Faux 2001, Tabb 2001, Stiglitz 2002, Vilas 2002).

Cultural Patterns

The debate over the relationship between globalization and culture is no less contentious than the economic or political discussions. Culture is in many respects the most direct, obvious, and visible way in which we experience the changing interconnections in our daily lives. Culture provides not only a "blueprint" to guide us in our daily lives but the means by which we can understand the world around us. Until the eighteenth century and the emergence of the modern nation-state and nationalist movements, however, most people lived out their lives in a network of highly localized or community-level cultures (Held and McGrew 2002, 25). Today, the signs of global culture are everywhere, reflected in the worldwide proliferation of consumer brands, such as Nike, Coca-Cola, and CNN.

So what does globalization mean for national cultures? Does it mean that people are no longer living out their lives within their own national cultures? Conclusions differ widely. From the neoliberal perspective, globalization is bringing the era of national cultures to an end. In a similar fashion, Marxists argue that globalization represents the homogenization of the world under the auspices of the United States or of Western culture and consumerism. Conversely, social democrats suggest that a global hybrid culture is emerging through an intense mixing of local cultures. In contrast to all three, realists insist that "global culture" is too thin and artificial to supplant national cultures (see Mann 1986, Anderson 1991, Huntington 1996, Featherstone 1995, Waters 1995, Barber 1996, Rothkoph 1997, Cowen 2002).

You may have noticed that these questions do not neatly fall into our basic skeptic/globalist categories. There is overlap between the Marxists and the globalists, for instance. Both see globalization as undermining local cultures, though for neoliberal globalists this is a positive development. Neoliberals theorize not only that globalization spreads democratic values but also that increasing cultural homogeneity translates into fewer global cultural (ethnic) clashes in the future (sort of a global melting pot). In contrast, Marxists understand cultural globalization as a process of imperialism that is reducing everyone to mere consumers of corporate mass-produced products and materialist values and ideas. Social democrats propose a more nuanced view, arguing that globalization will supplement, rather than displace, national culture, thereby producing a global hybrid culture. Only the realists clearly emphasize the tenacity and continued viability of local cultures. We lay out these basic positions in Table 3.4.

Skeptics: Culture

In general, skeptics understand cultural forms and institutions as deeply rooted in national (local) myths, memories, values, and symbols that are inexplicable at the global level. Skeptics work on the supposition that nations are based on a national culture that was built on the history and culture of communities within a particular territory. These local "ways of life" provided a *common* basis for codifying a national identity that later became essential to the forging of nation-states. Over generations, these identities served to *differentiate* one nation-state from another. Although the media is making us more aware of the diversity of lifestyles and values throughout the world, the media remains nationally regulated and nationally produced and, thus, reinforces the national identity (see Smith 2003). If anything, the growing awareness of cultures born of global communication networks may sharpen differences among cultures rather than nurture understanding.

Skeptics do not dismiss the globalists' argument that cultural patterns are historical products of international interaction. For Marxists, however, the fundamental issue is power. The distribution of global power is highly unequal and makes its presence felt in the intersection of cultures. As a result, cultural interchanges have never been equal. Rather, these interchanges evolve in ways consistent with the interests of the more powerful actor, in this case the United States and other Western societies. These interactions alter global tastes in ways that increase the demand for Western-style foods and consumer products.

Realists respond that even though many products and ideas that flood across borders originate in the United States and other Western societies, local cultures remain robust. Television and radio broadcasts retain strong national roots, and local cultural understandings continue to affect how

Table 3.4   Culture and Cultural Processes

	NATURE OF CULTURE	IDENTITY	PROCESSES
Globalists			
Neoliberals	Trend toward a homogeneous global culture and the decline of national culture. Globalization of culture will spread democratic values and create stability and community.	Decline of national political and cultural identities. Homogeneous cultural identities based on Western language and cultural attributes.	Technologically driven process; rapid and intense volume of global cultural communication.
Social democrats	Global culture supplements, but does not supplant, national- and subnational-level culture. Emergence of global pluralism.	Emergence of new global identities based on the subjective realization that all people share a common (global) fate. Global identity coexists with national- and subnational-level identities. Emerging notion of global citizenship.	Cultural borrowing and hybridization of different cultures, though increasingly shaped by global corporations. Growth of a transnational civil society.
Skeptics			
Marxists	Cultural imperialism. "Globalization" of Western values and consumer culture.	Identity of the world's population is increasingly compelled toward Western language and culture.[a]	Profit-driven process dominance of Western (mainly U.S.) capitalists. Imbalanced and unequal cultural flows.
Realists	Persistence of a national culture and identity.	Members of society continue to share a common political and cultural identity tied to the nation. Citizenship rights guaranteed and enforced by the state.	Resurgence of nationalism and inevitable clash of different cultural civilizations.

[a] Notice the similarities with neoliberalism. Both see the globalization of culture as leading to cultural homogeneity, but the Marxists see this as a negative outcome driven by the profit motives of global capitalists, while the neoliberals see this as positive, contributing to the restoration of community.

national audiences read and interpret foreign cultural products (Held and McGrew 2002, 30). Even McDonald's is "reinvented" when introduced into a different cultural context.

In the end, skeptics argue that there is no global cultural process comparable to the national one. There is no common global pool of memories, no common global way of thinking, and no common or universal global history upon which to create a global culture capable of uniting people. In other words, there is no *global* basis on which to create a *global identity* that could mirror *national identities*.

Globalists: Culture

Globalists do not dismiss the significance of nationalism or national-level culture. What the skeptics ignore, the globalists argue, is the constructed nature of culture. Local culture is a product of a multitude of interactions over thousands of years. With globalization accelerating the movement of images, ideas, data, and people across regions and intercontinental space, people are increasingly exposed to the ideas and values of other cultures. There may be inequities in these exchanges, as the Marxists insist, but that does not mean these processes are not happening; in fact, global communication networks are intensifying cross-cultural borrowing.

For globalists, a key to an emerging global culture is the information infrastructure. Global communications are severing the traditional links between the "physical setting" and "social situation." In other words, geographical boundaries are overcome and individuals and groups increasingly "experience events and developments far afield" (Held and McGrew 2002, 36). Moreover, globally sourced news and information intensifies our *subjective* awareness and understanding of world events. As we become more aware of global issues and global problems, we become conscious of how we are intimately connected to something larger than our immediate communities or even to the nation-state.

Central to the emergence of a global culture is a growing subjective awareness that is linked to the way in which globalization is creating a "risk society," a world in which biological and ecological risks are no longer confined to local areas but "endanger all forms of life on this planet" (Beck 1992, 22). With the spread of television, radio, and print media, we begin to understand that such problems as nuclear accidents, acid rain, and the destruction of the rain forests, severe acute respiratory syndrome (SARS), mad cow disease, and violations of human rights are not localized.

As we interact globally, sharing new understandings, commonalities, and frames of reference, local and national identities are transformed into a more complex global hybrid form. Thus, just as a national culture—nationalism— was essential to the building of the nation-state and the nation-state was essential to the operation of an international system, globalists argue that a process is under way which may create a global history and a transnational civil society critical to a global system.

Globalization and Inequality

As we suggested in the Chapter 1, one of the most heavily debated issues in the globalization literature is the effect of globalization on inequality. Three major points frame the discussion of inequality. First, there is little disagreement that patterns of wealth and income distribution are associated with the location and distribution of productive capabilities; what causes the distribution of these capabilities, however, is hotly disputed. A second point is the measurement of inequality that in most studies centers on the distribution of wealth and income, typically changes in gross domestic product (GDP) per capita over time. Social variables, such as education and health, are often ignored (notable exceptions include the United Nations Development Program's Human Development Index, or HDI). The scale of human tragedy caused by material inequalities (as well as social—i.e., health, education) is a third factor in the debate. These issues create a more complex overlapping dialogue among the four perspectives.

For the neoliberal globalists, inequality has been declining as a direct result of the free-market (neoliberal) strategy that has guided the process of globalization. Inequality and poverty still exist but can be solved by accelerating economic growth, which is itself a product of increased transnational investment, of the opening up of markets, and of increasing global integration (Ohmae 1990). Social democrats respond that inequality has actually increased due to the same free-market strategy, but since globalization cannot be reversed, new global institutions need to be created (and existing ones reformed—e.g., the United Nations) that are capable of altering the globalization process (Bradshaw and Wallace 1996, Castells 1997, Held 1997, Giddens 1999).

Skeptics agree with the social democrats that inequality is problematic, though they differ on why it exists or how to solve it. For realists, international inequality is inevitable in a world of competing nation-states with different resource endowments. At the same time, international inequality creates the basis for stability in the anarchical international system by "allowing" the most powerful states to enforce the rules of order on the system as a whole (Gilpin 1981, Krasner 1985). For the realists, inequality can be improved only by political policies at the *level of society*. The Marxists agree that inequality is generated as part of the system, though it is integral to the *capitalist* system (Burbach, Nunez, and Kagarlitsky 1997; Vilas 2002). Reducing inequality for the Marxists requires a new socioeconomic system.

Thus, in three of the four positions, local (within nation-states) inequality is a problem connected in some way to globalization and, among these three, only realists reject the idea that globalization exacerbates (between nation-states) inequality. Table 3.5 summarizes these basic positions.

Globalization as Beneficial

For neoliberal globalists, globalization is a harbinger of modernization and development (Ohmae 1990). Globalization diffuses the requisite wealth, affluence, and political values central to economic growth, democracy, and a more stable world order. As a result of globalization, global poverty has fallen more in the last 50 years than in the past 500, which has significantly improved the lives of people in almost all regions of the world (Held and McGrew 2000, 28). Moreover, the global spread of democratic values and

Table 3.5   Globalization and Inequality

	INEQUALITY AND POVERTY	LOCATION/SOURCE	SOLUTION
Globalists			
Neoliberals	Declining	Global system	Accelerate globalization
Social democrats	Increasing: central issue	Global system	Creation of a global social-welfare system
Skeptics			
Marxists	Increasing	Capitalist system and imperialism	New sociopolitical system
Realists	Increasing at the national level but inevitable at the international level	A function of national resource base and geopolitics	Increase the nation's economic, political, and military power; create national-level programs

free-market policies underlies the "third wave" of democracy that has swept across the globe. According to Razeen Sally of the London School of Economics, globalization is growth-promoting: "Growth, in turn, reduces poverty . . . [and] the liberalisation of international transactions is good for freedom and prosperity. The anti-liberal critique is wrong"; poverty and marginalization are in large part caused by not enough, rather than too much, globalization (see Porter n.d.). In general, the current wave of globalization, which started around 1980, has actually promoted economic equality and reduced poverty (Dollar and Kraay 2002). We see this specifically in South and East Asia, where increasing participation in the global economy has encouraged foreign investment, stimulated growth, raised income, and reduced inequality.

Globalization as Harmful

For the social democrat globalists and Marxist skeptics, economic globalization is directly responsible for an increasingly polarized world. Beyond this basic agreement, the two positions diverge. The globalization myth, Marxists argue, has been used to *reinforce* the global divide between the wealthy core societies and the poor peripheral societies. Social democrats warn that the *vertical* core–peripheral structure of stratification is transforming into a *horizontal* one. For these scholars, globalization is intensifying inequality *across* national political boundaries. Thus, levels of poverty and marginalization once confined to South Asia or Central America are increasingly present in the United States and Western Europe, while the prosperity once associated with the United States and Western Europe is growing in South Asia and Central America.

To solve the problem of increasing inequality, social democrats propose a new set of global rules, a global "new deal" which would reform the system and ensure a minimum standard of living. The new deal would rely on multilateral cooperation and coordination through a new set of global institutions to regulate the forces of economic globalization and ensure that markets work for people—not the other way around (Faux 2001, Derber 2002, Stiglitz 2002, Held 2004). Demand for a global new deal, according to the social democrats, is growing within an emerging transnational civil society, which includes labor organizations, environmental and gender-based groups, and progressive elites, among other social movements.

Realists and Marxists respond that such a new deal is utopian. Marxists point out that it is naive to believe that those benefiting from the system will consent to its reform (see Burbach, Nunez, and Kagarlitsky 1997). It is impossible to create a system of global governance that would solve the problem of inequality because the present system is *already* governed by the global wealthy and powerful. Marxists instead propose seizing state power in a number of societies and, through an international alliance among these societies, working at altering the process of "globalization." Thus, in contrast to the social democrats, Marxists consider the state the fundamental building block of the new order, as well as the object of the struggle and the ultimate source of change (Callinicos 1994; Burbach, Nunez, and Kagarlitsky 1997).

Globalization as Insignificant

For the realists, the recent collapse of state socialism suggests that the Marxist solution is equally a fantasy. Realists insist that inequality is a function of national factors—from resource endowments to economic policies—that determine the patterns of inequity (Gilpin 1987). The realists add a twist to the Marxist position by arguing that inequality is not only inherent in the international system but *necessary* to create international stability. Societies are ranked in terms of national-level economic, political, and military power. This inequality is the basis for international order as the most powerful nations enforce order throughout the system. Any attempt to resolve international inequality will destabilize the entire system.

Can inequality be solved for realists? Yes, but only at the national level. Recall that realists believe that the nation-state retains autonomy in the international system and can pursue its own political policies. Thus, states must take seriously policy alternatives as a means to alter the way in which society is inserted into the international system. As David Dollar and Aart Kraay (2002) argue, in cases where inequality has increased, shifts in inequality "stem more from domestic education, taxes, and social policies" than globalization. In general, higher growth rates in globalizing developing countries have translated into higher incomes for the poor. The cases of South Korea and Taiwan are illustrative: both were able to improve the problems of poverty and inequality through policy initiatives that essentially "renegotiated" their relationship with the global (international) system. Therefore, states (governments) matter and, unlike for the social democrats, the solution to inequality and poverty exists at the national level.

Conclusion

We began this chapter by pointing out that these four positions agree that the world was changing more rapidly and dramatically at the start of the twenty-first century than ever before. We can see these changes manifested in the emergence of new inequalities and growing economic interconnectedness reflected in new regional alliances (NAFTA and the European Union) as well as cultural changes. However, do these changes constitute "globalization"?

As you think through this question, you should keep these points in mind. First, despite occasional overlap between the skeptic and globalist positions, skeptical Marxists and realists reject globalization as a fruitful concept, while globalist social democrats and neoliberals believe it reflects fundamental economic, political, and cultural changes. Second, as Held and McGrew (2000) point out, we cannot reduce any position to rhetoric and/or ideology. All four positions illuminate important issues, situate the processes within the historical context, and identify important present trends. Third, the issues that drive this debate are fundamentally about how to create a more just, humane, democratic, and stable world. Because these issues are important, complex, and difficult, the literature on globalization is equally complex.

At this point, you may be thinking: OK, I understand the basic arguments of these positions, but what does all this have to do with reality? After all, we do not live in a theoretical, ideal-type construct but in the real world, where real people live with real problems. This is the basic question of assessment, or how will we know globalization when we see it. We take up this issue in the next chapter.

CHAPTER 4

The Globalization Debate

An Assessment

What is "global" about globalization? —skeptics
Power no longer resides in the locales in which it is immediately experienced. —globalists

As we discussed in the last chapter, the globalization debate poses fundamental questions regarding human justice, democracy, and the direction of future change. The above claims illustrate the basic positions in the debate. For skeptics, the concept reifies and mystifies a process that continues to be determined by struggles between classes or between nation-states; for globalists, existing concepts fail to capture the deep structural changes that are under way. In this chapter, we offer a more detailed examination of the issues raised in the globalization literature by exploring the nature of economic, political, and cultural change. Our intent is twofold: to present a more systematic means by which to judge the usefulness of globalization as a concept and to provide a context for our subsequent discussion of globalization, power, and inequality in the United States.

Globalization and Economic Change

In the last chapter, we noted that the debate over globalization and economics raises the issue of whether a global economy that subordinates national economies is emerging. To answer this question, we look at changes in global trade, the global division of labor, subcontracting and outsourcing, **foreign direct investment** (FDI), and the growth of transnational corporations (TNCs).

Foreign Trade

Weighing in on the comparison between globalization processes during the 1870–1913 (belle époque) period and today, a recent International Labour

Organization (ILO) study shows that, in contrast to the present period, trade liberalization and openness *did not* play a major role in promoting global integration between 1870 and 1913 (Ghose 2003, Chapter 2). Tariff rates, for instance, were reduced in some countries (mainly Europe) from 1860 to 1880 but remained high in others (the United States), and after "1880, tariff rates were growing in virtually all the countries concerned" (Ghose 2003, 16; see also Held et al. 1999, 158, Table 3.2; Perraton et al. 2000). Ghose concludes that, particularly during the 1880–1913 period, trade (and FDI, or investment in factories and land by foreign investors) grew *despite* declining openness, *not* because of increasing openness. The dramatically lowered cost and ease of transport were driving forces behind these changes.

These conclusions are generally consistent with the globalist position. Increasing openness is a characteristic that differentiates the present period from the belle époque. Also, advances in transportation have been integral to the long-term globalization process. Let's look closer at these changes. Using 1990 as a benchmark, Girvan (1999) shows that shipping costs have fallen by more than two-thirds since 1920, airline transportation costs have fallen by more than 60 percent since 1960, and the cost of an international telephone call has fallen by 90 percent since 1970.[1] Combined with the use of communication satellites, fiber optics, and the Internet, these changes are creating the possibility for rapid and inexpensive movement of goods, services, and information and a global economy that is increasingly capable of operating in real time (Castells 2000).

The efforts of the Bretton Woods Trio to liberalize global relations have further contributed to a more open and integrated global system. For instance, average worldwide tariffs as a percentage of total trade value dropped from 40 percent in 1947 to 5 percent in 1990 (Gabel and Bruner 2003, General Agreement on Trade and Tariffs 14) and GATT-based negotiations have significantly lowered overall barriers to trade in services since 1950 (Gwynne, Klak, and Shaw 2003, 113). The data in Figure 4.1, showing the relationship between trade and production, suggest that since the 1950s global trade grew faster than global economic production; the pattern, which accelerated after 1990, indicates a more open and globalized world economy.

Still, this tells us little. As you may recall, globalists argue that as the developing or Third World has become industrialized, there has been a shift in the global division of labor.[2] If this is the case, we should find evidence for an increase in trade of manufactures *from* these countries. Let's begin with the general world trends in trade since 1960. Data in Table 4.1 show that the developing world's share of merchandise and service trade has grown since 1990—with the greatest change in merchandise trade—while the developed countries saw their share of world merchandise and service exports decline.[3] If we look at merchandise trade, we see in Table 4.2 and Figure 4.2 that the most significant change since 1980 has been in the trade of manufactures. According to Table 4.2, trade in manufactures increased sharply, while trade in services rose initially and remained roughly at 19 percent of total world

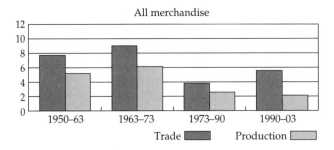

Figure 4.1 World merchandise trade and economic output: 1950–2001. Average annual percentage change. *Source*: WTO (2005, Chart II.1).

Table 4.1   Share of Merchandise and Service Exports

REGIONS	WORLD EXPORTS IN MILLION US$ AND SHARES IN PERCENTAGE BY COUNTRY GROUP					
	1960	1970	1980	1990	2000	2002
Merchandise						
World	130,135	316,428	2,031,219	3,500,278	6,426,893	6,414,058
Developing countries	24.7	19.2	29.4	24.1	32.0	31.7
Central/East European countries	10.6	10.1	8.0	5.0	4.2	4.9
Developed countries	64.7	70.7	62.6	70.8	63.8	63.5
Services						
World	—	—	385,352	824,724	1,511,935	1,610,608
Developing countries	—	—	17.9	18.1	23.1	22.6
Central/East European countries	—	—	—	—	3.6	4.2
Developed countries	—	—	79.1	79.7	73.2	73.2

Source: UNCTAD (2005).

Table 4.2   Structure of World Trade (Percentage Share)

YEAR	SERVICES	MERCHANDISE	MANUFACTURES	NONPETROLEUM PRIMARY PRODUCTS	PETROLEUM PRODUCTS
1980	11.0	89.0	49.7	23.8	15.5
1985	21.8	78.2	50.8	15.7	11.7
1991	21.4	78.6	58.7	12.9	7.0
1998	19.9	80.1	64.2	11.5	4.4
2003	18.6	81.4	63.0	12.7	5.7

Sources: Ghose (2003); data for 2003 are from World Bank (2005).

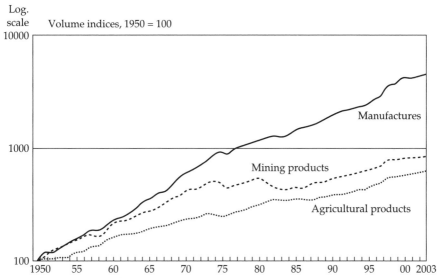

Figure 4.2 World merchandise trade by major product group: 1950–2003.
Source: WTO (2005, Chart II.2).

trade. The trade of primary agricultural products declined over the entire period—until the last few years (see also Ghose 2003, 9). By 2003, trade in manufactures accounted for nearly two-thirds of total trade in goods and services, up from one-half in 1980. Data in Figure 4.2 further show the growing importance of manufactures in world merchandise trade. Since 1950, there has been an almost continuous upward trend in the trade of manufactures and a growing gap between trade in manufactures and trade in agricultural and mining products. We should note that the current composition of trade contrasts with that of the belle époque when trade in primary products (e.g., agricultural and mining products) dominated international trade (see Ghose 2003, 16–17).

Yet, we still do not know the effects on the developing or developed countries. In other words, do the data reflect a process of deindustrialization in industrialized countries, as labor is transferred from the manufacturing to the service sector, while developing countries become industrialized, as the globalists contend? If the developing world is industrializing, we should find evidence of an increasing share of world manufacturing exports originating in these countries.

Data in Table 4.3 show that between 1980 and the late 1990s the developing world's share of world manufactured exports more than doubled from 12.0 to 26 percent, while the developed/industrialized world's share declined from 83 to 71 percent. According to the data, the share of manufactured exports in total merchandise exports increased for all countries, reflecting the general rise in the importance of manufactures in world trade, but the increase

Table 4.3   Manufactured exports: 1980–1982, 1996–1998, and 2004

	% SHARE IN WORLD MANUFACTURED EXPORTS		MANUFACTURED EXPORTS AS % OF MERCHANDISE EXPORTS		
	1980–1982	1996–1998	1980–1982	1996–1998	2003
Industrialized countries	83.3	71.2	71.6	79.9	79.0
Developing countries (Third World)	12.0	25.9	22.4	65.8	73.0
European transition countries	4.7	2.9	45.9	53.2	58.0

Sources: Ghose (2003);[4] data for 2003 from UNDP (2005).

was dramatic *only* in the case of developing countries (see also Perraton et al. 2000, 290–291). *Overall*, the percentage of manufactured exports from developing to industrialized countries continues to increase (see World Bank 2005), as reflected in the growing importance of manufactures in merchandise trade in developing countries (Table 4.3). This conclusion is supported by evidence from the United Nation's Conference on Trade and Development (UNCTAD) showing that the developing world's share of world manufacturing value increased from 14.4 to 23.7 percent during the 1990–2001 period, while the developed world's share declined from 76.7 to 73.6 percent (UNCTAD 2005).

We should note, however, that this is not a universal process, as the skeptics contend. For instance, in Taiwan, South Korea, Hong Kong, China, Singapore, and Mexico trade in manufactures accounts for 80 to over 90 percent of total trade, while for Indonesia, Argentina, Chile, and Brazil the figure ranges from 16 to 52 percent (World Bank 2000, 268–269; 2005). Moreover, for Taiwan, South Korea, Hong Kong, China, Singapore, and Mexico exports grew at an average annual rate of 13.2 percent between 1980 and 2002 (World Bank 2005). Specifically for China, this reflects a dramatic shift away from low-technology exports to high-technology exports since 1985. In Latin America, however, if we exclude Mexico and Brazil, primary exports constituted more than 80 percent of the region's total exports in 1998 (Gwynne, Klak, and Shaw 2003, 117).

Finally, Africa remains marginal to the shifting global division of labor, with only noticeable changes in northern and southern Africa and, to a lesser degree, western Africa. Manufactures as a percentage of total merchandise trade (data are for 2003) is significant only in Morocco (69 percent) and South Africa (58 percent)—the next largest exporter was Egypt, with manufactures constituting 30 percent of total exports—(World Bank 2005; also 2000, 268–269). Still, with the exception of South Africa, the total value of export manufactures in these countries remains small (World Bank 2005).[5]

Data on employment further support the globalist perspective of a changing global division of labor (see Ghose 2003, 17–19). In countries such as Taiwan, South Korea, China, and Mexico, employment in the manufacturing sector increased from 35.8 percent of total employment in 1980 to 53.0 percent in 1997. In industrialized countries, the percentage employed in manufacturing declined from 37.0 to 31.0 percent, while among other developing countries the percentage employed in manufacturing increased from 1.3 and 1.6 percent (Ghose 2003, 18). (Country categories are explained in note 4.)

Foreign Direct Investment, Global Capital, and Outsourcing

So far, the data suggest a transformation of the developing world within a changing global context, as the globalists would expect. The liberalization of capital flows due to the spread of the neoliberal ideology and the influence of TNCs, the International Monetary Fund (IMF), and World Bank policies have all contributed to these trends. FDI, for instance, increased rapidly after 1990: between 1992 and 1998, FDI tripled in East Asia and the Pacific region and quadrupled in Latin America and the Caribbean (World Bank 1991, 57; also Gwynne, Klak, and Shaw 2003, 120). FDI also increased in sub-Saharan Africa and the Middle East, though starting from a much lower base (World Bank 1991, 57; also Gwynne, Klak, and Shaw 2003, 120). By the beginning of the twenty-first century, China had become the most attractive destination of FDI in the world and India ranked third.

If we combine data on trade and FDI (see Table 4.4), we can draw several conclusions about the nature of the global economic change. First, in keeping with the skeptics' analysis, industrialized countries continue to account for a large proportion of both FDI inflow and total world merchandise trade— 62 percent in the 1996–1998 period, though a decline from 68 percent in the 1980–1982 period. Also in keeping with the position of the skeptics, industrialization has been limited to a small number of developing countries or regional economic zones.[6] Other developing countries continue to be marginalized by the process, specifically those in Africa and the Andean region of South America (see World Bank 2000, 268–269). Nonetheless, trends showing that developing countries have not only increased their share of FDI and of total

Table 4.4   Trade and FDI Flows: 1980 and 1998

	% SHARE IN GLOBAL FDI FLOWS		% SHARE IN GLOBAL MERCHANDISE TRADE	
	1980–1982	1996–1998	1980–1982	1996–1998
Industrialized countries	68.0	62.2	66.5	66.9
Manufactures exporters	19.5	25.8	13.7	23.3
Petroleum exporters	7.9	2.0	10.6	3.0
Other developing countries	4.6	5.8	4.0	2.8
European transition countries	0.0	4.2	5.2	4.2

Source: Ghose (2003).

global merchandise trade but also become important sources of FDI over time support the claims of the globalists. This FDI, according to Gwynne, Klak, and Shaw (2003, 151), is concentrated in manufacturing (secondly services), while investment in primary sectors declined significantly after the 1980s; by comparison, the bulk of FDI during the belle époque went into primary products (Ghose 2003, 16–17). These data suggest a more inclusive process of change and a shifting international division of labor away from the developing world's specialization in the production and export of primary products, which is consistent with the argument put forth by the globalists.

Finally, the data in Table 4.4 show that the developing world's share (the manufactures exporters) of merchandise trade grew more rapidly than its share of FDI. This suggests an important difference between the present process of globalization and globalization during the belle époque. If we narrowly focus on aggregate FDI as an indicator of globalization, we may overlook important changes. In comparison with the belle époque, the conditions we discussed in the previous chapter allow corporations to reduce their role as direct producers and specialize in the marketing of their products. Companies can now participate in what are being called "emerging markets" (formerly labeled the "developing world" or the "Third World") and achieve comparative advantage by subcontracting or outsourcing the production of goods and services.[7] Outsourcing to foreign subcontractors, however, *is not* captured by FDI data. Therefore, if Levi Strauss and Company transforms itself into a marketing company by closing its factories in the United States and Europe and subcontracts that same production through foreign producers in Indonesia, FDI data will not capture these changes and will underestimate the level of globalization.

The trend of increased outsourcing is not limited to manufacturing. Increasingly, whole buildings slated for construction in the United States are produced in places like Mexico and Singapore and shipped in sections to the United States. More common, however, is the outsourcing of services in the financial, insurance, legal, medical, and information technology (IT) sectors. Even the U.S. film industry is part of this trend. In 2003, for instance, of the 88 U.S. films made for television, only five were made in the United States (Dobbs 2004a, 81).[8]

According to Richard Trumka, secretary-treasurer of the AFL-CIO, over 500,000 service sector jobs are outsourced annually (Dobbs 2004b). Call centers are one major area of outsourcing; the bulk of these jobs go to India. For years we wondered "what all those fiber-optic cables laid around the earth at massive expense in the late 1990s would ever be good for, we finally have an answer: They're good for enabling call-center workers in Bangalore or Delhi to sound as if they're next door to everyone. Broadband's killer app, it turns out, is India"[9] (Fox 2003). Why? Indian knowledge workers who get those jobs are paid 80 to 90 percent *less* than similar workers in the United States.

Outsourcing is not only about call centers however.[10] India is also the world's leading producer of software engineers (Sernau 2001, 53). These workers typically earn one-sixth to one-eighth the wage of their counterparts in the United States or United Kingdom (Gwynne, Klak, and Shaw 2003, 177). In Bangalore, some 110,000 people are employed writing software, designing chips, running computer systems, processing mortgages, preparing tax forms, and doing other essential work for U.S., European, Japanese, and even Chinese companies. Outsourcing of professional service jobs involves a virtual Who's Who of major U.S.-based companies; the list includes Apple, Dell, Hewlett-Packard, Intel, Cisco, Oracle, Phillips, IBM, and SAS. Accenture, AOL, and Ernst & Young also have a major presence in Bangalore, as does General Electric, which employs more than 15,000 people in Delhi and other Indian cities.

A score of other Western corporations outsource work to Indian companies to answer calls from credit card customers, do accounting work, manage computer networks, research and develop new pharmaceuticals, and examine medical information. For instance, Massachusetts General Hospital sends X-rays and magnetic resonance imaging scans to India for examination. Some U.S. firms go so far as to outsource *actual* healthcare by sending employees to India for operations (Yi 2006).

In the financial world, a staff of 350 in Chennai (formerly Madras) designs the PowerPoint presentations that McKinsey consultants around the world show their clients. Morgan Stanley has been hiring equity analysts in Mumbai (formerly Bombay) to help cover U.S. companies from ten and a half time zones away. There are more than 350,000 people working in IT services and outsourcing in India now, and the number is expected to soon pass one million. While recent reports suggest that a few U.S. companies are moving some of their service operations back to the United States, the overall trend is toward more outsourcing of service jobs. A glimpse of this outsourcing process is provided in Table 4.5.

So what do all these data tell us about globalization and economic change? First, data on trade and FDI are supportive of the globalist position that a global economy is emerging and that national economies are increasingly subordinated to it. These data, however, do not support the neoliberal claims of a fully developed borderless global economy. Second, evidence regarding outsourcing supports the globalists' argument that the world economy is fundamentally different today in comparison with the belle époque or even in comparison to 30 years ago. Finally, data on trade, manufacturing, and growth are consistent with the globalists' position that the traditional global division of labor is changing. The scope of industrialization and outsourcing is limited, however, as the skeptics would argue, with most of Africa and sections of Latin America remaining marginal to the process.

Transnational Corporations

As we alluded to earlier, the central actors in the globalization process are the TNCs that outsource jobs, provide direct investment, and engage in global

Table 4.5 Outsourcing of Service Jobs to India

AREA	OUTSOURCING AND IT WORKERS	FOCUS	WHO'S THERE
Delhi	73,000	Call centers, transaction processing, chip design, software	GE, American Express, STMicroelectronics, Wipro, Spectramind, Convergys, Daksh
Kolkata (Calcutta)	7,300	Consulting, software	PwC, IBM, ITC, Infotech, TCS
Pune	7,300	Call centers, chip design, embedded software	Msource, C-Dac, Persistent Systems, Zensar
Hyderabad	36,500	Software, back office, product design	HSBC, Microsoft, Satyam
Bangalore	109,500	Chip design, software, bioinformatics, call centers, IT consulting, tax processing	Intel, IBM, SAP, SAS, Dell, Cisco, TI, Motorola, HP, Oracle, Yahoo, AOL, E&Y, Accenture, Wipro, Infosys, Msource
Chennai (Madras)	51,100	Software, transaction processing, animation	World Bank, Standard Chartered, Cognizant, Polaris, EDS, Pentamedia Graphics
Mumbai (Bombay)	62,050	Financial research, back office, software	Morgan Stanley, Citigroup, TCS, MphasiS, i-flex Solutions

Source: Fox (2003).

trade. TNCs are fundamental to the changing nature of the global economy and the shifting global division of labor. By definition, a TNC is any large company headquartered in one country with design, production, marketing, and service divisions in many other countries. three issues are important: these are extremely large corporations, their countries of origin are often obscure, and they underlie the shift in the spatial organization and dynamics of the global system.

Size

The growth and size of these organizations are exemplified in the following data. Today, there are over 65,000 firms with subsidiaries in other countries, up from about 7,000 in 1970 (Gabel and Bruner 2003, 31; ILO 2004, 33). Of the world's 100 largest economic entities, 54 are corporations (up from 51 in 2000) and 46 are countries (see Table 4.6). The world's largest corporation, ExxonMobil, ranked as the seventeenth largest economic entity in the world,

Table 4.6   Global Ranking of the Largest Economic Entities[a] (Companies in Bold)

RANK	COUNTRY/ CORPORATION[b]	GDP/SALES (BILLION US$)	RANK	COUNTRY/ CORPORATION	GDP/SALES (BILLION US$)
1	United States	10,984.5	38	Finland	161.9
2	Japan	4,300.9	39	South Africa	159.9
3	Germany	2,403.2	40	Ireland	153.7
4	United Kingdom	1,794.9	41	**General Electric**	**149.7**
5	France	1,757.6	42	Portugal	147.9
6	Italy	1,468.3	43	**Total Fina Elf**	**144.9**
7	China	1,417.0	44	Thailand	143.0
8	Canada	856.5	45	Iran, Islamic Rep.	137.1
9	Spain, Mexico	838.7	46	**ING Group**	**137.1**
10	Mexico	626.1	47	Argentina	129.6
11	Korea, Rep.	605.3	48	**Allianz**	**124.4**
12	India	600.6	49	**Mitsubishi Motors/ Industry**	**108.9**
13	Australia	522.4	50	**AXA**	**121.6**
14	Netherlands	511.5	51	**Citigroup**	**131.3**
15	Brazil	492.3	52	**Volkswagen**	**112.6**
16	Russian Federation	432.9	53	Israel	110.2
17	**ExxonMobil**[c]	**339.9**	54	**American Int'l Group**	**107.0**
18	Switzerland	320.1	55	Malaysia	103.7
19	**Wal-Mart**	**315.7**	56	**Nippon Telegraph**	**100.8**
20	Belgium	301.9	57	**Carrefour**	**98.6**
21	**Royal Dutch Shell**	**306.7**	58	Singapore	91.3
22	Sweden	301.6	59	**IBM**	**91.1**
23	**BP**	**285.1**	60	**Siemens**	**90.6**
24	Austria	253.1	61	Czech Republic	89.7
25	Turkey	240.4	62	**Generali**	**89.0**
26	Norway	220.9	63	**Hewlett-Packard**	**87.9**
27	Saudi Arabia	214.7	64	**McKesson**	**85.9**
28	Denmark	211.9	65	Venezuela	85.4
29	Poland	209.6	66	**Bank of America**	**85.4**
30	Indonesia	208.3	67	Hitachi	84.2
31	**General Motors**	**192.6**	68	**ENI**	**83.1**
32	**Chevron/Texaco**	**189.5**	69	Hungary	82.7
33	**Ford**	**177.2**	70	Egypt	82.4
34	**Daimler/Chrysler**	**177.0**	71	Pakistan	82.3
35	**Toyota Motor**	**173.1**	72	**Valero**	**82.2**
36	Greece	172.2			
37	**ConocoPhillips**	**162.4**			

Table 4.6 (*Continued*)

RANK	COUNTRY/ CORPORATION[b]	GDP/SALES (BILLION US$)	RANK	COUNTRY/ CORPORATION	GDP/SALES (BILLION US$)
73	Home Depot	81.5	88	HSBC	76.4
74	Fortis	81.5	89	Berkshire Hathaway	76.3
75	Matsushita Electric	81.3			
76	Crédit Agricole	81.1	90	Nestlé	76.1
77	Honda	80.7	91	Aviva	75.6
78	Philippines	80.6	92	Verizon	75.1
79	Nissan Motor	80.0	93	Chile	72.4
80	J. P. Morgan	79.9	94	AHOLD	70.6
81	New Zealand	79.6	95	IFIL	70.4
82	Samsung	79.2	96	Sinopec	70.3
83	Colombia	78.7	97	Altria Group	68.9
84	Deutsche Telekom	78.5	98	Credit Suisse	68.3
85	UBS	78.2	99	Sony	66.8
86	Cardinal Health	77.9	100	E.ON	66.7
87	Metro AG	76.5			

[a] Data are for 2003–2005.
[b] Does not include Taiwan, which by some estimates would rank between Russia and Switzerland.
[c] In 2005, ExxonMobil replaced Wal-Mart as the largest *and* most profitable company in the world.
Sources: *Fortune* (2006), *Forbes* (2005), UNDP (2005), World Bank (2006).

had a workforce of 83,700, sales of $328.2 billion, and profits of $36.1 billion in 2005. ExxonMobil, which replaced Wal-Mart as the world's largest corporation in 2005, was larger than the economies of *all but* 16 countries. In comparison, the world's largest company in 2004, Wal-Mart, had a workforce of 1.7 million, sales of $312.4 billion, and $11.2 billion in profits in 2005. By some accounts, TNCs account for over 70 percent of world trade (Steger 2003, 29) and a minimum of 20 percent of total world production (Perraton et al. 1997). In terms of sales, the top 200 firms (in 2000) were equivalent to 27.5 percent of *all* world economic activity, yet they employed *only* 0.78 percent of the world's workforce (Anderson and Cavanagh 2000).[11]

Obscurity

Despite being extremely large—or because of it—the country origins of TNCs are often hard to determine. A good example of this type of obscurity comes from one of the author's sisters-in-law. While living in Germany during the 1980s the sister-in-law had a disagreement with her German landlady over the country origin of Nestlé. The landlady insisted that Nestlé was a German company; the sister-in-law said that it was a U.S. company. Turns out they were both wrong: Nestlé is a Swiss company. (Ask your friends the country origin of Nestlé; chances are they will not know either.)

The Nestlé example illustrates an increasingly important issue in the global economy. Foreign companies often face risks that "local" companies do not and, thus, may encourage this kind of obscurity as a means to boost market shares or reduce security risks. If a company is perceived as "local," such campaigns as "buy American" or "compra Mexicana" will not negatively affect sales of what are actually TNCs (or become the target of nationalizing attempts or violent attacks). Would the now famous example of José Bové, the French farmer who destroyed a McDonald's construction site (see Morse 2002), have occurred if McDonald's had not clearly been a symbol of globalization?

A Global Transition?

What differentiates the present global phase from earlier ones, according to the globalists, is the shift in the spatial organization and dynamics of the global system. As Held and McGrew (2000, 25) summarize, in the present epoch "capital—both productive and financial—has been liberated from the national and territorial constraints, while markets have become globalized to the extent that the domestic economy constantly has to adapt to global competitive conditions." Transnational organizations are central to this "new" economy, and it is global capital, rather than nation-states, that exercise divisive influence over the organization, location, and distribution of economic power and resources in the present system (see Held and McGrew 2000, 23–27). For instance, TNCs are increasingly investing in, and exporting from, the newly industrializing countries (NICs) of East Asia and Latin America. Today, São Paulo is often referred to as "Germany's largest industrial city" (quoted in Held and McGrew 2000, 24). In fact, more than 60 percent of all manufactured imports to the industrialized world are coming from the developing world (UNDP 1998). Not surprisingly, the developing economies (e.g., Brazil, China, India) are currently driving the global economy. Aggregate gross domestic product (GDP) growth rates for the developing countries in 2005 were double those of the industrial economies (International Monetary Fund 2006, Petruno 2006).

Skeptics largely dismiss this argument, contending that the majority of the world's largest corporations remain headquartered in the United States, England, Germany, or Japan (see Burbach, Nunez, and Kagarlitsky 1997). In other words, the governments retain considerable control over TNCs by retaining control over access to national economic resources. To a degree, this is true; but as Susan Strange (1997) argues, control over national resources is not the same thing as control over a TNC. If a government places restrictions on foreign capital that are more severe than those of other governments—with similar resources—there is little chance of keeping up with the more welcoming governments for world shares of investment.

As the IMF, World Bank, and World Trade Organization (WTO) policies reduce trade and financial barriers through policies emphasizing privatization and deregulation, TNCs are made more mobile and can pull out of economies that do not offer conditions favorable to their interests. As a result, TNCs gain greater access to cheap labor and other resources in the developing world. Moreover, the leverage of TNCs—vis-à-vis national governments—is increased as governments in need of investment controlled by TNC will find it difficult to regulate economic activity and social conditions in ways that conflict with the interests of TNCs.

Finally, the organizational structure of TNCs has changed consistently with the globalist perspective. Many manufacturing transnationals have transformed themselves into **marketing companies**. Nike, for instance, subcontracts 100 percent of its goods production to 75,000 workers in China, South Korea, Malaysia, Taiwan, and Thailand (Steger 2003, 49). Recently, the CEO of Levi Strauss and Company closed six plants in the United States stating that Levi Strauss was becoming a "marketing company" with future production to be subcontracted to places such as Mexico, Bangladesh, and China (Dickey 2002, 16).

Globalization and Political Changes

Let's return to the question of how globalization is affecting politics. What have been the local political effects of economic globalization? How have global economic processes changed the distribution of political power, political participation, and ultimately democracy? Are these processes creating a democratic deficit that is reducing the ability of citizens to influence public policy while increasing corporate influence?

To begin, trends suggest that the ability of the nation-state to pursue locally (i.e., nationally) determined goals is increasingly constrained. In other words, democracy is eroded with the emergence of the neoliberal state. Thus, what once had been "Third World or developing world problems"—governments that are simultaneously ineffectual on the international stage and undemocratic —are now increasingly concerns for the First World. Even U.S. policy making has been affected by global economic pressures, as we discussed in the previous chapter. In 2003, the WTO found tariffs on imported steel imposed by the George W. Bush administration to be in violation of free trade rules; under the threat of global retaliatory measures, the administration eliminated the tariffs.[12] Or, as the Finns discovered with Nokia, the global strategy of TNCs is not necessarily consistent with the interests of the local community or society. In a little over a decade, Nokia grew from modest beginnings to ranking 136 in *Fortune*'s global 500 (2003), manufacturing 37 out of every 100 cell phones worldwide and connecting over one billion people in its global communications web. As Manfred Steger (2003, 51) writes,

... Nokia's gift to Finland—the distinction of being the most interconnected nation in the world—came at the price of economic dependency. Nokia is the engine of the Finland economy, representing two-thirds of the stock market's value and one-fifth of the nation's total exports. It employs 22,000 Finns, not counting the estimated 20,000 domestic employees who work for companies that depend on Nokia contracts. The corporation produces a large part of Finland's tax revenue, and its $25 billion in annual sales almost equals the entire national budget. Yet, when Nokia's growth rate slowed in recent years, company executives let it be known that they were dissatisfied with the country's relatively steep income tax. Today many Finnish citizens fear that decisions made by a relatively few Nokia managers might pressure the government to lower corporate taxes and abandon the country's generous and equalitarian welfare system.

These two examples are suggestive of two indicators we can use to examine the links between economic globalization and political change. If globalization is empowering corporations at the expense of national-level actors and dominating the national-level political process, we should see changes in tax incentives that encourage investors and corporations to invest in a particular region or country. Likewise, we should see legislation enacted that favors capital over labor and communities.

Taxes

According to the *Economist* (1997, 18–19), data from 17 industrial countries show that average taxes on wages and salaries have risen since 1980 while taxes on capital (corporations) have fallen. Focusing on the United States, an analysis by the Institute on Taxation and Economic Policy (ITEP) of the 250 largest and most profitable U.S. corporations found that these corporations paid only 20.1 percent of their profits in taxes in 1998, down from 26.5 percent a similar group of large companies paid in 1988. The standard federal corporate tax rate is 35 percent (ITEP 2000). By 2004, the average corporate federal tax rate had fallen further to 17 percent (Dobbs 2004b). Between 2001 and 2003, 82 major U.S. corporations paid no federal income taxes for at least 1 year (Dobbs 2004b); and in some cases, corporations pay *less than* zero taxes. Texaco, Chevron, CSX, Pepsico, Pfizer, J. P. Morgan, Goodyear, Enron, General Motors, Phillips Petroleum, and Northrop Grumman, for instance, had before-tax profits of $12.0 billion but actually paid less than zero in federal income taxes in 1998 because of rebates (ITEP 2000).

A snapshot of U.S. individual income tax rates shows a similar picture. In 2002, the average state and local tax rate on the wealthiest 1 percent of families was 7.3 percent before accounting for the tax savings from federal itemized deductions. After the federal offset, the effective tax rate on the wealthiest 1 percent declined to 5.2 percent. By comparison, the average tax rate on families in the middle 20 percent of the income spectrum was 9.9 percent before the federal offset and 9.6 percent after the offset. The poorest 20 percent of families pay 11.4 percent, the highest of all (McIntyre et al. 2003).

The conditions for globalization we discussed earlier also make "hiding" wealth much easier. Offshore financial centers (OFCs), for instance, allow corporations and individuals to evade national banking regulations and taxes. Offshore banking centers include the "traditional" locales, Switzerland and Luxembourg, as well as new locations in the Caribbean region, including Belize, Dominica, Grenada, St. Lucia, and St. Kitts. The Cayman Islands currently represent the world's fifth largest banking center (Gwynne, Klak, and Shaw 2003, 184–185). At least 20 Caribbean jurisdictions offer offshore banking services—more than any other region—that provide secrecy and asset protection among other "benefits" (Gwynne, Klak, and Shaw 2003, 184).

In 2000, it was estimated that the total proportion of the world's wealth based in OFCs was well over 60 percent (Hetherington-Gore et al. 2000). Inevitably, this number will rise, according to Hetherington-Gore et al. (2000) as the Internet introduces "a permanent shift in the balance of power between the taxman and his tax-paying corporate targets [because] countries are anchored in the physical reality of their territory, while companies will increasingly be free to locate large parts of their economic activity in low-tax areas."

Legislation

As we mentioned in previous chapters, the role of the regional and global rules of the North American Free Trade Agreement (NAFTA) and the WTO have a direct effect on legislation. Chapter 11 of the NAFTA charter (not to be confused with Chapter 11 of U.S. bankruptcy laws), for instance, states that no government may "directly or indirectly nationalize or expropriate an investment or take a measure tantamount to nationalization or expropriation" (Mooney 2001, Moyers 2002). The term *tantamount*, as Mooney (2001) and Moyers (2002) show, allows TNCs to subvert local democratic decisions. When California decided to phase out the use of methyl tertiary-butyl ether (MTBE) in its gasoline, the Canadian firm that produced MTBE sued the U.S. government for $970 million for profits *they might have earned* had California not enacted legislation; the company felt that California's decision was *tantamount* to expropriation.[13]

An example of how the WTO affects policy is the 1996 case in which the Brazilian and Venezuelan oil industries contended that U.S. Clean Air rules discriminate against foreign gasoline (Wallach and Sforza 1999, 28–30). The Brazilian and Venezuelan oil industries took their case to the WTO. After deliberations, the WTO dispute panel agreed with the plaintiffs and ruled that the U.S. Clean Air Act regulations adopted under 1990 amendments were in violation of WTO rules. The WTO instructed the United States to amend its gasoline cleanliness regulations to be consistent with WTO rules; the United States complied in August 1997.

These two examples are illustrative of the national/local political effects of transnational organizations: when democratically created legislation conflicts with corporate goals, corporations have a powerful tool to force changes in the legislation. The underlying issue is power and how the redistribution of power is eroding the effectiveness of local democratic institutions. Power is not only shifted *outward* as governments privatize public services but *upward* toward transnational capital and regional and global institutions. The shift in power atomizes citizens and creates tension between people in "their role as consumers and investors, who might benefit from globalization because of lower prices, wider choices and better income opportunities, and their role as citizens, which risks becoming less and less meaningful because of the declining opportunities for collective [local] self-governance" (Koenig-Archibugi 2003, 14). The result is to break the social bonds between people, to undermine the sense of community and community participation within the nation-state, and to devalue democratic participation that is manifested most vividly in decreased voting rates (see Derber 2002, Hertz 2001, Koenig-Archibugi 2003).

These trends support the basic point of the global social democrats. Democratic institutions and procedures remain in place, but they are increasingly ineffective or are being "hollowed out" by globalization. This institutional hollowing out creates a democratic deficit reflected in three political outcomes. First, "political participation" is redefined in terms of consumption patterns ("one dollar one vote"). Second, the ability of citizens to influence the political process is minimized, while corporate influence is maximized; many argue that this is why voting participation continues to decline (see Derber 2002, Hertz 2001). Third, the range of economic and social policy options declines due to the constraints imposed by global markets and by investors threatening to exit countries with "unfriendly" policies. We see this with the shift in the tax burden away from capital to labor, which reduces a government's ability to pursue democratically determined political policies.[14]

Solution?

So what now, you may be wondering? Are these trends inevitable, or is there some way to counter the negative political effects of economic globalization? Recall our earlier discussion of Karl Polanyi and his theory of the double-movement. With globalization, power is being shifted not only upward and outward but *downward*. Globalization may be altering the more established modes of political participation (e.g., voting) by weakening traditional movements (e.g., labor unions), but these same processes may create new forms of political participation. In the previous chapter, we cited data on transnational civic organizations and international non-governmental organizations (INGOs). Data show that the number of INGOs increased from under 20 in the 1940s to nearly 5,500 in the mid-1990s (Boli and Thomas 1997, 176; Held and McGrew 2000, 11). Similarly, the number of **transborder civic associations** increased from 1,117 in 1956 to 16,586 in 1998 (Scholte 2000a, 86). These groups and organizations, responding to the democratic deficit, point to a nascent movement from *below* that is attempting to alter the process of globalization, deepen democracy, and reinvigorate citizenship through increased mass participation in setting global policy.

The 1999, protest against the WTO meeting in Seattle revealed the possibilities of the countermovement using the tools of globalization to forge transnational connections between geographically dispersed groups (see Faux 1999, 2001; Urry 1999; Cockburn, St. Clair, and Sekula 2000; Nichols 2000; also Levi and Olson 2000). In organizing across borders on such issues as sweatshops, environmental problems, wages, working conditions, human rights, and the rights of women and children, these groups are constructing what Ronaldo Munck (2002) calls a "new internationalism."

As we discuss in later chapters, these groups are taking on the growing power of TNCs and declining power of local governments (i.e., the democratic deficit) through such strategies as guerrilla theater, boycotts, media campaigns, and **codes of conduct** to compel corporations to alter the way they produce goods and services. The effort to bring democratic control over corporations is a multidirectional process of organizing and sharing resources and strategies across geographical space that may create the conditions for a **global civil society** upon which a new form of global democracy can be constructed. Thus, in keeping with the position of the social democrats, politics, it appears, are being recast in the age of globalization (see Kazin 1999; Meyerson 1999; Brysk 2000; Evans 2000; Mandle 2000; Nichols 2000; Scholte 2000a; Alpert 2002; Brecher, Costello, and Smith 2002; Conroy 2002; Derber 2002; Hertz 2001; Stiglitz 2002; Armbruster-Sandoval 2005).

Globalization and Cultural Change

Cultural globalization involves the movement of objects, signs, and people across geographical regions (Held et al. 1999, 329). While culture has always shown a "greater tendency toward globalization" (Waters 1995, 124) than other forms (e.g., economic or political), what distinguishes this period from previous ones is the global reach and speed of cultural traffic.

Crucial to the process of cultural globalization, according to Michael Mann (1986), is the notion of *transcendence*, in which culture rises above the existing (local) ideological, economic, military, and political institutions. Mann argues that the movement of people and texts helps establish patterns of exchange and shared cultural beliefs between separate places and the possibility for cultural ideas in one place to influence those in another (see also Held et al. 1999). Culture does not "merely integrate and reflect an already established 'society'; indeed it may actually create a society-like network, a religious or cultural community, out of emergent, interstitial social needs and relations" (Mann 1986, 23).

Clearly, this argument is consistent with the globalist position that globalization is fostering a global culture. While we agree with this position, we are not arguing that globalization is supplanting national-level culture or leading to cultural global homogeneity. The skeptics are right that cultural forms and institutions are deeply embedded nationally (locally) and that culture remains strongly tied to local memories, values, and symbols.

The preeminence of local-level culture explains why corporations try to impart a local flavor on global brands. On its web page, the Hong Kong and Shanghai Banking Corporation calls itself "the world's local bank" that allows personal Internet banking "when you want from where you want."[15] Headquartered in London and with 9,500 offices in 79 countries, its slogan is designed to position the bank as a global brand while stressing its ability to operate as a local organization in each of its markets. Other attempts to manage the global-local nexus include McDonald's creating a mutton-based "Maharaja Mac" that replaces the beef burger on its menus in India (Scholte 2000b, 60), Teriyaki McBurgers in Japan, and McArabia sandwiches in the Middle East. Not to be outdone, Burger King includes *gallo pinto* (the traditional breakfast staple of black beans and rice) with breakfast in Costa Rica.

The globalization of culture is often portrayed as moving from the "West to the rest," as illustrated by indigenous leaders in the Amazon region of South America wearing Nike shoes or Palestinian youths wearing Chicago Bulls sweatshirts in downtown Ramallah (Steger 2003, 70–71). Culture flows in the other direction as well, however, as demonstrated by the popularity in the United States of the Japanese-produced Pokémon and Yu-gi-oh games and cards or television programs such as *Dragon Ball Z*.[16] As Ritzer (2004, 78) argues, globalization is creating the possibilities of eating Irish bagels, Chinese tacos, or kosher pizza in New York or Dublin.

These examples illustrate the hybrid nature of culture. Culture as a product of a multitude of global–local interactions is not recent, however, but dates back hundreds, if not thousands, of years. Navajo weaving, for instance, reflects a pattern borrowed from the ponchos and clothing of Spanish shepherds in Mexico, which in turn drew upon Moorish influences in Spain (Cowen 2002). This notion is captured in the preamble of the Convention for the Protection or Cultural Property in the Event of Armed Conflict of May 14, 1954, which argues that "each people makes its contribution to the culture of the world . . ." (quoted in Appiah 2006, 121). Yet, to say that cultural patterns are historic products of global–local interaction is not to argue that these interactions have been equal. To do so, as Benjamin Barber (2003) points out, is to miss the importance of power in this hybridization process. As the Marxists argue, inequalities of power mean that cultural interchange will evolve in ways consistent with the interests of the more powerful actor. The African slave trade may have revolutionized world music, but these exchanges and interactions were hardly fair or equal.

There is something else at work in this interaction. With changes in the information infrastructure, we now have access to a greater variety of values and ideas. At the same time, globally sourced news and information increase our subjective awareness of—or what we know, think, and feel about—world phenomena. Enhancing our subjective awareness is the fact that ecological risks are no longer confined to local areas or particular groups and classes: global warming, acid rain, mad cow disease, or severe acute respiratory syndrome (SARS) show no respect for geographical, political, or class boundaries. Beck (1992) coined the term *risk society* to describe these changes and in so doing contributed to the debate in three important ways. First, ecological risks associated with unregulated industrial growth can no longer be confined to a local area. This *extensification* of ecological risks forces people to become more aware that everyone inhabits the same planet or, as Beck (1992) argues, forces our subjective consciousness in the direction of globalization. Second, because ecological risks are increasingly not bound by any particular locale, solving them requires global cooperation and global solutions—e.g., strategic arms talks, global agreements on emissions reductions and global warming, agreements on banning the use of cancer-causing chemicals, an international court to bring human rights violators to justice, or even multilateral agreements on working conditions. Finally, increased risks and the realization that we all share a common fate create the basis for a global pool of memories (e.g., the Holocaust), which is a key component of global civil society.

Layered Culture

Still, these changes do not necessarily mean that globalization will result in a homogeneous global culture. This would be an oversimplification of the complexities of humanity and the culture we create; even within strong national cultures, there exist vibrant sub-cultures. The most likely cultural manifestation of globalization is a "layered culture," a kind of composite of local and global. The notion of a layered culture seems to be at the center of Roland Robertson (1994) concept "glocalization", in which there is a complex interaction between the global and the local.[17]

By "layered culture", we mean that people increasingly inhabit a cultural space that is simultaneously local, national, regional, and global, with *understandings* corresponding to these different levels.[18] Everyone has—and will continue to have—a "local life," but the subjective changes induced by globalization mean "the ways people make sense of the world are increasingly interpenetrated by ideas and values from many diverse settings" (Held and McGrew 2002, 36). If, for instance, you decide to buy a hybrid car because you wish to reduce the consumption of fossil fuels or reduce the impact on the ozone, you are acting locally out of concern for the global—a positive effect of subjective changes. At the same time, the increasing popularity of SUVs in Costa Rica—even though gas is double what it is in the United States and the streets are not built for SUVs—reflects a negative effect of subjective awareness (i.e., the local incorporation of globally generated ideas and values).

Finally, as work on multicultural changes and transnational communities suggests, globalization may actually be decoupling ethnicity from locality. Cities such as Los Angeles reveal the complex ways in which multicultural groups are forming beyond our existing explanatory categories. What does it mean culturally to have parents from Korea and Cuba while growing up in a predominantly African American community in Los Angeles? Our existing cultural categories and reference points are inadequate to understand the globalized world of the twenty-first century. Even the nation-state is being challenged in new and different ways, illustrated by Scotland's and Catalonia's attempts to seek independence within a new relationship with the European Union, rather than within the framework of a new state (Waters 1995, 139).

Culturally, globalization means that everyone everywhere is less and less living out their lives in a network of local cultures, yet the effects of globalization on identity and knowledge remain uneven and contradictory. They remain so because global processes take place within culturally local contexts. Culture then "has to be seen as a complex, overlapping disjunctive order" that cannot be understood in terms of simple dichotomies such as local and global (Appadurai 1996, 32), similarity and dissimilarity, or heterogeneity and homogeneity. Globalization may create homogenizing pressures, as Ritzer (1996) shows in his work on McDonaldization; but even McDonald's restaurants differ depending on the cultural setting. In the end, we must see cultural globalization as something both "out there" and "in here," a fusing of local and global elements through a process that is homogenizing and heterogenizing, multi-dimensional, and layered.

Conclusion

So is globalization a useful concept? We agree with Jan Aart Scholte (2000b, 40), who argues that there "is no reason to abandon the topic as a vacuous buzzword." Quite the opposite; when key issues of security, justice, and democracy are central to the debate, "social responsibility demands that researchers give globalization serious attention" (Scholte 2000b, 40). At the same time, we need to exercise caution: globalization is a process that suggests convergence, but adopting such a view is misleading, as the skeptics argue. Globalization has been both a homogenizing and a diversifying *set of processes*. It is this multidirectional unevenness that allows for multiple interpretations of the process and for skeptics and globalists to marshal supporting evidence for their respective positions.

As we have argued, globalization is an ongoing process involving political, economic, and cultural changes central to the way social life is (and has been) organized. Globalization is fundamentally about power, the way power is organized and exercised in an increasingly linked system. Decisions and actions by actors on one side of the globe have consequences for societies, communities, and groups on the other side. The stretching of power relations, Held et al. (1999) point out, means that sites of power and the exercise of power become increasingly distant from the subjects or locales that experience the consequences.

Globalization is changing the role of governments and affecting the ability of citizens to democratically influence the policies of their governments. Yet, almost simultaneously, globalization is creating the conditions for new forms of political participation. These forms are based on a "new internationalism" that is more transnational and may potentially create a global civil society.

Globalization is reconfiguring social space as we move from the three-dimensional geography of longitude, latitude, and altitude to adding a fourth dimension of global spaces (Scholte 2000b, 46–61). With globalization, there is the tendency to transcend territoriality, though clearly not to totally transcend territorial space, and there is a proliferation of social connections that are often detached from a defined territory. As economic, social, and political activities are stretched across the globe, what is local, national, or continental becomes reformed and is no longer coterminous with established legal and territorial boundaries (Held et al. 1999, 28). This reconfiguration means that not only transactions but also ecological risks are no longer effectively impeded by space or boundaries.

Globalization is potentially McDonaldizing the world, but it is also responsible for a dazzling array "of consumption possibilities from across the globe in terms of imported products" and imported cultural practices (Waters 1995, 142). Finally, global processes are interpreted through a culture that is local and local action is increasingly shaped by a people's collective understandings (Halford and Savage 1997).

Thus, in our view, the fundamental changes we are witnessing are consistent with the globalist social democratic argument. Powerful forces are shaping the process of change, and these changes reflect deep structural transformations—for the first time in history, we have a global economy capable of working as a unit in real time. Yet, as the social democrats argue, a fully *globalized* world does not exist, though we appear to be in the midst of a *globalization process* that remains incomplete and undetermined as to where it may go and how far it may proceed.

In the end, we need to avoid the tendency to see globalization as a closed-ended linear process that is reducible to universalism or convergence. To say that globalization has exacerbated inequality, for instance, should not be taken to mean that change had to assume this form: globalization is a multidimensional and uneven process significantly shaped by a conjuncture of factors and inscribed with many contradictions. As the "early globalists" Karl Marx, Max Weber, and C. Wright Mills may well have argued, the process of globalization remains a product *shaped* by human action and conditioned by the historical and social context.

CHAPTER 5

Globalization and Stratification

- Infant mortality rates vary from 3 per 1,000 in Norway, Japan, and Singapore to 182 per 1,000 in Sierra Leone (UNDP 2002).

- The percentage of the population living on $1.00 per day ranges from 0 percent in the United States to 82 percent in Ethiopia and Nicaragua (UNDP 2002). Overall, 1.3 billion people live on less than $1.00 per day, or about 20 percent of the world's population.

- Europeans spend about $2 billion a year more on ice cream than the estimated amount needed to provide clean water and safe sewers for the world's population (Crossette 1998).

- In the late 1990s, the world's richest three individuals had assets that exceeded the gross domestic product of the 48 least developed countries (Crossette 1998).

- The percentage of women in government at the ministerial level ranges from 55 percent in Sweden to 5.7 percent in Japan to 0 percent in Turkey (UNDP 2002).

- Carrier, the maker of air-conditioning and heating units, closes its Syracuse, New York plants and moves most of the 1,200 jobs to Singapore and Malaysia.

- IBM announces growth and new jobs creation in the United States and then outsources 90 percent of them—15,000 in all.

- Before Siemens in Orlando, Florida laid Patricia off, the company brought her Indian replacement to the United States so that Patricia could train her.[1]

What comes to your mind when you read these examples? You may be thinking that the world is a very unequal place. Or that inequality manifests itself in many different forms, such as economic, social, and political. You might ask yourself if, or how, these examples are linked to globalization. In this chapter, we concentrate on these kinds of questions by extending our earlier discussion of stratification and inequality. We begin by reviewing the basic concepts and then examine the theoretical links between globalization, stratification, and inequality.

Definitions and Concepts

Social Stratification and Social Differentiation

Recall from Chapter 1 that social *inequality* implies unequal access to valued resources, services, and positions in society, while social *stratification* refers to the institutionalization of these inequalities. It is important to keep in mind that social stratification is not simply a result of differences between people; rather, stratification reflects a system of valuation that determines who gets what and why. By comparison, the notion of "differences," or **social differentiation**, means only that people have distinct qualities and social roles, that people are different in terms of sex, skills, and occupations. As Celia Heller puts it, "positions may be differentiated from one another and yet not *ranked* relative to each other. For example, in our society the position of the adolescent is generally not considered superior to that of infant, merely different" (quoted in Kerbo 2003, 11). The key distinction is that these differences are not *ranked* in a hierarchical manner or *evaluated* as inferior or superior.

Biological factors such as sex, race, and age become relevant in patterns of social superiority or inferiority only when "they are socially recognized and given importance by being incorporated into the belief, attitudes, and values of the people in the society" (Eitzen and Baca Zinn 2004, 234). As we discuss in detail in Chapter 8, social scientists use *gender* to refer to the social meanings attached to the biological category of sex; however, we do not have separate words to differentiate between the biological categories and social meanings of race and ethnicity. Once biological characteristics are socially constructed as meaningful, they—along with class—locate individuals in positions within the social hierarchy that affect access to resources and opportunities. In other words, class, race, ethnicity, gender, and age are the macro-level structures that organize society as a whole (Eitzen and Baca Zinn 2004, 234–235). Depending on the combination of these attributes, individuals will experience a range of privilege and subordination, oppression and opportunity. Finally, the meanings attached to biological attributes vary historically and cross-culturally, indicating their relationship to other features specific to a society, such as culture, politics, and economics.

Wealth and Income

Of the many types of inequality, two fundamental forms are based on income and wealth. In class stratification systems, the distribution of wealth and income is crucial because both determine access to basic necessities of life (e.g., food, clothing, and shelter), other goods and services, and power.

Wealth and income are not the same. *Income* consists of a person's wages, salaries, and income transfers (governmental aid such as social security, welfare, and pension). *Wealth*, by contrast, is the value of a person's or a family's economic assets less any liabilities. Thus, wealth includes income as well as accumulated assets, such as personal property and income-generating property. These assets—which include stocks and bonds, for instance—can be used to generate income that in turn can be used to acquire basic goods and services as well as luxury items. Wealth can also be used to gain advantages over others through the "purchase" of greater opportunities (i.e., life chances) by acquiring such goods as greater safety for oneself and one's family, high-quality health care, high social prestige, political influence, and power (see Keister, quoted in Kendall 2003, 271).[2]

Power

One of the great advantages of wealth is its links to power. Within any stratification system, an individual's life chances (indeed, quality of life) are strongly shaped by how much power she or he has because power determines the range of options (or autonomy) and control one has. By *power*, we mean the ability to accomplish one's goals despite resistance from others. As you may suspect, accomplishing "one's goals" can be achieved directly by force or indirectly by getting others to think or believe in accordance with your interests (Eitzen and Baca Zinn 2004, 412). The latter is perhaps more insidious because of the potential to set the parameters of what is deemed possible in society. When A can get B to *think, feel,* or *believe* something and to place a positive value on certain things and a negative value on other things, A has successfully forced B to define his or her interests and priorities consistently with those of A (Parenti 1978, 41). Thus, by influencing or controlling the definition of interests and defining the agenda of issues in this manner, A is winning battles without having to fight them.

Power is also embedded in society's basic social institutions. These institutions in turn play a central role in legitimizing the stratification system. In the United States, for instance, we believe that hard work leads to success—the idea of "competitive individualism"—and that those who contribute more to society deserve proportionally greater rewards in terms of income and wealth. Both of these ideas are important aspects of our dominant culture, or our collective understandings that shape individual behavior and action. But where do we learn or internalize these beliefs or ideology? The answer lies in the way in which the basic institutions of our society (e.g., educational, political, economic, family) instill in each generation ideas about what is expected in society, what is possible, what is good, and what is bad (Eitzen and Baca Zinn 2004, 413–422). How many of you can remember a parent or adult telling you that to "get ahead in life you have to work hard" or a teacher saying "If you study hard and keep up with the reading, you will do well in this class"? All is possible if you work hard; after all, look at Abraham Lincoln or Bill Gates. These ideas serve to legitimize our stratification system by instilling in each generation the notion that everyone has an equal chance at success and that success (income and wealth) comes from hard work.

Furthermore, wealth determines who runs society's (and the world's) important political and economic institutions. The wealthy, as Domhoff (1998) shows, exert considerable influence over society through their dominance in industry, banks, policy-making institutions, councils for national and international affairs, the media, and the basic institutions of society, including schools. What happens, then, if power is concentrated in the hands of a few individuals, groups, or classes? Consider the debate over globalization and how our understanding of globalization has been shaped. Until recently, the neoliberal position has dominated the general perception of globalization. This position suggests that globalization is an inevitable market-driven process that will improve the living conditions and life chances of everyone regardless of geographical location, race, ethnicity, gender, income, or wealth.

Who has the power to define globalization in such terms? Who benefits from this conceptualization? When asked why neoliberal ideas dominate our understanding of globalization, Susan George (1999) referenced Antonio Gramsci: "If you can occupy peoples' heads, their hearts and their hands will follow." Neoliberals (among them major business, industry, and political leaders), she argues, have created a huge international network of foundations, institutes, research centers, publications, and public relations people to develop, package, and push their ideas. One result is the wide acceptance of the notion that governments are the problem and markets are the solution to our social problems. To question the importance of free markets is akin to asking why there are "waves in the ocean."

Both Domhoff and George raise the idea of power as influence, but power is not simply a result of wealth, as we see with the growth of the antiglobalization (or global justice) movement. In this case, people are organizing themselves in response to the contradictions of globalization and seeking to promote or resist specific forms of change, to reform and transform society at the local through the global levels. At the World Trade Organization (WTO) meeting in Seattle in 1999, for instance, the world became aware of a diverse and robust countermovement challenging the neoliberal notion of globalization. These groups contesting globalization are not wealthy, but through their transnational organizing efforts, they are gaining the *power* to alter or influence our understanding of globalization.

Class

One of the fundamental forms of stratification is class. When we talk about *class stratification*, we mean groups differentiated by income, wealth, and power. Earlier, we defined *class* as a group of individuals with similar political and economic interests who share similar life chances and possess similar material resources (income and wealth). Class involves the idea expressed by Karl Marx, which in its most basic formulation is a dichotomous model based on conflict between those who own property (the dominant capitalist class) and those who do not (the subordinate working class). But class conflict can also spring from divisions *within* classes, or **class segments**, whom globalization impacts differentially due to their different locations in the social structure (see Zeitlin 1984). The key point from a Marxist perspective is the central role of conflict and competition in class relations that derive from structural inequality. Thus, social class relations are constantly in flux, determined by the concrete historical circumstances and structures of relations that class conflict brings about; social classes then stand in relation to each other as well as to the private means of production.

Implied in Marx's idea of class is the notion that class location determines access to resources, including power. Here, Marx and Weber generally agree: for Weber (1978, 302–305), class position or situation shapes life chances, reflected in access to such goods as health care and education that affect an individual's options to live a better and longer life. Take life expectancy, for instance. Migrant farm workers have a life expectancy 30 years *below* the national average (Eitzen and Baca Zinn 2003, 405). At age 25, U.S. women with incomes above $50,000 can expect to live four years *longer* than women with incomes below $5,000; for men, the difference is 10 years (Newman 2004, 348). Health is another central feature of the quality of life. As we mentioned earlier, 64 percent of the over 41 million people in the United States under age 65 with no health coverage are the poor and near poor. These examples illustrate how class location or position translates into quality-of-life issues—specifically, how class affects an individual's health and longevity.

Weber further argued that class represents opportunities for income. By *opportunities*, Weber means the skill level possessed (or potentially possessed) by individuals. Skills locate people in specific class categories, such as working class or professional class. Moreover, access to wealth or income creates opportunities to acquire the skills, information, and expertise that can lead to upward social mobility. The critical issue is the link between social structure and class. The intersection of the skills an individual possesses and the skills demanded by the society influences class position. Likewise, changes in the kinds of skills needed by society influence social mobility and, hence, class position.

Think about this in the context of globalization and the United States. Globalization means industrial jobs are declining in importance, while technology increases in importance. Thus, those who have computer-related technical, engineering, and software designing skills (or the opportunities to acquire such skills) will be advantaged by globalization and obtain greater returns for their labor; those possessing traditional blue-collar skills (or lacking the opportunities to acquire such skills) will be disadvantaged. As globalization advantages or disadvantages individuals, global processes not only affect class stratification patterns but also potentially create or exacerbate existing conditions for conflict between and within classes. These conflicts in turn can affect the process of globalization and, thus, the patterns of class stratification in an ongoing dynamic.

Social Status

Stratification by **social status**, like class, determines an individual's position in the social hierarchy and includes expectations and restrictions on social interaction. Unlike *class*, however, social *status* refers to the cultural dimensions of inequality. As we noted earlier, social status is a form of "popularity" or respect accorded groups based on the value society places on certain characteristics. Those possessing "valued" characteristics—family name, geographical location, race, ethnicity, sex, age, or certain educational degrees—will be "granted" greater respect and honor in society. Social status, then, draws on our ascribed attributes—characteristics we have no control over, like sex, age, race or ethnicity—and our achieved attributes—those over which we have some control, such as occupation. You may note the overlap between class and status when we refer to such qualities as geographical location and education or skills.

The relationship between class and status is particularly interesting, specifically the effects of sex, race, and ethnicity on class. The interaction between status and class forms what Patricia Hill Collins (1991) calls a complex **"matrix of domination"** within which we all exist. Our location in the social structure dictates how we experience this matrix. People of the same race will experience race differently depending on their location in the class structure as upper, middle, or lower; their location in the gender structure as female or male; and their location in the age structure as elderly, middle-aged, or young (Eitzen and Baca Zinn 2004, 237).

The notion of a matrix of domination is useful to tease out the complex interplay between class and status; your status often affects your access to skills and power, while your skills and power affect your class ranking. Again, let's place this in the context of globalization. Leaving aside the normative issues, outsourcing of manufacturing jobs from the United States creates employment in places like Mexico and South Asia. Status and class factors strongly influence who will be employed in these factories: the typical employee is a poor, young, single woman. Similarly, as industrial jobs are replaced by service jobs in the United States, class and status will affect who ends up in which service occupation (e.g., engineers, managers, or receptionists). In both scenarios, structural changes interact with existing class and status characteristics to (re)shape stratification by class and status.

Stratification, Inequality, and Globalization

So how does globalization fit into the discussion of stratification and inequality? As you may have noted, our discussion thus far has emphasized the societal (or national) level; clearly, the immediate effects of stratification are experienced at the societal level. Increasingly, however, these societal-level structures are shaped by another, more macro-layer structure. Here is where globalization fits in: global structures and processes functioning "above" society affect the rankings of groups and the distribution of resources at the societal level. These global-to-local effects can be thought of as complex set of *indirect* and *direct* linkages.[3] One caveat: although we can analytically separate the indirect and direct effects of globalization, the two are really part of the same process.

Indirect: Globalization shapes our perceptions and goals as we become more cognizant of shifting occupational opportunities, fashion trends, global social problems, or political policies—such as tax breaks for corporations and wealthy individuals. The idea of indirect effects is consistent with our earlier discussion of the subjective effects of globalization, how global processes continually shape our subjective perceptions, values, and needs.

Direct: Globalization affects our opportunities as firms and companies attempt to adjust to the competitive global environment by downsizing, outsourcing, reclassifying, reengineering, and **deskilling** jobs and occupations. These are the objective changes that directly affect individuals.

The Indirect Influence of Globalization

Let's begin by stating that humans generally act according to a set of preferences, goals or ambitions, and tastes. If you have a goal to learn computer programming, for instance, chances are you will look for some place to learn this skill. In a similar way, our tastes vary from person to person and even from year to year. Some of us shop at Wal-Mart, others at Saks Fifth Avenue; some like Chevy others prefer Toyota or BMW. In each case, our goals and tastes will shape our actions, and our actions will affect the larger structures by changing consumer demand for competing goods (e.g., Toyota versus BMW) and services (e.g., computer classes).

Our goals and tastes do not simply pop into our heads spontaneously or through some random process however. Social scientists know that social conditions, norms, and personal experiences have much to do with what we desire. For example, many social scientists recognize that our preference for a particular action is swayed by the number of other people engaged in the act. Owning a BMW or attending college and taking computer classes can become an individual ambition because so many others own BMWs or attend college.

Globalization truly has become a key external influence on everyday decision making among individuals. Take the value of education and the decisions we make about educational choices. In the case of college students, we might argue that their actions reflect the desire for upward social mobility. If we combine this goal with existing information suggesting that globalization is creating jobs that require advanced skills, we can understand the emphasis on education. In this sense, globalization acts as a fundamental influence, meaning that globalization sets the context in which an individual makes choices about her or his future. The important point is that individual decisions are not made in a social vacuum; they are influenced by the social–historical context and social networks in which we live.

Increased global communication, the ease of travel, and the stretching of social networks across the globe improve our access to information and affect our perceptions and awareness of global social problems. In 1996, for example, the U.S. public discovered that Wal-Mart's Kathie Lee collection of clothing—endorsed by talk show host Kathie Lee Gifford, who was paid $5 million a year to do so—was produced by teams of Honduran children. Some of these children were only 13 years old, working for as little as 31 cents an hour (Hertz 2001, 117). As organizations like the National Labor Committee (and later the United Students Against Sweatshops) exposed the conditions under which imported products were produced, consumer preferences began to change, as reflected in demands to end sweatshops and the use of child labor.

At a more general level, consumer demand is shaped by citizen (or consumer) advocacy market campaigns that pressure major retailers to alter their buying strategies. Since 1995 the Forest Stewardship Council (FSC), a multilateral nonprofit organization founded in Canada and located in Chiapas, Mexico, has been certifying forest products that are produced according to a set of standards. These standards include conservation of old growth forests, reduced use of chemicals, and prohibitions on the use of exotic trees (Conroy 2002). Although these efforts are still modest, Rainforest Action Network and other environmental groups have succeeded in convincing a growing network of retailers to formally agree to buy only products certified by FSC, including Home Depot and other major do-it-yourself retail chains, Anderson Windows, Nike (for paper and cardboard), The Gap (for flooring and shelving), and Kinko's (Conroy 2002).[4]

As environmental, human rights, labor, gender, and other activist groups transmit information through e-mail campaigns and public demonstrations, they raise public awareness, shape perceptions, and affect norms. At the same time, as more and more organizations in which we daily participate are affected by globalization, as nationally based institutions such as schools globalize and internationalize their curriculums, and as the media expand their coverage of global events, our awareness of globalization also increases and affects our perceptions, decisions, and goals. John, the individual, fears global warming and decides to purchase a hybrid car and consume only certified forestry products. Or Julie, the CEO of a manufacturing firm, worries about losing market shares to her competition, so she decides to take her company global.

Globalization, then, indirectly affects our perceptions, which creates direct effects reflected in increased demand for environmentally friendly products or economic restructuring. When firms make decisions reflecting changing market conditions, individuals can in turn be directly affected in the process. As companies downsize the labor force, invest in technology, or outsource jobs, individuals "experience globalization" as their jobs change or disappear. This is important. While some individuals are advantaged by these changes —e.g., those working for FSC—others may not be so lucky. It may be that we *want* a well-paying high-tech job and even acquire the requisite skills and education. Nonetheless, *if* the objective conditions are not present—demand outstrips job supply—we may well be left out no matter how qualified or how much we want the job.

The Direct Influence of Globalization

As globalization has accelerated competition for domestic and international markets, the types of jobs available in the United States have changed. The U.S. automobile sector is a leading example. Until the 1980s Ford, General Motors, and Chrysler easily dominated the U.S. market. Now, market shares are split up among several large automobile manufacturers, many with foreign-based headquarters. With growing competition, CEOs of these firms are under tremendous pressure to reduce production costs and increase market shares. When companies add technology or send traditional blue-collar jobs offshore to stay competitive, the demand for and qualifications of U.S. labor are altered. Today, for instance, seven out of ten jobs are in the low-wage, low-benefit service sector, while the "typical" factory employee is more likely to be working at a computer than on the "line."

Thus, organizations are a basic direct link between individuals and globalization. As the U.S. economic institution is globalized, certain sectors of the economy (e.g., financial or manufacturing) and specific organizations (Citibank or Ford) within those sectors are advantaged and others are disadvantaged. These changes in turn increase competition and conflict among sectors of the economy, among specific organizations, and ultimately among individuals. This is the basic idea illustrated in Figure 5.1 using the economic institution. Take, for example, the apparel industry. With globalization, Levi Strauss and The Gap are thrust into greater competition to increase or maintain market shares, which in turn increases competition among individuals— complicated by class and status attributes—for existing well-paying jobs. Individuals may react to these changes by organizing and pressuring firms or industries to adopt policies that will mitigate the effects of globalization, such as anti-sweatshop policies or hiring practices. These effects are represented by the upward arrows in Figure 5.1. Finally, we should note that even those who do not work for a large formal (and globalized) organization such as Levi's or IBM are affected by global processes. Small businesses, for example, experience the effects of globalization through wage and price pressures originating with larger globalized firms, a reason that communities and small businesses see Wal-Mart as a threat.

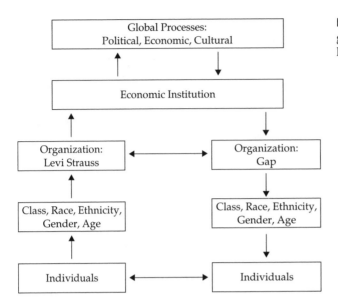

Figure 5.1 Direct global–individual links.

Blue- and White-Collar Transitions

Recall that one of the initial manifestations of increased global competition and stagflation in the 1970s was to accelerate the transformation of advanced industrialized (manufacturing) societies into service-based societies. In what we can call the "blue-collar" transition, major proportions of the manufacturing sector in the United States were shifted to less costly parts of the globe. Reflecting this transition, Wal-Mart became the largest U.S. employer in 1997 with 675,000 jobs, surpassing General Motors with 647,000.[5] Currently, a similar transformation—a "white-collar" transition—is taking place in the professional service sector as many middle-class professional occupations are being outsourced and computers and other technology are used to replace middle-management positions (Leicht 2001, 428–431) or to rearrange tasks within jobs.[6]

Three points are important. First, in both the white-collar and blue-collar sectors, labor demand does not disappear. There is no world without work. As Joseph Schumpeter ([1942] 1975) pointed out in the 1940s, social change (i.e., capitalism) involves a complex process of "creative destruction," a process that destroys some existing occupations, rearranges the characteristics of others, and creates new ones (including industries).[7] Today, however, the creative destruction process operates more intensively on a global scale than when Schumpeter was writing. Second, within the highly competitive global economy, the global reach of business means that these new occupations and industries will not necessarily be better in terms of wages and benefits or will be geographically accessible. Third, by outsourcing or relocating jobs, companies take advantage of the wide discrepancies in global wages and benefits (i.e., global stratification) that are products of social systems or country-specific class, race, ethnic, gender, and age stratification systems.

Blue-Collar Transition

According to the AFL-CIO, some 1.5 million jobs were lost in the U.S. manufacturing sector between 2000 and 2002. Today (2003) manufacturing represents only 12.7 percent of total GDP, down from 29.3 percent in 1950 (Philips 2006, 267). Recognizable factors have been at work: the low cost of manufacturing abroad—the "China price"—based on the availability of skilled labor and a business-friendly environment, the existence of global production and supply networks (*Business Week* 2004b, Bardhan and Kroll 2003), and the prevailing perceptions among CEOs discussed below.

Within the deindustrialization/industrialization process whereby societies like that of the United States lose manufacturing and "entry-level" jobs to societies such as that of China, status—gender, race, ethnicity, and age—and class attributes assume central roles. As Ursula Huws (2003, 176) points out, gender and race (and we should add age and ethnicity) are particularly important determinants of class identity in the formation of the new "cybertariate"; the typical worker today is not the highly flexible Silicon Valley programmer but the poorly paid young female call-center operator or factory worker in a Third World country.

Decreasing production costs by reducing labor costs typically involves reducing the skill level of jobs (deskilling) or by replacing human labor with machines. Today, there is a twist on this familiar set of processes. In contrast to earlier patterns of deskilling—most notably during the earlier Fordist period—the application of digitized information technology affects women more heavily than men (Munck 2005, 125). At the same time, the requirement of certain kinds of skills in labor-intensive industries means that replacing workers with machines is not always cost-effective. In these cases, we see high-cost labor (e.g., in the United States) replaced with low-cost labor (e.g., in El Salvador). The garment and electronics industries are two examples. In these industries, women are the employees of choice because, as Jill Steans (1998, Chapter 6) argues, women make the most "flexible robots of all." Thus, as the least unionized and poorest-paid workers (i.e., the least powerful), women have been particularly vulnerable to global restructuring.

When manufacturing jobs disappeared in the United States and the International Monetary Fund (IMF) and World Bank pushed export-led growth policies throughout the world, many of these manufacturing jobs reemerged in **export processing zones** (EPZs) in Central America and South Asia. EPZs are labor-intensive manufacturing centers that import components (or raw materials) for assembly (or production) into finished goods for export. Companies that locate in these special zones enjoy subsidies, tax exemptions, the suspension of certain labor legislation, union-free labor, and so on (Scholte 2000b, 77).[8] These policies, you may conclude, help facilitate globalization by making outsourcing more attractive.

How do women fit in here? Upward of 90 percent of the estimated 27–50 million workers in EPZs around the world are women, most between the ages of 16 and 25 (AFL-CIO 2004b, ILO 2004). Furthermore, the growth of low-paying jobs in EPZs is an important factor explaining why women, who make up 45 percent of the world's workforce, account for 70 percent of the world's population living in poverty. Reflected in these data is Patricia Hill Collins's matrix of domination; it is not just women but young, poor women of "color, particularly those in the Southern Hemisphere" who are most likely to be employed in the global factories (Powell and Udayakumar 2000). As companies respond to global competition by taking advantage of inequalities between countries and exploiting differences within countries, those producing goods for export are increasingly women—the **feminization of the labor force**—and the poor are increasingly female—the **feminization of poverty**.

So what about work in the United States? Increased investment in high-tech research, automation, and computer-integrated manufacturing systems that drives deindustrialization and restructuring has similar effects on women and on racial and ethnic minority groups in the United States. As we mentioned, the transformation of the U.S. economy within the context of globalization has dramatically altered the kinds of jobs available. In 1979, for instance, more than 50 percent of U.S. adults worked in either blue-collar or clerical jobs. Today, less than 40 percent of adults work in either of these two categories and many of these jobs now require at least some college education (Levy and Murnane 2004, 3). Initially, these changes affected men—in particular minority group men—more than women because men tended to monopolize the "old" good manufacturing jobs and women were concentrated in the service sector. Over time, however, the decline in traditional manufacturing jobs has increased the level of competition for "female" service sector jobs.

As the transformation of the U.S. economy shifted the skill prerequisites from an emphasis on physical to cognitive abilities—a process called "financialization"—differences in capabilities based on individual-level skills, levels of education, and access to technology became more pronounced.[9] These changes mean that the better educated and trained (or those able to acquire the requisite skills based on class) will have access to better jobs, benefits, and other opportunities; those lacking the requisite education and specialized skills will be disadvantaged in the new environment. For instance, in 1979, the average 30-year-old man with a bachelor's degree earned 17 percent more than a 30-year-old man with a high school diploma; today, the gap exceeds 50 percent (Levy and Murnane 2004, 6). Thus, as the traditional well-paying factory jobs disappear, those unable to compete for the **cognitive-intensive jobs** in the high-wage service sector or the "new" blue-collar production sector (e.g., computers and peripherals) are thrown into competition for low-wage, low-benefit service jobs. Yet, rather than connecting these outcomes to changes induced by globalization, they are often interpreted as a result of "unfair" competition due to affirmative action programs, "out of control immigration," or unfair global competition, perceptions that can increase global- and national-level tension and conflict between class and status groups.

Historical and contemporary inequalities in access to education and technology are exacerbated by the bifurcation of the economy; an economy that, according to Amy Dean of Silicon Valley's South Bay AFL-CIO Labor Council, is best described as an "hourglass economy" with high-end employment, low-end employment, and very little in between (Rayman-Reed 2001, 32). Between 1980 and the mid-1990s, for instance, the fastest job growth took place in jobs paying minimum wage while the second fastest growth was in jobs paying around $25 per hour.

The "hourglass" phenomenon is expected to continue. Today, roughly 20 percent of jobs have advancement potential, are high-paying, and have high prestige, such as engineering and finance (Eitzen and Baca Zinn 2004, 203), while 70 percent are low-paying and low-prestige jobs with little or no potential for advancement.[10] With few exceptions—most notably, physician assistants, registered nurses, and postsecondary teachers—the latter are those the AFL-CIO and the U.S. Department of Labor project will generate the most growth through at least 2012: retail sales, customer-service representatives, food preparation/fast food workers, cashiers, janitors and cleaners, general managers, wait staff, and nursing aides and orderlies. Other studies indicate that office support occupations—nonsecretarial office positions with an average wage of $13 per hour—are at the greatest risk of the next stage of outsourcing (see Shulman 2003, 101–108; also Bardhan and Kroll 2003, U.S. Department of Labor 2003). Given these structural changes in the U.S. economy, it is not surprising that 65 percent of laid-off full-time workers experience downward social mobility as they end up in a job that pays less than their previous one. Nor is it surprising that the U.S. Department of Health and Human Services found that the annual median income of people leaving welfare (including program participants) was between $8,000 and $12,000 or that the Urban Institute found that only 23 percent of these workers have health care provided by their employers (Hytrek and Davis 2002).

White-Collar Transition

Although outsourcing and job loss have typically been associated with blue-collar workers, clerical workers and the professional service and informational sectors are not immune to these pressures. We mentioned the decline in clerical workers above, which are the service sector jobs that have been most affected by new technologies and corporate reorganizing and reengineering strategies (see Levy and Murnane 2004). More recently, the professional and business services and information sectors have also experienced job losses, shedding some 850,000 jobs between 2001 and 2004, according to the AFL-CIO (2004a, 2004c; also Dobbs 2004a). While many of these jobs were outsourced, as noted previously, others were lost through the same mechanisms that have eliminated clerical jobs: application of the new information technologies, reengineering, and reorganizing attempts designed to improve a firm's competitiveness.

During the 1980s and 1990s, corporations began eliminating middle-management positions in a strategy that became known as the "flattening of organizational hierarchies." In some cases, clerical jobs were reorganized to include traditional management responsibilities (see Appelbaum, Bernhardt, and Murnane 2003); in other cases, CEOs added informational technology that allowed one manager to do the work of several. In both situations, firms reduced the need for "overpaid" middle managers and eliminated layers of middle management. When combined with other corporate reorganizing strategies, these changes led to deteriorating working conditions in firms that had long been known for benevolent and paternalistic worker–employer relations. Increasing numbers of employees began to experience "**job spill**" as technology blurred the line between work and home, benefit packages shrank, and the growth of temporary workers served to remind permanent employees that they too could be replaced. Yet, even as the changes in the white-collar workplace began to mirror those in the blue-collar world, white-collar workers believed that their level of skill and knowledge would shield them from a fate similar to that of those working in factories.

How quickly the white-collar transition materialized is suggested by Jill Fraser's book *White-Collar Sweatshop*. Writing in 2001, Fraser argued that the deterioration of working conditions in the world of big business would limit the ability of these firms to recruit, hire, and retain the best white-collar workforce the United States could offer (Fraser 2001, 205). As a result, companies would be forced to alter their "sweatshop"-like conditions in order to attract the best job candidates. Scarcely 2 years later these same firms seemed little concerned with hiring U.S.-trained white-collar workers as they outsourced everything from financial services to radiology to software programming. The work that is being sent abroad has increasingly climbed the skill ladder to include workers such as aeronautical engineers and scientists engaged in pharmaceutical research and development as educated workers from China, Russia, and India have rapidly entered the global labor market. So too is the case with, Central and Eastern Europe, who appear to be increasing their participation in the global service sector at the expense of Asia. "All of a sudden you have a huge influx of skilled people . . . ," pointed out Craig R. Barrett, chief executive of Intel, the computer chip manufacturer (quoted in Uchitelle 2003).

Both the direct and indirect effects of globalization are illustrated by these changes—that is, directly through the actual outsourcing of jobs and increased competition and indirectly through the growing *perception* of what might happen if a CEO does not take the company global. Driven by what has been called the "Indian price," CEOs believe that they must match the prevailing wage in India to remain competitive; the easiest way is to outsource jobs to India. C. Michael Armstrong, CEO of AT&T, sums up the prevailing wisdom among industry leaders: "In the future there will be two kinds of corporations; those that go global, and those that go bankrupt" (Gabel and Bruner 2003).

Some data suggest that this may not necessarily be an accurate statement, that companies can remain competitive without resorting to a "sweatshop" strategy (see Fraser 2001) or to outsourcing jobs—whether in the white-collar or blue-collar sector.[11] Under conditions of uncertainty, however, CEOs will look to the actions of others to help define the situation; therefore, what is important is one's perception of reality. As the Thomas theorem in sociology holds, if people define situations as real, they are real in their consequences. So, when the chief executives of Hewlett-Packard, Dell, IBM, and other companies believe that restrictions on outsourcing would imperil their companies, they will act according to this construction of reality. "What we are basically saying is that if your competitors are doing this, you will be at a disadvantage if you don't do it too," remarked Harold Sirkin, a senior vice president at the Boston Consulting Group (Uchitelle 2003). Thus, by acting under this assumption, companies can create their own self-fulfilling prophecy. Companies globalize and downsize because they fear losing market shares to competitors, which compels their competitors to globalize and downsize in an ongoing cycle.

One final point before we conclude this chapter: The issue of perception is important, but we do not want to leave you with the impression that globalization is merely an issue of perception. It is not. While perception is part of the indirect and subjective aspect of globalization, the objective conditions manifested in low wages, poor working conditions, and status inequalities around the globe strongly attract jobs from higher-cost production areas to lower-cost ones. In other words, we can think of the indirect effects as perceptions that lead to action and the direct effects as the outcomes of these actions.

Conclusion

Globalization means that we need to rethink our ideas of stratification, poverty, wealth, and inequality and to analytically incorporate global structures and processes into our examination of these issues at the societal level. This does not mean, however, that societal-level factors are no longer important. Globalization operates through existing societal class and status inequalities to reinforce and exacerbate these inequalities, while generating new patterns of inclusion and exclusion. As globalization reshapes the occupational structures of society, for instance, those with access to material capital, educational capital, and **social capital** networks will be in a better position to adapt to the changing labor markets than those lacking such resources.

The transformation of the U.S. economy has not been kind to older workers, middle-management workers, those with few skills, those with little education, or those coming off welfare. Globalization-induced changes will affect most severely those groups that have historically been denied access to quality education and have been overrepresented in production jobs currently being reengineered by technology, being reorganized by CEOs, or on the verge of disappearing.

Finally, the societal-level effects of global processes are products of multiple indirect and direct links. Globalization indirectly shapes and reshapes the perceptions, values, norms, and needs that affect action and directly causes change as policies of outsourcing and downsizing are implemented. Essentially, there are feedback loops between the two, as we noted, in which perceptions can change or reinforce the direct effects of globalization and vice versa. When individuals decide to pursue educational opportunities because it will make them more competitive in the changing global market, they will invest more time and resources in pursuing that ambition and potentially affect their ranking in the stratification system. Likewise, learning that children are producing apparel or toys may well alter a person's existing ideas about certain companies, stores, or products. In both situations, shifting consumer demand will affect the market for competing products and eventually the strategy of corporations.

We have argued in this chapter that corporate strategies designed to address the highly competitive global economy affect U.S. society in three fundamental ways: (1) the shift to services, specifically the rapid growth of low-wage, low-prestige jobs combined with cognitive-intensive ones; (2) the shift to high-tech production, which requires greater (often specialized) skills; and (3) the shift toward flatter organizational hierarchies as corporations reorganize and reduce the size of middle management (Hytrek and Davis 2002). In Part II, we examine in more detail the issues raised in this chapter. Our specific focus is on patterns of inequality reflected in three salient issues: class (income, wealth, and poverty), immigration, and gender.

Dimensions of Inequality

CHAPTER 6

Globalization and Work

- An individual with a college education in 1979 started his or her work life making 25 percent more than a typical high school graduate; in 2000, the difference was almost 70 percent.
- Every day in the United States, 85,444 people lose their jobs and are forced to compete for jobs that pay 21 percent less than the job they lost.
- In the past 3 years, 2.9 million well-paying U.S. manufacturing jobs have disappeared.
- Experts estimate that 14 million white-collar jobs in the United States will be shipped *permanently* overseas in the next few years.
- After losing a job, the average time a person spends out of work increased from 13 weeks in 2003 to 18 weeks in 2005 because of changes in technology and the fact that there are three job seekers for every one job.

Contemplating what to do after high school or college or whether or not to change jobs is a daunting task. As the above data from Mishel, Bernstein, and Allegreto (2005) and the AFL-CIO (n.d.c., 2004a) suggest, we are truly living and working in a new age. Analyzing such changes led the authors of the 2001 Economic Report to the President (2001, 19) to conclude that "over the last eight years the American economy has transformed itself so radically that many believe we have witnessed the creation of a New Economy." Gone is the predictability of the fixed Keynesian model; flexibility, innovation, and risk rule the day. In the twenty-first century, we must be well educated and we must be flexible enough to change where we live, where we work, and what work we do at the drop of a hat. What happened?

Economic globalization and the attendant political policies accelerated competition, which along the way restructured and transformed the U.S. economy and the occupational structures. At the dawn of the twenty-first century, we are more individualized, more educated, more competitive, and more unequal than ever before. In this chapter, we examine the way in which globalization has altered the workplace and intensified class inequality (income, wealth, and poverty) in the period since the Second World War.

The Context: Fordism to Flexibility

The three decades after World War II were hopeful times for many in the United States. When the war ended, soldiers came home anxious to return to their jobs and resume their daily lives. Factories that had been producing war-related products were retooled to produce commodities for domestic consumption (e.g., cars, household appliances, etc.) and export. Jobs that paid living wages were relatively plentiful, and labor unions were active; poverty rates declined, and income distribution became more equal. For many—mainly the white working and middle classes—the "Ozzie and Harriet" image of the family was an attainable goal. Our present notion of the traditional family emerged in this period: living in the suburbs with a car in the driveway and a balance of work and personal life that included being home for dinner at five, taking yearly family vacations, and saving for the children's college education.

As the competitive environment changed in the 1970s and U.S. firms went "global," the restructuring of the U.S. economy created a more flexible and uncertain job market. New workers were no longer entering predictable work settings; rather, they, along with displaced workers from declining industries, were confronting more intense global and national competition for jobs that either paid too little or required specialized training and education. The globalization of the U.S. economy was altering the location of production as well as the mix of jobs *between* and *within* the U.S. manufacturing and services sectors. Over time, the U.S. occupational structure shifted from one resembling a diamond, with a large middle sector, to one in the shape of an hourglass, with cognitive-intensive jobs at one end and low-wage jobs at the other. The way in which globalization transformed the blue- and white-collar sectors is central to explaining the shifting patterns of inequality and stratification in the United States.

U.S. Workers in the Globalized Economy

Flexibility, as we have noted, is a fundamental aspect of globalization. From the position of the corporation, firms must be flexible in order to react quickly to market changes and remain competitive. Technology is a central factor in the globalization process, functioning as the mechanism that coordinates the flexible global production process, replaces human labor, and creates new forms of technology–human collaboration. Research shows that computers can *substitute* for human labor or they can *complement* human labor (see Levy and Murnane 2004). Because computers excel at processing information through the application of rules, computers will complement humans working in jobs characterized by complex perceptual problems and requiring contextual knowledge. For example, a cardiologist complements her experience and her patient's medical history with an echocardiogram to arrive at an accurate diagnosis; without the aid of the echocardiogram, her task would be much more difficult.

New information technology can also complement human labor and enhance competitiveness by speeding up and adding flexibility to the production process. Boeing, for instance, launched its 727 passenger plane in 1962 after an 81-month development process. In 1994, Boeing used a computer-aided design (CAD) system developed by Dassault, a French engineering company, to complete its new 777 passenger plane in only *52 months* (Levy and Murnane 2004, 31–32). Even in labor-intensive industries, such as textiles, CAD systems can reduce the design time for a garment from weeks to minutes. Already by the late 1980s, Nike could specify a shoe design in Oregon and send these plans by satellite to a CAD firm in Taiwan, which in turn could fax the plans to engineers in South Korea. In other words, information technology and CAD systems allow firms to easily and quickly change designs to "tailor-make" products and meet rapidly changing individual consumer demand.

By contrast, computers will substitute for humans in jobs governed by rule-based logic. Jobs that can be fully and easily described by rules, such as many blue-collar and clerical jobs, are the most likely candidates for substitution by a robot or computer.[1] Assembly line jobs and those involving tax preparation or financial bond trading are good examples of jobs where human beings have been replaced (substituted) by robots and computers (Levy and Murnane 2004, Chapter 3).[2]

For positions in which technology cannot easily substitute for human labor, such as security guards or janitors, a large pool of available workers keeps wages low. For other non-rule-based jobs, such as textiles and electronics, technology facilitates a different type of substitution through outsourcing and subcontracting. Take the example of the textile industry. The sewing of garments remains labor-intensive, but information technology allows the repositioning of these jobs in the global production line through outsourcing and subcontracting (see Chapter 4). The creation of the global production process enhances flexibility by allowing the substitution of U.S. jobs for ones (outside of the United States) that are nonunionized, cheaper, and highly mobile.

Yet, not all corporations are moving offshore, and thus, there are alternative strategies that corporations use in an effort to cut costs and increase flexibility. Manufacturers, for example, routinely rely on **just-in-time production** strategies, whereby goods are ordered via computer direct from the factory (which is often located in another country) and shipped immediately to retail establishments (located in yet another country). This eliminates the need to warehouse goods and the second-guessing associated with product supply and demand. Firms are also creating a **just-in-time labor force** based on nonstandard part-time, temporary, or **contingent labor** that allows firms to meet increased demand or to finish specialized projects—just in time—without the costs and long-term commitments that come with full-time or permanent workers.

The shift to **nonstandard work arrangements** throughout the 1980s and 1990s not only enhanced flexibility but also reduced labor costs (by decreasing health-care benefits, vacation, sick pay, and pensions). The average part-time worker, for example, gets paid 60 percent of the average wage rate of a full-time worker. And 25 percent of part-time workers earn minimum wage compared to 5 percent of full-time workers (Williams 2000). Over the 1980s and 1990s, temporary work doubled each decade (Mishel, Bernstein, and Boushey 2003), with low-wage workers hit the hardest by these changes (Belous 1997). Of the 2.4 million workers employed by temporary help agencies in 1996, six out of ten did work on the lowest end of the corporate job ladder (Belous 1997). By the late 1990s, however, nonstandard arrangements had spread throughout the occupational ladder to include white-collar professional occupations (e.g., lawyers, accountants, physicians, technicians, college and university professors, among others) and firms known for their long-term employment policies (e.g., IBM, AT&T).

Thinking about these kinds of changes in the context of our discussion in the previous chapters, what are the effects on working women and men in the United States? Recall that neoliberals argued that these changes would create a new economy with virtually endless growth potential and increasing wealth through the generation of high-skilled and high-wage jobs. Let's look more closely at labor market changes and, more specifically, at what Schumpeter calls the "creative destruction process."

Changing Mixture of Employment Opportunities: The Manufacturing Sector

Manufacturing, we noted in the previous chapter, has been hardest hit by globalization. Between 1979 and 2001, employment in goods-producing industries declined from 29.5 to 19.0 percent (Mishel, Bernstein, and Schmitt 2001); in manufacturing, the U.S. industry lost more than 3 million jobs from 1998 to 2003, reducing this sector to its pre-1958 size (Bivens 2004). During this period, 14 states lost more than 10 percent of their manufacturing workforce—with ten states losing at least 65,000 manufacturing jobs—which accounts for more than half of the total U.S. job losses. Five states—California, New York, Pennsylvania, Texas, and Ohio—accounted for 30 percent of the loss (AFL-CIO n.d.a).

Significantly, corporations did not fire employees "here and there"; rather, they instituted **mass layoffs** in the process of restructuring their operations by adding technology or moving offshore. The transportation equipment, primary metals (e.g., steel), apparel, computer and electronic products, and food manufacturing industries were the hardest hit by mass layoffs and plant closures. For example, 33 steel companies filed for bankruptcy and/or ceased operations between 2000 and 2002, affecting more than 73,000 steelworker jobs. Similarly, the textile industry saw 150 textile plants close since 2000—116 during 2001 alone—with North Carolina, South Carolina, and Georgia accounting for two-thirds of the losses (AFL-CIO n.d.a). These trends continued in 2002 and 2003 with 39,240 mass layoff events that prompted 4.1 million people to file for unemployment benefits (Brown 2004).

The way globalization is shaping the job mix in the manufacturing sector is illustrated by the U.S. automobile sector. Several trends are apparent. First, the sector has eliminated most entry-level, labor-intensive, assembly line jobs in the United States and increased job growth in the parts sector, jobs that assemble modules such as seats and climate control systems for final assembly elsewhere. Since the early 1980s, the parts sector has added over 220,900 jobs versus 25,300 assembly sector jobs. Hourly wages in the parts sector average $17.91, or 75 percent of the $24.25/hour pay in the assembly sector, declining from rough parity as late as 1978 (Sturgeon and Florida 2004, 55). Second, following the parts sector in job growth have been positions in research and design, engineering, and administration. Finally, while jobs in the parts sector are located throughout the world, the research and design, engineering, and administrative jobs typically remain in the United States.

The employment outlook for high-tech workers is no less problematic; in this industry, the number of jobs shrank by 18.8 percent to 1.7 million positions from mid-2001 to mid-2004 (Srivastava and Theodore 2004). Again, we find research and development jobs maintained in the United States while assembly jobs are relocated offshore. In the hard disk drive sector, for instance, U.S. firms produced 80 percent of the world's hard drives in 1999 but assembled fewer than 1 percent in the United States, with 70 percent assembled in Southeast Asia (McKendrick 2004, 145). As late as 1985, 55 percent of hard drives were assembled in the United States; in 1995, over half of those working for U.S. firms in this sector were employed in Southeast Asia (McKendrick 2004, 145).

Jobs in software occupations within the manufacturing sector shrank even faster than overall manufacturing jobs. Between 2000 and 2002, total manufacturing jobs fell by 12 percent, while software jobs within manufacturing dropped by 19 percent. From mid-2001 to mid-2004, while the U.S. manufacturing sector shed 15 percent of its jobs, the software-producing industries lost 16 percent (Economic Policy Institute 2003).

Where did these manufacturing and high-tech jobs go? Figure 6.1 provides a partial picture. The software sector, one of the key sectors in the global economy, exemplifies the process by which U.S. jobs are outsourced to other places (in this case, India) in the global economy (see also Table 4.5). Other jobs have been casualties of technology. In 1980, U.S. Steel employed 120,000 workers; by 1990, the firm had cut 100,000 jobs yet maintained the same output of steel. On Ford assembly lines, robots do 98 percent of the spot welds on such cars as the Taurus. In addition, the advent of certain technologies, such as CAD, has changed the skill requirements for numerous jobs. As the motor vehicle industry suggests, the typical assembly line worker was more likely sitting at a computer than at the line by the new millennium. The point

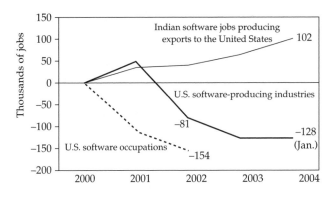

Figure 6.1 Changes in software-related jobs since 2000. *Source*: Mishel, Bernstein, and Allegreto (2005).

here is that technology not only accelerates the pace of job change; it also raises the value of verbal and quantitative literacy.

Changing Mixture of Employment Opportunities: The Service Sector

Reflecting the general structural transition of the U.S. economy, the service sector accounted for over 80 percent of the jobs at the end of the twentieth century (increasing from 70 percent in 1979 to 81 percent in 2001). Between 1969 and 1999, the fastest-growing service sector occupations were the low-paying categories (those non-rule-based, difficult to outsource jobs, such as janitors, cafeteria workers, and security guards). In this same period, high-paying professional, managerial, and technical sectors and middle-range service jobs (e.g., administrative support workers) showed the greatest *decline* (Levy and Murnane 2004, 42, Figure 3.2). Other service sector jobs experiencing decline include the geographic information systems services for insurance companies, stock market research for financial firms, medical transcription services, legal online database research, customer-service call centers, and payroll and other back office–related activities, to name a few.

The forces at work in the service sector are the same ones shaping the manufacturing, high-tech, and software production jobs—specifically, advances in the information infrastructure, the emergence of a global "24/7" economy capable of operating in real time, as well as institutional convergence as many parts of the world adopt common accounting and legal systems.[3] Still, outsourcing these service jobs would be difficult without the presence of another global process—cultural globalization. Increasingly, English is the accepted medium of communication and business throughout the world, and there is a steady and copious supply of technically savvy graduates, many of whom leave their native countries to study in the United States and later return home to work in globalized firms (see Bardhan and Kroll 2003).

These transformations are aptly illustrated by trends in the software sector. The transfer of service activities in this sector to offshore locations has created a critical mass of expertise and resources in concentrated locales (e.g., the city of Bangalore in India; see Table 4.5). Firms involved with software services outsourcing and **business processing outsourcing** (BPO) are rapidly gaining ground in places such as the Philippines and Malaysia (call centers and other back-office BPO), China (embedded software, financial firms, back office BPO, some application development), Russia and Israel (high-end customized software and expert systems), and Ireland (packaged software and product development). At the same time, the higher value-added, better-paying jobs in management, finance, marketing, and research and development have been retained in the United States, as we found within the manufacturing sector. Estimates suggest these outsourcing trends will continue. Forrester Research predicts that $151.2 billion in wages will be shifted from the United States to lower-wage countries by 2015, while Dobbs (2004a) argues that this trend will affect some 3.4 million white-collar service jobs in 550 of the 700 service job categories in the United States in the coming decade.

The changes in the software industry are consistent with the arguments of neoliberals and Marxists alike[4]: that the United States will shed low-wage jobs and retain the higher-end, more profitable ones. For the neoliberals, the transition is a temporary one that will eventually lead to better jobs and higher income; for the Marxists, the results are not so benign. We might even ask how much it matters if those bearing the majority of the costs today will be better off in the *long run*. When confronted with a similar situation many years ago, J. M. Keynes replied that in the long run no one benefits. With this in mind, what are the ramifications of all these changes for class inequality in the United States?

Patterns in Class Inequality

Income

As we mentioned in Chapter 5, differences in income, wealth, and poverty are central indicators of class stratification. How, then, have the structural shifts—from manufacturing to services and changes within the manufacturing and service sectors—affected class stratification in the United States? In general, the nature of these shifts has contributed to a widening in the income gap in the United States, which many suggest is wider today than at any time since the Great Depression. Data from the Center on Budget and Policy Priorities and the Economic Policy Institute, for instance, indicate that the income gaps have widened in 45 states over the past 20 years (Bernstein et al. 2002). But not all have experienced declines in income. Professional, administrative, and technical workers have experienced the greatest returns for their labor, as shown in Table 6.1.

Table 6.1 Changes in Hourly Wages by Selected Occupation (Males),
1973–2001 (2001 Dollars)

	1973	2001
White-collar occupations		
Managers	$22.08	$27.53
Professional	$22.12	$26.31
Technical	$18.80	$21.38
Other services	$12.49	$11.42
Blue-collar occupations		
Craft	$17.18	$16.21
Operatives	$13.47	$13.05
Laborers	$12.34	$10.75

Source: Mishel, Bernstein, and Schmitt (2001, 125).

While these data are consistent with the occupational shifts described above, they likely underestimate the earnings of professional workers, which often include bonuses and stock options. For instance, those in the top 5 percent of income earners saw their income increase the most after the 1970s. Part of this story is the often ignored issue of CEO compensation. During the 1990s, CEO compensation soared to unprecedented heights. Data from United for a Fair Economy (2001, 10) show that "if the minimum wage, which stood at $3.80 an hour in 1990, had grown at the same rate as CEO pay over the decade, it would now be $25.50 an hour [2001], rather than the current $5.15 an hour." According to *Business Week* (2004a), the pay gap between an average blue-collar salary and the CEO of a large company was 531-to-1 in 2000 and remained more than 300-to-1 in 2003 compared 42-to-1 in 1982 (also Gill 2001).[5] For the average blue-collar worker, wages did not keep up with inflation after the 1980s, which supports another finding: the severing of the historical link between rising productivity and rising median family income. Historically, the two tended to rise together, but from 1973 to 2003 median family income grew less than one-third as fast as productivity (Mishel, Bernstein, and Allegreto 2005).

Thus, it is not surprising that the median annual real income per worker *fell* from $25,896 in 1979 to $24,700 in 1995 (Table 6.1). By 2003, the average worker was taking home $517 in the weekly paycheck; the average CEO collected $155,769 weekly. We might note that the average worker probably makes less than these figures suggest. According to the Economic Policy Institute, the hourly wage for (male) blue-collar workers as a group declined from $15.02 per hour in 1973 to $14.32 per hour (2001 dollars) in 2001 (Mishel, Bernstein, and Schmitt 2001, 125). Yet, for (male) laborers—a subcategory of blue-collar workers—the hourly wage declined from $12.34 to $10.75 (2001 dollars) during the same period. The hourly wage decline was even greater

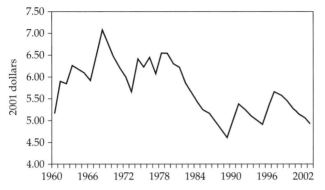

Figure 6.2 Real value of the minimum wage (2001 dollars), 1960–2002. *Source*: Mishel, Bernstein, and Boushey (2003, 197).

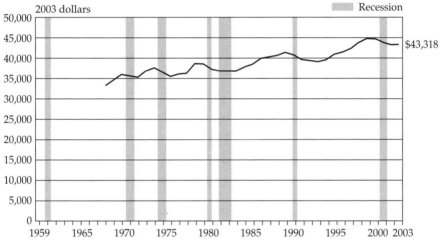

Figure 6.3 Changes in real median household income, 1967–2005.
Note: The data points are placed at the midpoints of the respective years. Median household income data are not available before 1967. *Source*: DeNavas-Walt, Proctor, and Lee (2005, 3).

for those working at minimum wage (7 million adult workers in 2000), as Figure 6.2 shows. The changes are reflected in that fact that by the year 2000 the average income for the top 1 percent of the population was 88.5 times that of the lowest 20 percent, an increase from 33 times since 1979 (Mishel, Bernstein, and Allegretto 2005).

The sum of these changes is reflected in income trends since the 1950s. To begin, data in Figure 6.3 indicate that as a nation we are much richer in terms of household income since the late 1960s. Compared with 1967, the first year for which household income statistics are available, real median household

Table 6.2   Change in Family Income by Quintile and the Top 5 Percent,
1947–1979

	BOTTOM 20%	SECOND 20%	MIDDLE 20%	FOURTH 20%	TOP 20%	TOP 5%
1979 Income range	Up to $9,861	$9,861–$16,215	$16,215–$22,972	$22,972–$31,632	$31,632 and up	$50,746 and up
1947–1979 Income change	+116%	+100%	+111%	+114%	+99%	+86%

Table 6.3   Change in Family Income by Quintile and the Top 5 Percent,
1979–2001

	BOTTOM 20%	SECOND 20%	MIDDLE 20%	FOURTH 20%	TOP 20%	TOP 5%
2001 Income range	Up to $24,000	$24,000–$41,127	$41,127–$62,500	$62,500–$94,150	$94,150 and up	$164,104 and up
1979–2001 Income change	+3%	+11%	+17%	+26%	+53%	+81%

Sources: Data for Tables 6.2 and 6.3 are from United for a Fair Economy, n.d.

income is up 30 percent. Median income peaked in 1999, was unchanged in 2000, and declined over the next 2 years (Mishel, Bernstein, and Allegretto 2005).

If we look at changes within the aggregate data, a different picture emerges. Data in Tables 6.2 and 6.3 reveal a stark difference in the trends before 1970 and those after 1980—precisely the point at which the United States became more integrated into the global economy. Leading up to the 1970s, the data indicate a growing *equality* as the share of total income grew more rapidly for the lower and middle quintiles than for the top quintile. After 1979, however, the trend reversed itself as the share of total income going to the top quintile accelerated and growth dramatically slowed for the lower and middle quintiles. Overall, U.S. society has become *more unequal* since the late 1970s. In other words, the distribution of income reflects the polarization in the occupational structure—or the hourglass phenomenon—with growth in the low- and high-income quintiles and a shrinking in the middle.

Wealth

Wealth is a better indicator of inequality for the reasons we mentioned in Chapter 5 (e.g., links to power, opportunities to generate additional income, greater life chances, among others). Existing data on wealth reveal trends that are not unexpected. Recall that by *net worth* we are talking about total assets less any liabilities. Data in Table 6.4 and Figure 6.4 indicate the trend since the

Table 6.4 Distribution of Net Worth (by Population Segments—Quintiles)

WEALTH CLASS	1983	1989	1992	1995	1998
Top 1%	33.8	37.4	37.2	38.5	38.1
Next 4%	22.3	21.6	22.8	21.8	21.3
Next 5%	12.1	11.6	11.8	11.5	11.5
Next 10%	13.1	13.0	12.0	12.1	12.5
Next 20%	12.6	12.3	11.5	11.4	11.9
Middle 20%	5.2	4.8	4.4	4.5	4.5
Bottom 40%	0.9	−0.7	0.4	0.2	0.2

Source: Wolff (2000).

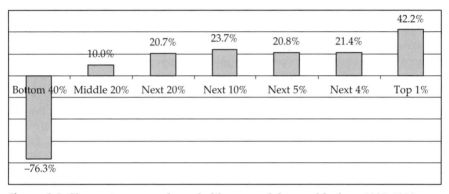

Figure 6.4 Change in average household net worth by wealth class, 1983–1998. *Source*: Wolff (2000: Table 3).

early 1980s. Note that in 1989 the bottom 20 percent of the U.S. population actually had a *negative* net worth! Overall, however, we can see that by the late 1990s the top 1 percent of the U.S. population controlled almost 40 percent of the total assets of the United States, while 90 percent of the population shared 29 percent of the total assets. Has this changed since 1983? Yes: The top 1 percent has *increased* its control from 34 percent, while the bottom 90 percent of the population has *lost* 2.8 percent. Overall, the bottom 40 percent of the population suffered the greatest decline, which is precisely what we would expect given the changes in the U.S. economy since the end of the 1970s (see Domhoff 1998, 2002).

Finally, the data on income and wealth are suggestive of another, more hidden trend: the rapid growth of millionaires and billionaires in the United States. Between 1997 and 2005, the number of millionaires grew from 1,800,000 to 7,500,000, while in the 10 years after 1996, the number of billionaires increased from 179 to over 400 (Lynch Capgemini Consulting 2000, Figure 3; 2001; Christie 2005; *Forbes* 2006).

Poverty

As the number of millionaires and billionaires increased, so too did the number of children in poverty: up from 3.4 million in 1979 to 13 million in 2004 (Eitzen and Baca Zinn 2003, 182–183; Children's Defense Fund 2004). And 8.9 million of these children are in working families—an increase of 623,000 since 2001 (Children's Defense Fund 2004). Today, people under the age of 18 have the highest **poverty rate** of any age group, with one in six children in the United States living in poverty (DeNavas, Proctor, and Mills 2004). The point? When we discuss wealth and the rich, we imply that there are individuals who are not rich—the poor. The most common indicator of the *lack of wealth* is poverty.

What do we mean by poverty? We can think of poverty in two ways: relative and absolute. By **relative poverty**, we mean an individual's economic position relative to the prevailing living standards of the society. From this perspective, an individual may be able to buy her or his basic necessities (e.g., food, shelter, and clothing) but unable to maintain the *average standard of living* for members of that society. By **absolute poverty**, we mean that an individual lacks the minimal requirements to sustain a healthy existence (e.g., the basic necessities of food, clothing, and shelter). To reduce relative poverty, the gap between the wealthy and the poor must be reduced (the distributional question); to reduce absolute poverty, the income of the poorest needs to be raised above the poverty line—or the annual amount of income a family requires to meet its basic needs. Thus, it is possible to have no absolute poverty with an extremely unequal distribution of income or high relative poverty.

In the United States, we use the absolute method, with the poverty line determined by the government and adjusted to reflect family size and annual inflation.[6] We included data for the years 2000 and 2004 in Table 6.5 to give you an idea of what the poverty line looks like in the United States. By using the poverty line, we can identify the percentage of the population that is "officially" poor, or the poverty rate. Trend data for the poverty rate and the number of poor in the United States are provided in Figure 6.5. The data suggest two points. First, the trends in the poverty rate reflect changes in the distribution of income: poverty declined through the mid-1970s, began to increase until the mid-1990s, and once more began to increase after 2000. Second, the trend is consistent with the overall transformation of the U.S. economy within the context of globalization.

Inequality and Poverty by Race and Ethnicity

How do race and ethnicity fit in here? In general, the data suggest patterns quite similar to the polarizing trends in the economy as a whole. Data on income in Table 6.6 show that the income gap has increased across all racial groups relative to whites since 1983. Moreover, the gap grows even wider

Table 6.5 U.S. Poverty Thresholds by Family Size and Year

2000		2004	
FAMILY SIZE (PERSONS)	POVERTY THRESHOLD ($)	FAMILY SIZE (PERSONS)	POVERTY THRESHOLD ($)
1	8,794	1	9,645
2	11,239	2	12,334
3	13,739	3	15,067
4	17,603	4	19,307
5	20,819	5	22,831
6	23,528	6	25,788
7	26,754	7	29,236
8	29,701	8	32,641
9 or more	35,060	9 or more	39,048

Note: Poverty thresholds are used to calculate the poverty rate, while the Department of Health and Human Service's poverty guidelines are used to determine financial eligibility for certain programs. To compare the two, see the data at http://aspe.hhs.gov/poverty/04poverty.shtml.
Source: U.S. Bureau of the Census (2000; 2004).

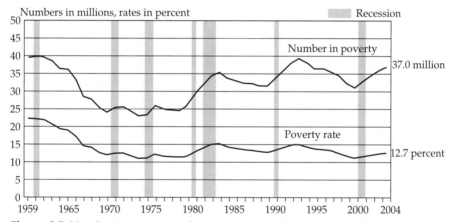

Figure 6.5 Number in poverty and poverty rate, 1959–2004. *Note*: The data points are placed at the midpoints of the respective years. *Source*: DeNavas-Walt, Proctor, and Lee (2005: 13).

when we adjust income for wealth. The data for African Americans show a wealth gap with whites that is larger than the income gap; since 1983, both the mean wealth-adjusted income and income gaps have grown wider. Looking at the data for Latinos, there was a steep drop in wealth-adjusted income and income relative to whites from 1983 to 2001 (e.g., median wealth-adjusted income dropped from 0.61 to 0.50 and median income declined from

Table 6.6 Family Income by Racial and Ethnic Groups

	1983		1983 RATIO TO WHITES		2001		2001 RATIO TO WHITES	
	MEDIAN	MEAN	MEDIAN	MEAN	MEDIAN	MEAN	MEDIAN	MEAN
Non-Hispanic whites								
Income	38,540	51,658	1.00	1.00	43,586	72,860	1.00	1.00
Wealth-adjusted income[a]	42,243	62,013	1.00	1.00	52,591	97,108	1.00	1.00
African Americans								
Income	21,474	29,231	0.56	0.57	24,683	36,321	0.57	0.50
Wealth-adjusted income	22,324	31,093	0.53	0.50	25,714	39,356	0.49	0.41
Latinos								
Income	25,693	32,912	0.67	0.64	25,711	39,494	0.59	0.54
Wealth-adjusted income	25,719	34,523	0.61	0.56	26,365	41,709	0.50	0.43
Asian and other races								
Income	38,356	51,619	1.00	1.00	34,967	61,544	0.80	0.85
Wealth-adjusted income	40,156	55,303	0.95	0.89	38,508	75,514	0.73	0.78

[a] Money income minus property income (sum of dividends, interest, and rent) plus income from home and non-home wealth.
Source: Wolff and Zacharias (2006).

0.67 to 0.59). This may reflect the characteristics of Latino immigration during the 1980s and 1990s that, as we discuss in the next chapter, was driven by an insatiable need for low-wage labor. The outlier, at least initially, was the Asian population, which had a virtual parity with whites in wealth-adjusted income and money income in 1983. By 2001, however, the ratios slipped, with wealth-adjusted income declining to three-quarters and income dropping to 0.80 (median) and 0.85 (mean) compared to whites. Similar to the Latino population, one possible factor is the large Asian immigration and expansion of the Asian population in the intervening years.

Other evidence supports the data in Table 6.6. According to Mishel, Bernstein, and Allegreto (2005) and United for a Fair Economy (2006), the average income for white families has risen 34 percent since 1995 while African American and Latino family income has risen 25 percent. Still, this masks the fact that African American and Latino families *lost* income between 2001 and 2003 at a rate faster than did white families: a negative 1.5 percent for African Americans and a negative 2.3 percent for Latinos compared to a negative 0.5 percent for whites. In terms of wealth, the median African American family saw no growth in net worth from 2001 to 2004; yet, mean African American net worth grew sharply, up 37 percent, reflecting growing inequality among African American families. In fact, income growth among the top 5 percent of African American families increased by 61 percent from 1979 to 2001, while the bottom 20 percent saw an increase of only 1 percent. Finally, poverty rates for African American and Latino families have remained roughly twice that of white families since the 1970s (in 2003 the rates were 24 percent, 22 percent, and 10.2 percent, respectively, according to U.S. Bureau of the Census data). For Asian families, poverty levels have been roughly on par with white families.

Working Hours

Given the nature of the changes in the U.S. economy, inequality and poverty rates might have been even higher had the average U.S. worker not increased his or her working hours. By the year 1997, U.S. workers were logging the greatest number of hours of all industrialized nations, averaging 1,966 hours per year, *up* from 1,942 hours in 1990 (it was 1,978 in 2000). In comparison, the average Japanese worker—long known for working the longest hours—put in 1,899 hours per year in 1997, *down* from 2,031 in 1992. Comparative 1997 figures for Norway and Sweden are 1,399 and 1,522, respectively (ILO 2001).

Although U.S. Bureau of the Census interviews show that the average male worked 43.5 hours a week in 1970 and 43.1 hours a week in 2000 and the average female worked 37.1 hours in 1970 and 37.0 hours in 2000, these averages are misleading (Gerson and Jacobs 2004, 30). To begin, more workers are putting in over 50 hours per week and more workers are logging fewer than

30 hours per week. Additionally, today, when the dual-income family is the norm, we find that 60 percent of couples (parents and nonparents alike) work more than *80 hours* per week—compared to 71 hours in the United Kingdom and 69 hours in Sweden—and 12 percent of U.S. families work in excess of *100 hours* per week (Gerson and Jacobs 2004).

There are several immediate explanations for the changes in work hours. First, when faced with declining wages and insecure employment, workers must put in more hours (sometimes at multiple jobs) in order to survive economically. Second, while the average workweek for individuals has decreased, it has increased for couples as more women are working. For instance, in 1970, one-third of all married-couple families had two wage earners; by 2000, this had increased to two-thirds (Gerson and Jacobs 2004, 33). A third factor is that increasingly employers are expecting more hours, which is particularly true in the white-collar sector of the economy.

Average work hours in the professional service sector have steadily increased over time to the point that currently over 25 million Americans work more than 49 hours each week and some log a good deal more. Nearly 12 percent of the workforce (about 15 million people) report spending 49–59 hours weekly at the office, and 8.5 percent (11 million) spend 60 or more hours there (Fraser 2001). Here, we need to keep in mind the re-organization of the workplace we mentioned earlier, which has increased the workload and job spill for millions of workers. Most of these people are white-collar professionals—corporate managers, marketing staffers, investment bankers, office administrators, software designers, lawyers, editors, engineers, accountants, business consultants, and the secretaries, word processors, computer programmers, and back office clerks who support their activities (Fraser 2001). Fraser (2001) argues that in some industries, among them the technology and financial services sectors, the norms—everyday expectations about just how much time people should spend at the office each day—have become so extreme that a 12-hour workday can seem "positively lightweight."

The Working and the New Poor

The trends in the income, wealth, and poverty data are consistent with what we would expect given the structural changes induced by globalization: the shedding of traditional manufacturing jobs, the growing numbers of both high-wage professional jobs and low-wage service and industrial jobs, and the reorganization of jobs and changes in requirements in both the service and industrial sectors. As firms continue to outsource, downsize, and introduce technology, they *directly* affect the number and type of jobs available in the United States and create a more polarized labor force. This is reflected in a growing number of working and **new poor** (Barrington 2000; Thurow 1987; Harrison and Bluestone 1988; Mishel and Bernstein 1993; Mishel, Bernstein, and Schmitt 2001).

Data, for instance, show that jobs in expanding occupations pay 21 percent less per year than jobs in contracting ones, suggesting links between globalization and the **working poor** (see Dobbs 2004a, Ettinger and Chapman 2004). The official definition of *working poor* is anyone working 27 weeks per year who falls below the poverty line. Moreover, 22 percent of jobs in the United States were in occupations that paid below the poverty level in 2000 (U.S. Department of Labor 2004). In the states of Alabama, Arkansas, Florida, Louisiana, Mississippi, Montana, New Mexico, North Dakota, Oklahoma, South Dakota, West Virginia, and Wyoming, more than 30 percent of the jobs were in occupations that paid below the poverty level in 2002 (AECF 2004). Not surprisingly, 7.4 million of the 34.6 million persons officially defined as poor in 2002 were classified as the working poor (about 560,000 more than in 2001), according to the U.S. Department of Labor (2004). Of these 7.4 million workers, 29.3 percent worked in the service sector; yet, only 2 percent of those in such service occupations as managers and professionals were classified as working poor. Even more troubling is the fact that 11.5 percent of the poor worked *full time and year round* in 2004—9.4 million compared to 7.7 percent in 1978 (U.S. Bureau of the Census 2006).

If we break down these numbers by race and ethnicity, we find that 30.4 percent of black workers and 39.8 percent of Hispanic workers earned poverty-level wages in 2003 (Mishel, Bernstein, and Allegreto 2005). As a result, we find that African Americans and Latinos are heavily represented among the working poor: 10.5 percent of African Americans and 10.4 percent of Latinos were classified as working poor compared to 4.5 percent of whites and 4.6 percent of Asians (U.S. Bureau of Labor Statistics 2004). Consistent with the overall changes in the economy—and leaving aside issues of discrimination—we find fewer African American and Latino workers among the poor and working poor as we move up the educational ladder or into managerial, professional, and related occupations (U.S. Bureau of Labor Statistics, 2004).

Many of these workers are also categorized as part of the new poor— or those people displaced by new technologies or mass layoffs and plant closings who have difficulty moving out of poverty. The poor of previous generations had hopes and opportunities to experience upward social mobility, but the new poor are not so fortunate. About 15 percent of the "tens of millions of Americans" who have lost their jobs in the past two decades because of these changes could not find employment (Eitzen and Baca Zinn 2003, 188).

A related category of the working and new poor are displaced older workers (see Helyar 2005). Between 1970 and 1998, for instance, the **labor-force participation** of men aged 55–65 declined from about 79 percent to roughly 70 percent (Carnoy 2000, 28). More recent evidence suggests that globalization via increasing competition and the use of technology is also rapidly affecting younger workers—those over 40 (Fraser 2001; Helyar 2005).

Looking once more at the software industry, 5 years after finishing college, about 60 percent of computer science graduates are working as programmers;

at 15 years, the figure drops to 34 percent, and at 20 years—when most are still only age 42 or so—it is down to 19 percent (Fraser 2001, 139). "Older" workers in the software industry suffer longer bouts of unemployment when laid off, where each additional age of a "mid-career" programmer (mid-forties) seeking a new job translates to three additional weeks of unemployment (Fraser 2001, 137). The employment tend is toward new and recent college graduates who command less salary, cost less in terms of benefits, and are more likely to work large amounts of unpaid overtime. Changing technology raises skill requirements, which younger workers are more likely to have; and because training and retraining costs are high, employers tend to shun poorly educated workers, especially older workers. Although this argument is not new, a study by William Baumol and Edward Wolff (quoted in Koretz 1999) shows a positive correlation between the lengthening of jobless spells and research and development outlays and spending on computers per employee. The most significant factor for longer jobless spells for older workers is the increase in computer outlays (Koretz 1999).

A View from the Bottom: Insecurity and Vulnerability

The direct effects of globalization are clearly evident in increased income and wealth inequality, which alter the well-being of individuals and families in the United States and across the globe. We need to keep in mind that the consequences of our class position, as Beth Shulman (2003) argues, are "about more than money" and affect our life chances—where we live, what we eat, the type of health care and schools we can afford for our children, and our access to transportation. Within the context of tighter, more competitive global labor markets, U.S. workers find themselves in jobs that are increasingly competitive, demanding, and insecure.

The need for employer flexibility, as we noted, is closely connected to these outcomes. Yet, in what might be called the "workplace paradox," most employees work in jobs characterized by *inflexibility*; employers want the flexibility to determine when, where, and how their employees will work, without the state or labor unions regulating employee–employer relations. Yet, among low-wage workers, only 13 percent are able to adjust their start and finish time at work when necessary (Galinsky and Bond, forthcoming). In these cases, any delay in getting to work—even 5 minutes—can result in disciplinary action, a cut in pay, or dismissal. Employers typically do not hesitate to rid themselves of workers in such cases, especially those in low-wage jobs in which employers have invested little time or money in such things as worker training. In 1996, for instance, 53.5 million workers—40 percent of the total labor force—worked in jobs that required only short-term on-the-job training (Silvestri 1997). Similarly, if jobs require little skill and workers are quickly and easily available, employers will not think twice about replacing workers.

Moreover, the impact of declining union power on workers, their families, and communities cannot be overstated, especially for those at the lower end of the wage spectrum (Card 1998). Some estimate, for instance, that unions increase wages for workers at the lower-wage sectors of the economy as much as 30 percent and a unionized high school graduate earns 21 percent more than the equivalent nonunion worker. When other types of compensation ensured by unions are considered, however, the total compensation is much higher (Mishel, Bernstein, and Schmitt 2001). Health-care insurance coverage, for example, is 35 percent higher in union than nonunion establishments (Belman and Heywood 1991, Fosu 1993).

These data are particularly meaningful when analyzed within the changing context of work. Unionized employees are also more likely to have retirement plans and to gain access to worker protections such as wage and work-hour guarantees, promotional procedures, due process in firings and layoffs, and unemployment insurance (Freeman 1980, Belman and Heywood 1991, Fosu 1993, Budd and McCall 2004, U.S. GAO 2000). Such benefits provide short- and long-term security for workers and their families. Without such benefits, the prolonged illness (or injury) of a family member, a bout of unemployment (even a temporary one), or the reduction of work hours can be devastating.[7]

Particularly vulnerable are those who have little savings or economic assets (wealth) to fall back on. Personal savings in the United States have declined drastically from 10 percent of personal disposable income in 1980 to 2 percent in 2003 (U.S. Bureau of Economic Analysis 2004). A Gallup survey conducted in 2003 reported that four in ten Americans say they could survive without a job for only about a month before "experiencing significant financial hardship" (Jacobe 2005). For families of color, savings is even more problematic, with more than twice as many African American households (30.9 percent) as white households (13.1 percent) having zero or negative net worth in 2001. In fact, while nearly three-quarters of whites owned their homes, less than half of African American or Latinos were homeowners in 2003—white, 72 percent; African American, 48 percent; Latino, 46.7 percent (Mishel, Bernstein, and Allegreto 2005).

Related to this, consumer debt has been steadily rising since 1970 (Board of Governors of the Federal Reserve System 2003). As one might expect, the debt burden is highest for those at the lower end of the income hierarchy. In 1998, for example, the debt burden was highest for those families earning less than $10,000 a year and the next highest debt burden was typically carried by families with incomes between $25,000 and $49,999. This growing burden of debt means increasing financial insecurity for most households, particularly families of color (Mishel, Bernstein, and Allegreto 2005). Personal bankruptcies shot up from 330,000 in 1980 to 1.4 million in 1990 (Henwood 1999) and in 2002 hit a record of over 1.5 million (Redmond 2003).

As more and more working individuals and families struggle to balance their responsibilities on the job and at home, people are working longer hours and multiple jobs to offset what have been reductions in pay and benefits. The effects of these changes on the family are particularly ominous. Carnoy (2000) argues that these changes are a major reason that young adults are increasingly unwilling to enter serious relationships until late in their twenties. Marriage remains a goal of most young adults, but they are waiting to get married and, once married, delay having children (Carnoy 2000). One result is an increasing number of families that care for not only young children (and young adults) but older parents or relatives as well. Yet, these may be the fortunate families; families lacking "built-in child care" must often patch together child care in ways that leave parents anxious and may potentially put their children in jeopardy (Presser 2003, Han 2005).

Faced with such challenges, parents adopt a variety of strategies to ensure economic survival and to provide for the health and well-being of their families. As we noted above, there has been a steady increase not only in the average number of individual work hours but also in the number of hours worked by all family members since the 1970s (Bernstein and Kornbluh 2004, Gerson and Jacobs 2004). While such strategies increase family wages, the day-to-day lives of individuals and their families often suffer. More than one-quarter of working women, including mothers, for example, spend at least some of their nights and weekends at work, and nearly half of all women who are married or living with someone work different schedules from their spouses or partners (AFL-CIO n.d.b).

The stress effects of such work arrangements on marital relationships can undermine otherwise healthy relationships (Rubin 1995). As couples struggle to juggle money, time, and child care, they have less quality time together, less leisure time, fewer meaningful conversations, and engage in fewer, if any, social or community activities. Combine this with the finding that 40 percent of U.S. workers describe their jobs as "very" or "extremely" stressful and we have a recipe for disaster. Living under these conditions takes a toll on workers' health and day-to-day family lives. The National Institute for Occupational Safety and Health, for instance, records that self-reported "stressed" employees incur health-care costs that are 46 percent higher—an average of $600 more per person per year—than employees who are not stressed (Healy 2005). For children, rising stress levels are even more hazardous. According to research from the Children's Defense Fund (2005), children who live in families with annual incomes less than $15,000 are 22 times more likely to be abused or neglected than children living in families with annual incomes of $30,000 or more. The culprit, according to the research? Stress. There is a great deal more stress in lower-income families.

What does this mean for the family? Clearly, the family is changing, and trying to manage a complex matrix of work, personal, and family lives can have devastating effects on mental and physical health. As market forces unleashed by the policies that have been instituted since the crisis of the 1970s continue to individualize and atomize our society, workers and families increasingly confront these market forces alone. How we respond to the heightened vulnerability and insecurity will determine the future health of our families as well as that of our communities.

Conclusion

In this chapter, we have examined how the economic changes in the United States have affected class stratification. As the global economic environment becomes more competitive and unions become less central to the lives of U.S. workers, the U.S. economy and occupational categories have been dramatically transformed. Contrary to the predictions of neoliberal globalists, however, globalization has *increased* the share of lower-wage employment in the United States, not decreased it. Globalization has created conditions of *greater* insecurity, not less. Globalization has *widened* the margin of inequality, not narrowed it. African American, Latino, and white families structurally located in the blue-collar sector have been particularly hard hit by the transformations, which involved the outsourcing of good-paying manufacturing jobs and a corresponding decline in wages. Still, few workers have been immune to these changes. Middle-class and professional workers also saw many of their jobs disappear or take on qualities that left less money and time for themselves and their families. For the poor and working poor, globalization has transformed them into our society's major philanthropists, greasing the wheels of economic growth by cleaning the rooms of the globe-trotting capitalists, delivering the food to the Wall Streeters burning the midnight oil, and neglecting their own children to care for the children of others (see Ehrenreich 2001).

Globalization has not created the conditions for widespread upward social mobility (or even those needed to get out of debt!). Not only have U.S. workers been increasingly *substituted* with low-paid labor in developing countries (outsourcing) and/or by technological advancements but the jobs that remain in the United States require workers to be flexible, competitive, and educated. The irony is that the demand for a *flexible* labor force has resulted in a tremendous *inflexibility and insecurity* for workers at all levels of the occupational hierarchy.

In the end, all workers are confronting heavier demands on their time, their money, and their other resources (medical care, unemployment benefits, etc.). What does this mean for the future of our communities and our society when we have less time for our families and communities and fewer opportunities to acquire the requisite skills to improve our positions in the global labor market? What does it mean for our society when the middle and upper classes ignore or are too economically insecure to care about the poor and working poor? How might we reverse these trends? These questions have taken on a renewed sense of urgency as the globalization of the U.S. economy continues under a political and ideological framework that deifies individualism and markets.

CHAPTER 7

Globalization and Immigration

- Undocumented migrants now comprise one-third to one-half of new entrants to most developed countries, including the United States—up from about one-fifth a decade ago.
- In 2000, women and girls accounted for almost 49 percent of all international emigrants.
- Today, more than 140 million people—nearly 1 in 40 of the world's population—live outside their countries of birth, and immigrants comprise more than 15 percent of the population in over 50 countries.

These data from the National Intelligence Council (2001) and Hania Zlotnik (2003) underscore the magnitude of human mobility throughout the world. In the United States, "the nation of immigrants," virtually everyone is connected to the immigration process. Your parents, grandparents, great-grandparents—someone in your family—made the decision to move to the United States. You may have even recently moved to the United States or to the present city or town you call home. People have always moved—some more often than others—but the magnitude and dispersion of people on the move particularly since the mid-1980s has led Castles and Miller (1998) to observe that the closing years of the twentieth century and the beginning of the twenty-first may well be understood as the "age of migration."

Skeptics of globalization dispute Castles and Miller's assertion, arguing that the era of the greatest openness and movement of people was the 1870–1913 belle époque (Hirst and Thompson 1999). Although data suggest that recent relocation trends do not compare in magnitude to those of the turn of the twentieth century, globalization has altered the nature of the flow of humanity among countries and has ushered in what we can justifiably term a new era in the history of migration. In this chapter, we consider how globalization and global processes have encouraged and sustained migration flows to the United States and the role of immigrants in the United States and the challenges they face.

Overview

Global Immigration Patterns

During the belle époque, labor migration was dominated by unskilled and low-skilled workers who moved from "north to south" and from "east to west." In other words, low-skilled labor moved from the more developed European nations to less developed areas such as the United States and South America. The flow of capital paralleled labor migration, moving north to south and east to west (see Ghose 2003).

Current patterns of labor migration reflect the complexity of the multi-faceted process of globalization. To begin, contemporary migration is geographically more extensive and involves a truly global labor force consisting of both high-skilled and low-skilled labor. Not only are more countries affected by migration but, as Massey, Goldring, and Duran (1994) show, the movement is mainly south to north and in the *opposite direction* of the movement of capital. Evidence also suggests that an increasing number of high-skilled laborers are moving from less developed areas around the world to the United States and Europe and that those who migrate are more likely to return to their place of birth or move on to a third country. These new trends can be attributed to declining migration costs (due to declining costs of transportation and communication), the growing gap between the richest and poorest countries of the world, and greater access to information (Ghose 2003, 87; UNDP 2004, 87). These same factors also affect low-skilled migration, but, as Ghose (2003) shows, the dominant trend continues to be migration between geographically proximate countries (e.g., migration from Turkey and North Africa to Western Europe and Mexican and Central American migration to the United States). Finally, we should note that women are immigrating in greater numbers—comprising one-half of all international migrants—among (and within) countries as tourism, global trade, and greater wealth concentration throughout the world have led to the explosion of the low-wage service and manufacturing sectors. While women used to migrate primarily as dependants, they are increasingly doing so on their own as breadwinners in what some call the **feminization of migration** (UNDP 2004, 87).

Beyond these general trends, patterns vary. Taking into account high-skilled migration, or what some call "elite" migration, globalization has created a bidirectional movement. Many of the estimated 25 million high-skilled workers (Munck 2005, 108) who emigrate are white males born in the United States (or Europe); they work as managers, consultants, information specialists, and high-tech specialists for U.S. (or European) transnational firms abroad (see McKendrick 2004). The movement of high-skilled workers also includes female nurses (from the Philippines) as well as male and female engineers, medical doctors, and scientists migrating to the United States and Europe from places such as India and China.[1] Later in this chapter we return to this issue of "brain drain," or the migration of educated and high-skilled workers to the United States and Europe, which augments the human capital stock of countries receiving immigrants (the United States) and depletes the human capital stock of countries sending immigrants (India and China).

U.S. Immigration Patterns

Focusing on the United States, the data show that the United States receives a significant percentage of total global migration flows (Ghose 2003, 83–90). Although significant numbers of people migrated to the United States throughout the twentieth century, it was not until after the 1990s that migration flows spiked (Table 7.1). During the 1990s, one out of every two new workers was an immigrant (Sum, Fogg, and Harrington 2002) and nearly 40 percent of new U.S. jobs, including those for software engineers, were filled by immigrants (National Intelligence Council 2001).

Throughout the 1990s, the United States experienced record-high immigration, with more than 13 million people entering the country (Center for Immigration Studies 2002). By 2005, the foreign-born population reached 35.2 million, or 12.1 percent of the total U.S. population. This compares to a historic low of 4.7 percent in 1970 and 6.2 percent in 1980. Today, almost one in eight U.S. residents is foreign-born, the highest percentage in over 80 years. If this trend continues, within 10 years the foreign-born share of the population will match the all-time high of 14.8 percent reached in 1890 (Center for Immigration Studies 2002).

Who are these migrants? Consistent with the new trends, contemporary migration to the United States combines both high-skilled and low-skilled

Table 7.1 Size of the Foreign-Born Population and Foreign-Borns as a Percentage of the Total Population: United States, 1890–2000

YEAR	NUMBER IN MILLIONS	PERCENT OF TOTAL
2005	35.2	12.1
2003	33.5	11.7
2000	28.4	10.4
1990	19.8	7.9
1980	14.1	6.2
1970	9.6	4.7
1950	10.3	6.9
1930	14.2	11.6
1910	13.5	14.7
1890	9.2	14.8
1850	2.2	9.5

Sources: The 2000, 2003, and 2005 data are from the U.S. Bureau of the Census; all other data are from Gibson and Lennon (1999).

labor that is overwhelmingly *non*-European in origin. Two-thirds of post-1960 immigration to the United States originated in the highly globalized Pacific Rim region: 52 percent from Latin America and the Caribbean (28 percent from Mexico alone) and another 15 percent from South and East Asia (Indochina, the Philippines, and China). Contrary to the stereotype that immigrants are primarily men, women alone or in families represent an increasingly significant factor, constituting half or more of some immigrant groups (Houstoun, Kramer, and Barrett 1984; also see Foner, Rumbaut, and Gold 2000).

What Motivates Migration to the United States?

Sassen (1990) argues that migration to the United States often follows previous flows of U.S. investment, military actions, or implementation of foreign policies. Investment affects migration in several ways. On the one hand, when a U.S. firm establishes a foreign subsidiary, skilled workers from the United States emigrate to work in these firms. On the other hand, investment creates conditions for the future migration of local engineers and scientists to the United States. Local professionals may acquire specialized training under the discipline of the U.S. labor system and even learn about better employment opportunities in the parent company through daily contact with U.S. managers and coworkers (Alarcón 2000). Still, professionals and technical workers seldom migrate because of unemployment in their country of origin; nor are they typically motivated by the gap between potential U.S. salaries and those at home. Rather, as Portes and Rumbaut (1996, 18) found, "the gap between available salaries and work conditions *in their own countries* and those regarded there as acceptable for people with their education" motivate migration. Thus, the globalization of cultural standards can figure into these decisions: if professional and technical workers *perceive* that their standard of living is inconsistent with their status and class, they are more likely to migrate.

Low-skilled migration is also encouraged by what is really an incomplete form of Schumpeter's creative destruction process (see Chapter 5). Recall that Schumpeter argued that investment often destroys some existing occupations, while rearranging the characteristics of others and creating new ones that offset those jobs lost. Today, however, foreign investment into the Third World destroys and rearranges existing occupations *without* a corresponding increase in new jobs to offset those lost. Because foreign investment typically involves the heavy use of technology and automation, production is increased at the expense of employment in countries that have an abundance of low-skilled labor. Finally, military actions and U.S. foreign policy objectives may fuel emigration. One recent example is the U.S.-sponsored wars in Central America during the 1980s that created tremendous social, political, and economic disruptions, which in turn created the conditions for migration to the United States during the 1980s and beyond.

Global Processes and Immigration

How does globalization more specifically affect migration? The conditions for globalization (e.g., advances in the information infrastructure, transportation, and neoliberal political policies) mean that firms can more easily relocate in order to take advantage of differential production costs between countries. These same conditions also mean that workers throughout the world have greater access to information about job opportunities in other countries. As globalization increasingly integrates the world and creates disruptions that manifest as unemployment, poverty, and marginalization, people are often left with few alternatives except to move.

The North American Free Trade Agreement (NAFTA) provides a good illustration of this process. When implemented in 1994, proponents of NAFTA promised that the liberalization of relations among Mexico, the United States, and Canada would create thousands of new high-wage jobs in the United States and in Mexico and that the standard of living in the United States, Mexico, and Canada would dramatically improve. Some 10 years later, these promises have yet to be fulfilled (see Faux 2006).

In Mexico, government policies that opened the economy to greater foreign investment have led to the loss of over 1.5 million rural jobs since 1994. Declining rural employment and the growing emphasis on agricultural production for export have distorted Mexican society. As thousands of newly unemployed rural workers migrate to Mexico's already overcrowded cities— where job growth is insufficient to absorb these new workers—the surging labor pool puts downward pressure on wages. Since the passage of NAFTA, for instance, the minimum wage has declined 20 percent, from approximately $5 per day to around $4 per day (Jordan 2003). Estimates by the Mexican government show that over one-half of the population earns less than what is required to cover the cost of basic necessities: food, clothing, housing, health care, public transportation, and education (Gallagher and Wise 2002). Equally important, rural job loss is heaviest among those producing foodstuffs for domestic consumption, which in turn increases the cost of food that, according to estimates by Public Citizen (2004), has increased 257 percent since 1994.

Caught between declining incomes and rising food costs, many decide to make the perilous journey to the United States in search of work. Data indicate that migration from Mexico to the United States has more than doubled since the introduction of NAFTA (U.S. Bureau of Citizenship and Immigration Services 2003). Increasingly, migrants are coming from the southern part of Mexico—the region most affected by NAFTA—rather than the traditional sending areas farther north. It is thus not surprising that the hotbed of resistance is in the most affected area: south Mexico, where the Zapatista rebellion emerged in 1994 and where other rural social movements have surfaced, such as *El campo no aguanta más* ("The Countryside Can't Take Any More"), which brought 100,000 protesters to Mexico City in 2003.[2]

Destination and Social Capital Networks

If someone makes the decision to migrate to the United States, does she or he choose a random destination, or is there a more structured process at work? Historically, people migrating to the United States have headed for the major metropolitan areas. If we focus on current immigration, we find a similar pattern whereby migration has flowed into the urban areas of six gateway states. In 2000, according to Meyers and Yau (2004), over two-thirds of the nation's total foreign-born population lived in six states: California (28 percent), New York (12 percent), Texas (9 percent), Florida (9 percent), New Jersey (5 percent), and Illinois (5 percent). This pattern may be changing, however, as increasing numbers of immigrants from Mexico and Central America—one of the most important sending regions—are settling in nontraditional destination states in the Midwest and deep South, such as Nebraska, Alabama, and Georgia (Mohl and Knudsen 2000; Duran, Massey, and Charvet 2000; Hernández-Léon and Zúñiga 2000; Gouveia 2000; Saenz 2004; also Hytrek and Wheat, unpublished data).

Current research shows that Latinos from Mexico, Guatemala, Honduras, Nicaragua, and El Salvador have become ubiquitous in both isolated rural localities (e.g., O'Neill and Lexington, Nebraska, or Dalton and Vidalia, Georgia) and metropolitan areas (e.g., Omaha, Atlanta, Memphis, and Birmingham) of these new destination sates (see Gouveia and Stull 1997; Mohl and Knudsen 2000; Hernández-Léon and Zúñiga 2000; Sassen and Smith 1992; Stull, Broadway, and Griffith 1995). During the 1990s, for instance, the Latino population increased 155 percent in Nebraska (Saenz 2004), 278 percent in Tennessee (Schenk 2003: 7, table 1), and over 300 percent in Georgia and Alabama (Georgia State University 2000). Yet, as recently as the early 1990s, it would have been highly unusual to encounter Latinos in places like the southeast or small midwestern towns. Today, it is not surprising to see immigrants in the Atlanta airport having just arrived in the United States on their first trip away from their family and village. While these immigrants arrive in Georgia speaking little or no English, they are embedded in transnational friendship or kinship **social capital networks**. It is a system that connects immigrants with labor contractors or employers looking for workers to fill jobs in factories, poultry plants, and the fields harvesting crops. Thus, migration is not a random process; it is structured by emerging and existing social networks.

Latino migration to the new destination states in the Midwest and Southeast reflects the creation of the above-mentioned ethnic communities and social capital networks beyond the gateway states. These social capital networks (see Chapter 9) refer to trust and norms of reciprocity, as well as other features of social organization, such as friendship and kinship networks and mutual assistance. As is the case with communities and networks in traditional receiving areas, immigrants rely on social capital networks to provide monetary and emotional assistance as well as information about jobs and daily life (housing, schools, legal issues, and so on) in their new country—i.e., the receiving country (see Massey et al. 1987, Massey and Espinoza 1997). We should note that immigrant communities and social networks have always been an essential feature of the migration process. Turn-of-the-century European immigrants, for example, sent letters home telling of their experiences and opportunities in the United States, thus motivating further migration. Yet, difficulties of communication and territorial distances separated these immigrants from their homeland. As a result, their bonds with "home" existed mainly in the imagination rather than in actual regular interaction (Scholte 2000b, 171).

Today, in contrast, the conditions of globalization (e.g., the information infrastructure) significantly enhance the capacities of immigrant groups to construct and maintain trans-territorial networks. Relatively inexpensive and immediate supraterritorial communication, such as e-mail, instant messaging, cell phones, and calling cards, allows for frequent and consistent contact. Latinos in Georgia, for instance, talk about how phone cards help sustain social networks by easing the process of sharing information about job opportunities with friends and relatives in other parts of the United States, Mexico, and Central America (Hytrek, unpublished data). In these emergent Latino communities, new immigrants are able to create and maintain a vibrant cultural life based on concrete realities that include food, kinship activities, sport, musical traditions, and Spanish-language newspapers—a cultural life centered in the home, restaurants, grocery stores, music and dance clubs, soccer leagues, and holiday festivals (Mohl and Knudsen 2000, 15).[3]

Occupational Location of Immigrants in the United States

By accelerating the flow of investment capital and information, globalization has contributed to migration pressures in places like Mexico and Central America, but what of the other side of the equation: the receiving areas? Immigrant job opportunities and experiences—like those of all workers—are shaped by the conditions of the labor market itself (i.e., economic prospects, stages in the business cycle, demands for specific kinds of labor, and so on). The same global processes restructuring Mexican society are reorganizing and transforming the U.S. economy and its occupational structures. Immigrants to the United States thus enter an economy characterized by polarized wage and skill differentials (see Chapters 5 and 6): the hourglass economy characterized by large numbers of low-wage jobs, moderate numbers of high-wage jobs, and few in the middle. Reflecting these structural characteristics and the human capital attributes of the immigrants, we find that one-quarter of foreign-born workers are employed in managerial and professional specialty jobs, while almost one-half are employed in low-wage service and blue-collar work (see Figure 7.2).

Table 7.2   Immigrant Shares and Earnings in Selected Occupations: 2002

OCCUPATION GROUP	PERCENT FOREIGN-BORN		MEAN EARNINGS OF FOREIGN-BORN WORKERS ($)
	ALL WORKERS (%)	LOW-WAGE WORKERS (%)	
All occupations	14	20	33,700
Private household	42	44	13,000
Farming, fishing, and forestry	37	44	15,500
Machine operators and assemblers	22	34	21,500
Administrative support, incl. clerical	9	10	27,400
Service, except protective	23	24	17,800
Precision production, craft, and repair	17	30	29,400

Source: Capps et al. (2003: table 3).

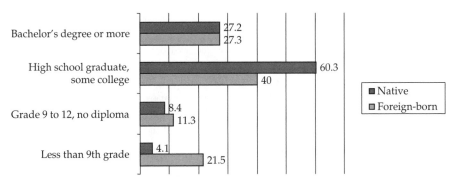

Figure 7.1 Population by educational attainment and nativity: 2003 (as a percentage of each population, 25 years and over). *Source*: Larsen (2004: 5).

The Brain Drain

Fix and Passel (1994) argue that while immigrants are more likely than natives to have very low educational attainment, a significant percentage have advanced degrees. Data in Figure 7.1 show that 67 percent of immigrants over the age of 25 have graduated from high school, while 21.5 percent have less than a ninth-grade education. This compares to 87.5 percent and 4.1 percent of native-borns, respectively. On the other hand, the percentage of immigrants with a bachelor's degree or more (27.3 percent) was not significantly different from that of the native-born population (27.2 percent).[4]

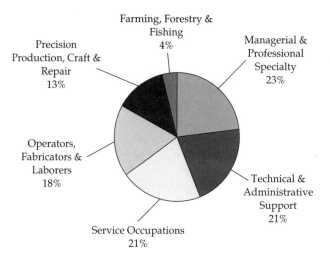

Farming, Forestry &
Fishing
4%

Precision
Production, Craft &
Repair
13%

Managerial &
Professional
Specialty
23%

Operators,
Fabricators &
Laborers
18%

Technical &
Administrative
Support
21%

Service Occupations
21%

Figure 7.2
Occupation of
employed foreign-
born workers in the
United States: 2002.
Source: Migration
Policy Institute
(2004: 3).

Immigrants with at least a bachelor's degree reflect, in part, the brain-drain phenomenon mentioned earlier. Many of these migrants to the United States enter the high-wage end of the job spectrum. According to the data in Figure 7.2, 23 percent of foreign-born workers are employed in managerial and professional specialty occupations and 21 percent are employed in technical, sales, and administrative positions (U.S. Bureau of Labor Statistics 2002). Immigrants also account for 42.2 percent of all physical scientists and 38.6 percent of all life scientists working in the educational and health services (Paral and Johnson 2004). Other data show that in 2002 the foreign-born accounted for 16.6 percent of all scientists and engineers, exceeding their 11.1 percent share of the U.S. population as a whole (Paral and Johnson 2004). Similarly, immigrants with doctoral degrees comprise 51 percent of engineers and 45 percent of life scientists, physical scientists, and mathematical and computer scientists (Paral and Johnson 2004).

Low-Wage Work

At the other end of the "hourglass," over half (56 percent) of all foreign-born workers are employed in blue-collar jobs—operators; fabricators and laborers; production, craft, and repair workers—and in service occupations (Figure 7.2). Table 7.2 disaggregates these categories. Accordingly, we find immigrants dominating the occupations of private household workers (42%); farming, fishing, and forestry (37%); machine operators and assemblers (22%); and service workers (23%).

These data are suggestive of the U.S. dependence on low-wage labor to produce, harvest, prepare, and serve our food; manufacture our clothing, furniture, and carpets; and landscape and maintain our properties. These labor demands are fulfilled through numerous mechanisms, including social networks, globalized information networks,[5] and recruitment by employers. While this may change in the near future, employers typically incur few supplemental employment costs or few recruitment costs and, until the 1980s, existing law specifically exempted employers from any liability for hiring undocumented workers.[6] Low-wage jobs also require little investment in worker training. In fact, employers often benefit from the social networks of the workers themselves, who are often willing to recruit, train, and manage other immigrants.

The characteristics of these jobs—low-skill requirements, low pay, and few benefits—keep large numbers of immigrant workers among the working poor. According to a study sponsored by the Urban Institute, one in nine U.S. residents is an immigrant but *one* in *five* is a low-wage worker. In 2001, for instance, the average low-wage immigrant worker earned $14,400 and over 48 percent of all immigrant workers earned less than 200 percent of the minimum wage—compared to 32 percent of native workers (Capps et al. 2003). Looking at Table 7.3, a couple of patterns are evident in the poverty data. To begin, poverty rates among immigrant workers are higher than among native-born workers. As with the general population, however, poverty rates for immigrants have declined since the early 1990s. Recall from Chapter 5 that part of the decline is explained by increased working hours and multiple jobs rather than higher wages. Finally, the current poverty rate for immigrants remains considerably higher than that for the native-born group (17.1 and 12.1 percent, respectively).

Table 7.3   People in Poverty by Nativity: 1993–2004 (Percent)

YEAR	ALL PEOPLE	NATIVE	FOREIGN-BORN[a]
2004	12.7	12.1	17.1
2003	12.5	11.8	17.1
2002	12.1	11.5	16.6
2001	11.7	11.1	16.1
2000	11.3	10.8	15.4
1999	11.9	11.3	16.8
1998	12.7	12.1	18.0
1997	13.3	12.5	19.9
1996	13.7	12.9	21.0
1995	13.8	12.9	22.2
1994	14.5	13.8	22.6
1993	15.1	14.4	23.0

[a] Includes naturalized citizens and noncitizens.
Source: U.S. Bureau of the Census (2005c).

Work in the Low-Wage Sector

Contributing further to low earnings among immigrant workers is their concentration in jobs where labor law violations are more likely and punishment of employers is more unlikely (especially among the undocumented).[7] The restaurant industry, a leading occupational niche for migrants, illustrates these problems. A recent study of New York's $8-billion restaurant industry showed that workers face not only low wages characteristic of many service sector jobs but also high levels of insecurity and vulnerability. Most of the 165,000 workers surveyed earned less than $20,000 per year, 59 percent reported overtime violations, and 73 percent said that they had no health insurance. At least 36 percent of the city's restaurant workers are undocumented immigrants (see Greenhouse 2005).

A similar pattern is evident in the apparel industry, also a major occupational niche for immigrant workers. Employment in the apparel industry has steadily declined since the mid-1970s, from 2.5 million workers in 1973 to 703,000 workers in 2004 (Rees and Hathcote 2004, 3). Nonetheless, the industry remains an important component of the U.S. manufacturing sector in such urban centers as Los Angeles. In the southern California region, an estimated 119,400 people held textile and fashion-related jobs in the mid-1990s, representing $15 billion of the regional economy (Torres 1995 also Vazquez 1981). Immigrant labor is the backbone of the industry; in Los Angeles, for instance, immigrants constitute 93 percent of all personnel in the garment-manufacturing sector (Light, Bernard, and Kim 1999). Los Angeles is also home to the nation's single largest garment plant, the American Apparel, Inc., factory that is located in downtown Los Angeles and employs 3,800 workers, of whom 90 percent are Latino (Hiltzik 2006). With the exception of American Apparel, Inc., which pays an average of $12 an hour (Hiltzik 2006), apparel jobs are typically characterized by labor law violations, high turnover, job insecurity, and low wages—ranging from $5.00 to $7.00 per hour. With the phasing out of apparel quotas on January 1, 2005, and the increasing dominance of Chinese producers in the apparel industry, the future of the industry in the United States is uncertain.[8] One thing is certain, however: given Chinese minimum-wage levels, which are reported to be as low as US$55 per month (or even lower), there will be tremendous pressure to reduce production costs in the United States, to relocate factories to low-wage areas, or to reintroduce quotas in the United States.[9]

Globalization, Rural Restructuring, and Latino Migration

While expansion of the low-wage sector has spurred the growth of Latino immigration into the United States since 1980, changes in rural America have contributed to the dispersion of Latinos throughout the country. Often, we neglect the rural areas when discussing globalization and restructuring, but rural America is tightly integrated into the global economy and is being transformed by the same forces responsible for urban changes: increasing global competition and changing consumer tastes and demands. The links among globalization, rural restructuring, and migration are apparent in agriculture, as well as the meatpacking, poultry, and carpet industries.

The Midwest

A phase of tremendous upheaval and restructuring in midwestern agriculture, the 1980s reversed the trend toward increasing specialization in this industry. In Nebraska, a traditional grain- and beef-producing state, new crops, such as potatoes, began to emerge. Today, the state produces over 986 million pounds of potatoes (ranking twelfth in the United States). Much of the labor for this crop—for production, storage, and processing—is provided by Latino immigrants. A similar pattern is evident in meatpacking. Responding to increasing competition and the rural crisis, globalized corporations such as Iowa Beef Packing and ConAgra relocated plants to rural communities. Over time, these plants became heavily dependent on Latino labor—even more so than in general agriculture—and the Latino population has grown rapidly within the context of rural crisis and restructuring (Gouveia 2000).[10] We can see these economic and demographic changes in potato production in small communities, such as O'Neill (population 3,733); in sugar beets in medium-sized communities, such as Scottsbluff (population 14,732); and in meatpacking in medium-sized communities, such as Lexington (population 10,011) and Norfolk (population 23,516).[11] While the food-processing industry is a major occupational niche for Latinos in Nebraska, the average hourly wage in this sector is one of the lowest in the food-processing industry nationwide (see Nebraska Department of Economic Development 1999).

The Deep South

Rural crisis, restructuring, and demographic change are not restricted to the Midwest but are found also in the food-processing and carpet/textiles industries in the Southeast.[12] Dalton, Georgia (population 21,761), for instance, produces over one-half of all the carpet in the United States. Faced with a tight labor market, Latino workers have meant the survival of the industry, according to Dalton's carpet executives (Engstrom 1999, 44). With the average wage in Dalton's carpet factories at $8.20 per hour (in 2000), these are considered the "good jobs" in the region and a sign of upward mobility (Hernández-Léon and Zúñiga 2000, 57–58). As in the Midwest, southern agriculture has also seen Latino labor come to dominate production and processing jobs. In south Georgia, production of the world-famous Vidalia sweet onions relies almost exclusively on Latino immigrant labor, as does production of tobacco, greens, beans, cabbage, and sweet potatoes. Immigrant and migrant labor is also crucial to forestry, peaches, carrots, and other occupations that are characterized by low wages (essentially minimum wage without benefits) and physical and emotional burnout.

Latinos are particularly important to the southern poultry industry and fill the industry's insatiable demand for labor. These are brutal and physically demanding jobs that "consume workers." With average hourly wages between $6.00 and $7.00, it is not surprising that there is an extremely high turnover rate (Guthery 2001, 62; also Hytrek, unpublished data). In Gainesville, Georgia (population 17,885—known as the poultry capital of the world in the 1970s), for instance, exports of broiler meat grew from $200 million to $1.9 billion between 1985 and 1997 (Guthery 2001, 62). At the same time, the Latino population increased by 300 percent, and the position of poultry production-line worker was one of the fastest growing jobs in the United States in the 1990s. Is this a coincidence? Unlikely. As one plant manager remarked, "At the beginning, we had only white folks. Then blacks. Then Vietnamese people. They are [mostly] gone now." A supervisor concluded that "if there weren't Hispanic workers, nobody in America would be eating chicken" (Guthery 2001, 61).

These changes reflect the same global processes that have led to outsourcing in other industries; one of the principal differences between the food-processing and other industries, say automobile manufacturing (or many service sector jobs), is that labor moves to jobs rather than jobs to labor. This may change, however, as immigrant labor increases the possibility of certain industries, such as automobile manufacturing, to relocate factories in the United States. Is it an accident, we might wonder, that Hyundai's recent investment in the United States includes an assembly plant not in a "traditional destination" city like Detroit or Flint, Michigan, but in Birmingham, Alabama? Thus, as global processes restructure the Midwest and South, these same processes are bringing a transnational, low-wage Latino labor force to the heart of Dixie—and the heart of the U.S. "heartland" (Stull, Broadway, and Erickson 1992; Capelouto 2000; Griffith 1995; Gouveia and Stull 1995, 1997; Mohl and Knudsen 2000; Murphy, Blanchard, and Hill 2001; Saenz 2004; Stull, Broadway, and Griffith 1995; also Hytrek as well as Hytrek and Wheat, unpublished data). While these emerging immigrant communities contribute to the survival of these sectors and of these communities, they also bring a cultural hybridization. How these shifting demographics play out in places not accustomed to dramatic change is a story currently being written in places like Vidalia, Georgia, and Norfolk, Nebraska.

Explaining Patterns of Immigrant Integration

Recall that one key difference between migration patterns during the current period and the belle époque is the degree of diversity. Immigrants today bring with them a greater range of material resources and human capital skills (e.g., money, education, training, and language abilities) that in turn condition how they are integrated into society. Those highly educated and proficient in English (and who migrate legally) often enter into well-paying, high-status jobs that positively affect life chances. Certain skilled workers can also migrate under the skills category (called H1-B visas) of U.S. immigration policy and are advantaged in the labor market relative to other immigrants.[13] In contrast, immigrants with less human capital are generally "assimilated" into the low-wage sector of the economy.

Human capital, however, is not the sole determinant of how immigrants are integrated into U.S. society. The "context of reception," or the political, social, and economic environments into which they enter, also influences patterns of incorporation (Portes and Rumbaut 1996). Political policies in the receiving country (i.e., whether they are welcoming, neutral, or exclusionary) can impact an immigrant's ability to find employment, housing, and other resources needed to survive, regardless of other human capital resources.

The social context likewise profoundly shapes the process of integration. Immigrants may enter a social context within which they are often "typified" or stereotyped based on their status as immigrants and/or as members of particular racial/ethnic groups. Patterns of discrimination, for example, may cause a particular group to be confined to low-wage or menial labor (i.e., "Mexican work" or "women's work"). Here, we can see how class and status intersect in what Patricia Hill Collins (1991) calls the "matrix of domination" (discussed in Chapter 5). Nonwhite immigrants and immigrant women, for instance, experience greater discrimination and are often integrated into jobs with little opportunity for upward social mobility (Healey 2001, 233). In urban centers such as Los Angeles, Latina immigrants are concentrated in some of the fastest-growing and lowest-paid sectors of the economy, in particular garments, electronics, and the low-wage service sector (Zentgraf 2001). By being confined to the low-wage labor market sector, these immigrants are vulnerable to job instability and unemployment—characteristics of these sectors.

Finally, social mobility is shaped by the nature of the community into which immigrants settle. Social capital networks provide important survival mechanisms that protect immigrants from the impact of cultural change, outside prejudice, and initial economic challenges. As we noted above, ethnic communities are often characterized by high levels of social capital networks. Immigrants sharing the same ethnicity (or race) who move to these communities can tap into important sources of information about jobs and other opportunities, as well as advice and resources. Cuban immigrants to Miami and Asian immigrants to southern California, for example, enter established ethnic economies whereby newly arrived immigrants find employment with Cuban or Asian business owners and entrepreneurs (Portes and Bach 1985, Light and Bhachu 1993, Light and Gold 2000). In many cases, initial low earnings give way to higher incomes as immigrants learn the tools of the trade and set up businesses of their own. We should note that social capital networks can also work in the reverse manner and reinforce low income and poverty. If, for instance, a new immigrant enters an ethnic community whose members are concentrated in a low-wage sector of the economy, it is likely that the social networks into which she or he will be incorporated will perpetuate class inequality and limit upward social mobility.

Immigration and Political and Civic Engagement

Arjun Appadurai (1990, 5) argues that globalization has created a complex, overlapping, and disjunctive cultural order. One dimension of burgeoning global cultural flows, he suggests, is what he terms the "ethnoscapes." An **ethnoscape** is "the landscape of persons who constitute the shifting world in which we live: tourists, immigrants, refugees, exiles, guest workers, and other moving groups" that constitute an essential feature of the world and "appear to affect the politics of (and between) nations to a hitherto unprecedented degree." Appadurai's argument is that immigrants bring their entire culture with them. This culture not only exerts influence on the existing culture but also has economic, social, and political effects. While we may see this quite easily in terms of elite migration, it is characteristic of all socioeconomic strata.

In the United States, immigrants from all socioeconomic strata are actively engaged in their communities and participate in schools, churches, local businesses and organizations, and larger political movements. The most obvious form of civic engagement is citizenship, and according to the 2000 U.S. Census, 40.3 percent of all foreign-born people were U.S. citizens (Grieco 2002). Another form of civic engagement is political participation, including voting, grassroots organizing, volunteering for campaigns, or donating money. Latino immigrants, for instance, are especially politically active. Barretos and Muñoz (2003) found that when considering nonelectoral political participation, foreign-born Latinos are more likely to be active than the native-born; among the foreign-born, noncitizens are just as likely to participate as naturalized citizens.

We can see the effects of political and community participation on two interrelated levels. First, there has been an increase in Latino candidates making serious runs for political positions and winning major offices (e.g., Los Angeles and San Antonio), and 2005 witnessed the appointment of Alberto Gonzalez, the first Latino U.S. attorney general. Second, Latino workers have helped breathe new life into the U.S. labor and civil rights movements. In what Harold Meyerson (1999) calls "liberalism with a new accent," immigrants are working to create a dynamic and globally focused movement. The Justice for Janitors campaign and the 2006 May Day Walkout ("A Day Without Immigrants") are only two examples of how Latino and Latina immigrants and workers are building upon shared work experiences and existing social networks to mobilize for fair wages and working conditions and against racist legislation. Because many migrants from Mexico and Central America bring with them considerable political organizing skills and expertise, they have become important actors in the labor movement (and community-based organizations) in the United States. The role of Latinas and Latinos in the labor movement is exemplified by the significant role of labor organizers such as Maria Elena Durazo and the late Miguel Contreras, who took over leadership of the Los Angeles AFL-CIO in 1996 and revived "a moribund union movement at a time of rapid demographic change" (Morin and Hall 2005).

Remittances: Completing the Global Cycle

In what is a continual cycle of global change, immigrants shape the receiving country and, by remitting million of dollars, shape the sending countries. While the remitting of money—or the sending of money back to the "home" country by immigrants—is not a new phenomenon, supraterritorial communication greatly accelerates the transmission of funds that are used in a variety of consumptive and productive ways in the countries of origin. For instance, in 2001, an estimated $111 billion was remitted worldwide and about 65 percent of this went to developing countries (O'Neil 2003).

Almost one-third of the world's total remittances are destined for communities in Latin America and the Caribbean, countries that constitute one-half of the U.S. foreign-born population. Over three-quarters of these remittances originate in the United States. From 2000 to 2002, remittances to Mexico, Nicaragua, El Salvador, Honduras, and Guatemala grew 39 percent, from $10.2 to $14.2 billion (Suro 2003). By 2004, the money transfers reached $23.8 billion, almost $68 million per day (*Los Angeles Times* 2005b, 2005d). In 2005, Latin America as a whole received roughly $55 billion, mainly from the United States (*Los Angeles Times* 2005b, B18; 2005d, B18; Bourdreaux 2006, A1; Williams 2006, A1). Increasingly, money transfers take place through automatic teller machines—and new financial forms are being created to facilitate the movement of money—rather than the more typical wire transfers. Much of the money is used to finance local development, paying for street paving or lighting, as well as productive enterprises that create local jobs (*Los Angeles Times* 2005c, B18; Bourdreaux 2006, A1; Williams 2006, A1; Paddock 2006, A1; Wilkinson 2006, A1).[14] Given these numbers, it is not surprising that remittances in 2000 augmented the gross domestic product of such countries as El Salvador, Jamaica, Jordan, Nicaragua, and Yemen by over 10 percent (cited in O'Neil 2003).

Conclusion

The UNDP (2004, 87) states that "globalization is quantitatively and qualitatively reshaping international movements of people." Immigration to the

United States reflects these changes. By the start of the twenty-first century, unskilled and low-skilled workers from Europe no longer dominated immigration to the United States; rather, immigration has been characterized by non-European, highly educated and skilled workers combined with those having little education and few skills. No longer confined to major urban areas in a few gateway states, immigrants from Mexico and Central America are finding their way to rural areas of the Mid-west and Southeast. By considering the impact of social networks and other noneconomic factors in an analysis of immigration, it becomes easier to understand these kinds of changes and the complex interaction between global political and economic processes and decisions made by individual immigrants. As predicted by the social democrats, globalization appears to create porous borders with respect not only to the movement of goods, services, and ideas but to the movement of people as well.

Examining immigration from the vantage point of globalization, we illustrated how immigration from Latin America is being driven in large part by the global restructuring of the U.S. economy that has created a dependence on low-wage workers as well as economic disruptions in the sending countries. At the same time, competitive pressures mean an increasing demand for highly educated workers, including computer scientists, physical scientists, and engineers from India, China, Hong Kong, and Taiwan. Ease of travel, greater access to information, and existing social networks strongly shape individual decisions about migration, although these factors appear to have a stronger effect on those who are highly educated and have the greatest resources. The brain-drain phenomenon is one of the most problematic issues. In the long run, the brain drain will mean a widening of the already huge gap in the human capital endowment among countries, and this will only increase global inequality (Ghose 2003, 113).

As large-scale migration continues, current immigrants will follow in the path of their historical counterparts: they will have children, buy homes, invest in businesses and communities, and become citizens. In contrast to the last major wave at the beginning of the twentieth century, however, the supraterritorial communication and ease of travel that have accompanied globalization allow immigrants to remain in close contact with their home countries and to create (transterritorial) global communities. Thus, while immigrants actively engage in their new society, they often maintain tight transnational links with their countries of origin. These connections may well create significant cultural changes in the host society or greater cultural hybridization, as we mentioned in Chapter 4.

Yet this cultural mixing will not be unproblematic. Cultural uncertainty is one outcome of any society experiencing a transition to a multicultural society. These feelings can fuel anti-immigrant and racist reactions as immigrants are blamed for declining wages, higher unemployment, and depleted social-welfare funds (education, health care, and social insurance programs). In many countries, a combination of trade unions attempting to defend jobs and conservative political parties promoting xenophobic agendas is pushing for stronger restrictions on immigration (Halliday 2000). All of this raises some interesting and largely unanswered questions about the future of globalization and migration. In a larger global context, how much political will or political power will nation-states have to control migration, either into or out of their countries? Will global economic and political institutions come to play a larger role in regulating international migration? Will national borders and national citizenship become increasingly meaningless? These are only some of the central questions we face in current debates over globalization and migration.

CHAPTER 8

Globalization and Gender

> In every society of the world, gender is a basis for social stratification. In no society is gender the sole basis for stratifying people, but gender cuts across *all* systems of stratification—whether slavery, caste, or class (Huber 1990, quoted in Henslin 2004: 170).

Is Joan Huber exaggerating the importance of gender to social stratification? Reflect for a moment on the following examples. We live in a world that is "missing" an estimated 100 million women—women who would be alive if not for infanticide, neglect, or sex-selective abortions (UNDP 2002, 37). It is a world in which 544 million of the estimated 854 million illiterate adults are women and 60 percent of the 113 million children who never attend primary school are girls (UNDP 2002, 36). Ours is a world in which men earn more than women in *every* society (Henslin 2004, 170). In the United States, less than 7 percent of all working women earn more than $75,000 a year, while 37 percent earn less than $25,000 per year (AFL-CIO 2005). While these data may support Huber's claim, what about globalization? What are the links between gender inequality and global social, economic, and political processes?

Although the influence of globalization on inequality has been a matter of intense debate, much of the globalization literature addresses the impact of global processes on gender inequality only in developing countries. Questions about globalization and gender in the United States are met with the same "deafening silence on gender" that Spike Peterson suggests typifies the critical international political economy literature (quoted in Munck 2005, 81). Our aim in this chapter is to explore the interactive effects between globalization and gender: that is, how gender inequalities facilitate the current globalization trajectory and how global processes in turn affect those inequalities. We begin with a brief overview of some basic concepts, followed by an examination of how globalization is incorporating women into the global system. We conclude with a discussion of globalization, restructuring, and gender inequality in the United States.

Sex, Gender, and Ideology

Sex and Gender

Huber points to the power our ascribed statuses (e.g., sex, race, and ethnicity) can have on the quality of our lives. Unlike class, which may change over a lifetime, sex is a status ascribed at birth and, like race and ethnicity, the society's cultural values and beliefs determine its meaning. To emphasize this, social scientists distinguish between *sex* as a biological feature and *gender* as the social, cultural, and psychological aspects of femaleness and maleness that vary by history and culture. This distinction is an important one.

Separating biological issues from social ones allows us to examine the cultural and historical specificity of gender roles and to consider how changing gender roles can affect life chances. This framework also elucidates how capabilities or behaviors do not automatically spring from biological differences between the sexes (Newman 2004, 142). Finally, the concept of "gender" allows us to analyze why men continue to prevail over women in terms of power, privilege, and prestige. For examples, we need only look at the gender distribution in political offices and top management positions in business or at who controls wealth and property. In terms of prestige, men are more likely to be considered experts and to garner more respect in both domestic and occupational spheres than their female counterparts.

Gender Ideology

When we discuss **gender stratification**, we are referring to the persistent unequal access to power, resources, and opportunities of women. While not all men are treated equally, nor are they equally *advantaged*, the structural dominance (or privilege) of men over women is universal. Because of existing **patriarchal** relations, men are born into positions of advantage relative to those of women. Globalization did not create this structure of inequality; before the onset of the accelerated phase of globalization in the 1970s, gender subordination had "a long history and had become embedded in most social contexts across the world . . ." (Scholte 2000b, 250). Nonetheless, globalization shapes patterns of inequality (and the lives of women and men) as it alters the nature of production and consumption, the composition of the workforce and occupational categories, and wages. Understanding how these changes affect women requires us to think about **gender ideology**, which is our collective cultural understanding of gender.

Recall that global processes are filtered through local cultures and that these cultures operate as an intermediate variable between globalization and local outcomes. As elements of culture, our collective understandings of gender (as well as of class, race, and ethnicity) influence the local manifestation of global forces. For instance, as globalization alters the mix of high- and low-paying jobs, our ideas about gender (and race and ethnicity) influence who ends up in which position. Moreover, these collective understandings are society-specific products that serve as mechanisms to explain and justify inequalities in that society.

Using the United States as an example, think for a moment about how our cultural beliefs about racial superiority—reflected in jokes, slurs, and even certain scientific theories—legitimize racial subordination.[1] As another example, recall from Chapter 5 how the idea of competitive individualism informs our understanding of class relations by explaining economic success and failure because of individual effort. Gender relations are also governed by a set of beliefs about masculinity and femininity that are used to justify gender inequality. In the United States, gender ideology begins with the assumption that there is a natural **sexual division of labor**. Accordingly, men are physically stronger, more rational, more assertive, and more competitive, while women are more emotional and have a greater capacity for affection and nurturing. As a result, it is assumed that men and women are *by nature* better suited to different tasks. Men function in the public realm as the economic provider and protector of the family; women are relegated to the private sphere, where they are responsible for nurturing and socializing children. The idea of a "natural" sexual division of labor has defined men as the primary wage earners in the family. If women venture into the public sphere, they are seen as supplementary contributors to the family income (see Enloe 1989, Elson 1995, Marchand and Runyon 2000).

From this ideology, it is but a small step to **gender stereotypes**. In terms of the workplace, gender stereotypes dictate that women work in occupations that take advantage of their "natural" abilities and mimic the roles they play in the home. Occupations in this category include preschool teacher, day-care provider, and private house cleaner, among others (Fuentes and Ehrenreich 1983, Mies 1986, Lee 1998). These jobs, often referred to as "pink-collar," tend to be low-paying and unstable and to provide few benefits or opportunities for upward mobility (see Enloe 1989, Elson 1995, Marchand and Runyon 2000, Muñoz 2004). Within the context of globalization, global capitalists *appropriate* or *subvert* local gender ideologies, stereotypes, and traditions in an effort to incorporate women into the labor market. As factory production increasingly requires less physical labor, for instance, old arguments about "natural" abilities are modified to fit the new reality. Women are suddenly viewed as a perfect fit for assembly line work because they possess the "natural" dexterity and nimble fingers that are vital to current production methods. As a result, employers in country after country prefer women for these jobs. Yet, the demand for female production workers is less about "natural" abilities than about containing costs; by defining these skills as *natural* rather than *learned*, employers can reduce the significance and the level of compensation for these skills (Steans 1998).

Engendering Globalization

Neoliberal policies of deregulation and privatization that facilitate the global reorganization of production and the shrinking of the welfare state all shape and are shaped by gender relations. Economically, women fill the crucial, albeit low-wage, industrial and service positions on which the global economy depends. Politically, the restructuring of the nation-state affects everyone, but the social costs of the transition from a fixed to a flexible economy are disproportionately assumed by women.

For poor countries, global incorporation involves economic openness, greater foreign investment, the scaling back of existing public support for health care and education, and the elimination of government spending that subsidizes food and water. In countries where women are the main producers, economic openness means an increase in imports of subsidized agricultural products and consumer goods that ultimately undermines the livelihoods of female producers and reduces family incomes. Reducing subsidies or outright privatization further increases the financial burden on families. Lower subsidies for water put an increased burden on women and girls, who spend much of their day retrieving water from public wells that are a great distance from the home—and, worse still, are often contaminated. Less government support for health care means fewer clinics and fewer medical providers, increased costs for supplies and drugs, and greater care responsibilities for women. With a reduction in government support for education, girls are forced to go to work so that families can afford to send their son(s) to school.

In the United States, a similar dynamic exists. The occupational changes reflected in the transition to neoliberalism place downward pressure on wages and family incomes. Politically, declining (or absent) public support for health, education and after-school programs, child care for working mothers, medical and maternity leave, and other programs produces additional financial pressures. As in poor countries, these changes add up to more care responsibilities and more stress for women as the principal caregivers of the family.

Today, in both rich and poor countries, few households can rely solely on one income (Ehrenreich and Hochschild 2002), and struggling families adopt a number of strategies to shore up family income. For women this means entering the labor force or increasing their working hours. Often, women face formidable barriers when attempting to enter the new sectors created by globalization, driving them into the low-wage manufacturing and service sectors that "prop up" the global economy. Even though large numbers of women are entering the labor force and providing substantial financial support to their families, they continue to work a second shift, performing virtually all the nonpaid labor in the home.

The essential question we are posing here is how women contribute to the unfolding of neoliberal globalization. Without bringing gender into the analysis, we cannot fully comprehend globalization, nor can we understand the daily lifestyles and consumption patterns of middle- and upper-class women and men. Gender inequalities not only determine how women are incorporated into the global system but also *engender* neoliberal globalization. In addition, working-class women and women of color throughout the United States and the world are providing products and services essential to the viability of neoliberal globalization (Mills 2003). We see this in the economic sphere, where women provide low-paid factory and service labor for transnational corporations; in the social realm, where women fill the majority of positions of low-paid care workers for families of high-wage professional workers; and, perhaps most troubling, in the sex industry, in which girls and women serve as unpaid or low-paid "entertainment" workers for global tourists.

The Global Assembly Line

As competition accelerated in the 1970s, the information infrastructure combined with the International Monetary Fund (IMF) and World Bank export-led growth policies in the developing world created the conditions for production in flexible and decentralized global assembly lines. The shifting global division of labor involves the rapid growth of textile, electronic, and other jobs in the developing world as transnational capital relocates production facilities to export processing zones (EPZs) in Mexico, Central America, and South and Southeast Asia. Existing gender-based inequalities have been an additional enabling factor for capital mobility to enhance flexibility, "productivity, management control, and ultimately profits" (Castells 1997, 157–162). As a result, labor in these production facilities is predominantly female, with women constituting anywhere between 70 and 90 percent of the workers (Fernandez-Kelly 1983, Ong 1991, Wolf 1988, Enloe 1995, Safa 1995, Freeman 2000, Burn 2000, Connor 2002).

Launched in the early 1960s, EPZs or *maquiladoras* (assembly factories) in Mexico reached an all-time high in 2001 with 3,735 factories employing over 1.3 million workers. In the 1990s, women made up over 90 percent of all workers in these factories. Today, the overall percentage is nearly 50 percent —which represents a "masculinization" of the workforce in these factories— although women continue to comprise 70 percent of the workforce in certain sectors, such as electronic parts assembly. As in other countries, including Indonesia, Israel, Vietnam, China, and Malaysia, industrial employers in Mexico prefer to hire young female workers (between the ages of 16 and 30) without children. Women in this group are some of the most vulnerable and least powerful members of society and, thus, constitute a workforce that is more passive, compliant, and accepting of low wages (Fernandez-Kelly 1983, Ong 1987, Wolf 1988, Drori 2000).

Working conditions and wages in these industries reflect the subordinate position of women more generally. Women worldwide work in settings that, according to the Maquila Health and Safety Support Network (n.d.), are extremely authoritarian. Women routinely face sexual harassment and are forced to undergo routine pregnancy tests and to quit if they become pregnant. Moreover, women are regularly exposed to dangerous conditions that result in illness, physical disabilities, loss of eyesight, loss of limbs, or even loss of life (see Athreya 2003). Work in Chinese export factories, for instance, involves girls as young as 13, who toil in an almost precapitalist working environment that consists of long hours with low pay, locked factory doors, and residence halls without heat (Kahn 2003, Ni 2005).

China is only one of the many countries where power and profits meet poverty; recall Maria Guadalupe and Sadisah from Chapter 1. In the 1980s, at the age of 16, Maria started working in a Mexican maquiladora, earning $27 for a 48-hour workweek (Guadalupe 1999). Maquiladora workers across Mexico still often work 10-hour days, 6 days a week, for wages averaging 50 cents per hour, which is far less than the estimated minimum weekly income of $175 needed to survive (Instituto Nacional de Estadistica 2000). In Indonesia, Sadisah earned 14 cents an hour and worked 10.5 hours a day, 6 days a week, for Nike in the early 1990s (Bradshaw and Wallace 1996). Wages in Indonesia continue to be extremely low, with women in the garment industry earning 16 cents an hour and working 70 hours a week (AFL-CIO n.d.c).

Finally, the global assembly line not only extends horizontally across societies but vertically into households as well. Households are connected to the global production process through informal networks of jobs that are not part of the official (formal) mainstream economy. These household activities form part of what is called the **informal sector** and include handicrafts, home-based piecework (often subcontracted apparel and footwear work), small-scale retail trade, petty food production, or domestic services (Sen and Grown 1987, 36–37). It is important to note that informal sector activities are not marginal to the global economy, as some argue, but an integral part of the global economic system. The transition to a flexible economy—a key element of globalization—is responsible for the dramatic growth of the informal sector (Steans 1998); informal (mainly female) home-based workers produce a large proportion of the products destined for formal global markets (see Moyers 2003).[2] What differentiates informal jobs from formal employment is the absence of security and benefits and their invisibility—they exist outside of any legal regulations.

The upside of the global assembly line, as neoliberals point out, is more jobs for women. In Indonesia, many women see working in an export factory as preferable to working in the village rice fields. Airline ticket processors in Barbados, for example, earn low wages, have few benefits, and are subjected to high levels of surveillance; but they see themselves as professionals (Freeman 2000). Women have also benefited from expanding call centers and new computer-related white-collar jobs—mainly data processing—in Malaysia (Ng and Yong 1995) as well as from the thriving financial sector in India, where educated women have made significant gains (Ng and Yong 1995,

Gothoskar 1995). Even informal sector employment has advantages; women working at home can combine earning income with their family and household responsibilities. Although wages and working conditions in most of the jobs are less than ideal, employment allows women to engage in new kinds of consumption, experience "modernity," and gain a greater degree of economic independence and autonomy not previously possible. Critics of neoliberal globalization, such as the National Labor Committee (NLC), echo these conclusions, arguing that "almost any worker in the world will tell you that it's better to be exploited and have a job than to have no job at all" (Kernaghan 2001, 190). In contrast to neoliberals, who see these jobs as an end in themselves, organizations such as the NLC want to alter globalization and in the process transform these jobs into ones with dignity, respect, and justice (Kernaghan 2001, 191).

The Global Care Line

Women are also the "employee of choice" to fill the growing demand for **social reproductive labor** in the expanding global care line (see Glenn 1992, Chang 2000, Hondagneu-Sotelo 2001, Parrenas 2001). Social reproductive jobs entail responsibilities such as household tasks, caring for children and the sick and elderly, and other "emotional labor" and "kin work" associated with meeting the needs of family members. While much of this labor has been provided by unpaid mothers, wives, and significant others, increasingly these tasks are performed by paid employees. What globalization has wrought, Hochschild (2001, 131) argues, is a global care line that is really "a series of personal links between people across the globe based on the paid or unpaid work of caring." When a Mexican woman goes to work in a Los Angeles household or an Eastern European woman comes to Paris to work as a domestic, she effectively becomes part of the global chain providing care services (Munck 2005, 84). The emergence of the global care line is a major factor for the growing number of women as part of the global flow of migrants (see Chapter 7).

Historically in the United States, care-giving positions were filled by American-born women from racial and ethnic minority groups; now, it is immigrant women from Asia and Latin America who do this work (Fernandez-Kelly and Sassen 1995, Sassen 1998, Vernez 1999, de la Luz Ibarra 2000, Lopez-Garza and Diaz 2001). As globalization dramatically changes the nature of work for many families, housecleaning and caring for children has "left the hands of wives and mothers and has entered the global marketplace" (Hondagneu-Sotelo 2001, xii).

Here is where the two ends of the U.S. hourglass economy meet. Globalization, as we have noted, accelerates competitive pressures manifested in heavier workloads for employees and a blurring of the line between work and home. In order to meet these demands (and to buttress stagnating real family incomes), women (and men) are increasing their participation and/or hours in the workforce. With less time for home and family, a growing number of these families hire low-wage domestic help (see Browne and Misra 2003, Zentgraf 2001). We see this in the United States, where Latina immigrants provide the flexible and relatively inexpensive labor pool of household and family-care workers. Yet, within the global care line, female domestic workers are often forced to neglect their own families to care for the children of other women. If she is fortunate, such a worker may hire a local woman to take care of her own household responsibilities when she immigrates to another city or another country or works during the day in another part of the city.

Clearly, some families have the resources to better address their work/ household dilemma, while others are able to increase participation in the labor market toward the same end. In both cases, women (and men) rely heavily on working-class and racial/ethnic minority women to replace them in their homes. Mothers, however, encounter the added stress of securing appropriate child care and of coordinating domestic help and the logistics of transporting children to non-live-in child-care locations.

The Global Sex Line

As with inequality in general, global forces did not create sex workers. The globalization of tourism is, however, transforming large numbers of women and girls into sexual commodities for the burgeoning sex trade industry (Castells, quoted in Munck 2005, 93). The global sex line is a highly diverse business that ranges from the more "respectable" mail-order bride business to the world of sex slavery. Low estimates indicate that over a million women are sex trafficked *each year* from the former Soviet Republics, Southeast Asia, South Asia, Latin America and the Caribbean, Eastern Europe, and Africa (Farr 2005, 4). The forces driving this industry are the same ones responsible for accelerating the outsourcing of jobs and the changing patterns of production more generally: policies of privatization and market liberalization; existing global gender inequalities combined with cheap and easy travel and communication especially the Internet (Farr 2005). Today the global sex line has become institutionalized, as illustrated by international hotel chains and package-holiday firms specializing in "esoteric sexual services" (Steans 1998).

Among the 93 countries for which the Coalition Against Trafficking in Women has data, the intersection of gender, age, and wealth is most visible in those in Southeast Asia. Increasingly, children are drawn into the industry as a response to the message that the "market place is open to all and that globalization provides great opportunities for those who will grasp them" (Munck 2005, 92). An estimated 1.2 million children are trafficked from their homes to foreign cities or countries *each year* (Farr 2005, 231); India, Thailand, and the Philippines alone have an estimated 1.3 million children in their sex trade centers. In India, girls as young as 9 years old are auctioned off to wealthy Indian and Arab males. In Cambodia, young girls are sold to "produce" leaches for sale as delicacies on the global market: girls are bound and submerged for hours in ponds filled with leaches; once the leaches are fat with blood, the girls are lifted out and the leaches removed and sold (see Ferraro 2003; Coalition Against Trafficking in Women n.d.).[3]

The booming sex industry in South Asia is run largely by the Chinese and Japanese mafias for the benefit of tourists from Japan, the United States, and other wealthy societies (AFESIP 2004a, 2004b). The sex tourist industry in Thailand grew from around 2 million tourists in the 1980s to over 7 million in 1996 (cited in Thompson and Hickey 2005, 248). In the Philippines, tourists in the late 1990s could "sign up" for Philippine Adventure Tours—$1,645 that covered round-trip airfare, lodging, and guided tours to the bars where men could purchase sex. As a marketing ploy, tour owner and operator Allan Gaynor promised potential customers that they would "never sleep alone" on the tour (Coalition Against Trafficking in Women n.d., see also Lim 1998, Nagel 2003, Pyle 2001, Pyle and Ward 2003).

The global sex line represents the dark extremes of neoliberal globalization—grinding poverty forces individuals to sell themselves and parents to sell their children (for as little as $15) as a means of survival. In some of the poorest West and Central African countries, an estimated 200,000 children have been sold into slavery by their parents (Eitzen and Baca Zinn 2003, 68). How many of these children ultimately end up in the sex industry is unknown. What we do know is that this industry reflects the more disturbing consequences of a system that reduces everything to a commodity, including the most private and precious aspects of human life and human dignity. We might ask if it is a mere accident that cities like Bangkok and Manila, which are experiencing massive growth in prostitution, are also major centers for transnational corporations and regional centers for global organizations (see Steans 1998). Unfortunately, with the deregulation and the shrinking of the nation-state (i.e., the emergence of the neoliberal state), poverty is growing, illegal activities are harder to control, and protection of the world's most vulnerable is more difficult. As supply and demand increasingly govern social relations, the most impoverished "exotic Oriental" and other non-Western women and children are incorporated into the global system in ways limited only by imagination and wealth.

Globalization and Gender Inequality in the United States

The above discussion illustrates the complex relationships between gender inequality and global processes. While the global–local dynamic and forms of gender inequality may differ in the United States from Asia, Latin America, or Africa, gender is no less important. In the United States, the most entrenched form of inequality remains in the workplace, where the average woman earns 79 percent of the average man (data for 2004), although this represents an improvement over the 1979 figure of 62.5 percent (U.S. Bureau of the Census 2004/2005b). Women are also more likely to be in poverty (the concept of the feminization of poverty): 13.7 percent of all women live below the poverty line compared with 11.2 percent of all men (data for 2003). Statistics on poverty by household type show an even greater disparity: 28.0 percent of all female-headed households were below the poverty level in 2003, in contrast to 12.1 percent for male-headed households and 5.3 percent for married couples (U.S. Bureau of the Census 2004/2005a).

Gender and Work

Women are subject to the same globalization-related factors that affect male earnings and life chances: the increase in flexible and insecure employment conditions[4] (see McCall 2001, Chapter 6) and the growth of low-wage service jobs. The principal difference between men and women is that women start from a subordinate position in the employment hierarchy, as demonstrated by their overrepresentation in contingent, casual, and nonstandard jobs as well as in the low-wage service sector.

In Chapter 6, we discussed some of the effects of globalization on the U.S. economy. Deindustrialization, changing job requirements, and increasing numbers of low-wage service and industrial jobs have shaped inequality in several ways. The decline or stagnation of wages for men since the 1970s has put a downward pressure on family incomes. As a result, we noted in Chapter 6, both men and women have increased their work hours and a growing number of women have entered (or reentered) the labor force. Throughout the post-1980 period, families have come to depend on women's paychecks to stave off declines in real income and even to ensure their very survival (McCall 2001, 188).

By 1997, U.S. workers were annually logging more hours than workers in any other industrialized country, but women experienced the greatest increase in hours. Data complied by Mishel, Bernstein, and Allegretto (2005) show that wives in families of two parents increased their annual working hours by an average of 10.2 weeks from 1979 to 2000 (see also Gerson and Jacobs 2004). These data represent women from *all* socioeconomic strata. A similar upward trend is evident in female labor-force participation, or the proportion of the women either working or actively seeking work.[5] The percentage of women in the paid labor force, regardless of marital status, educational level, or presence and age of children, increased from 46.3 to 59.5 percent between 1975 and 2000 (U.S. Bureau of the Census 2004, Table 578). If we look at women aged 25–55—the prime child-rearing years—nearly three out of four were in the paid labor force, either looking for work or working at least part time (data for 2000). Among women with children under 6 years of age, those who worked outside the home increased from 49.3 percent in 1980 to 68 percent in 2003; if we include women with children under age 17, this number increases to 75 percent (U.S. Bureau of the Census 2004, Table 579). These changes are not surprising. As we discussed in Chapter 1, having a child is now the single best predictor that a woman will end up in financial collapse (Warren and Warren Tyagi 2003). The trend is worrisome but even more so if we consider that the average U.S. woman who works full time outside the home spends an additional 33 hours a week on housework compared to 18 hours for her working significant other (Newman 2002, 393).

How did the shifting economic structures affect women as they assumed a greater role in the labor market? As we might expect, the data show a concentration of women in the low-wage sector, with only a slight expansion of the number of females in high-paying jobs (McCall 2001). Women, like many men, may lack the requisite education, credentials, or training for high-wage jobs; however, women also confront subtle—and not so subtle—obstacles that prevent them from moving into better jobs.

Focusing on the low-wage sector, data indicate that women are heavily employed in two subsectors that comprise the flexible economy: nonstandard or contingent jobs and low-wage pink-collar service occupations (McCall 2001). In 2001, 26.6 percent of all U.S. jobs involved some type of nonstandard employment, such as subcontracting, involuntary part-time work, and informal self-employment. Strikingly, 31 percent of all women worked in one of these jobs compared to 22.8 percent of men (Wenger 2003). If we look at the service sector, we find that while 60.4 percent of all service workers are women, women account for 97 percent of all secretaries, 95 percent of all child-care workers, 92 percent of all teachers' aides, 92 percent of all bookkeepers, and 89 percent of all bank tellers (U.S. Bureau of the Census 2004, Table 597).

Examining the high-wage sector, we find a growing number of women in traditionally male-dominated professions. Thanks in large part to the passage of legislation, such as the 1964 Civil Rights Act, the 1963 Equal Pay Act, and Title IX, which made it illegal to discriminate in employment, wages, or postsecondary education, growing numbers of women have been able to enter positions in management, medicine, law, and engineering.[6] Throughout the 1980s and 1990s, many women (generally middle-class) experienced unprecedented opportunities for managerial and professional employment. In 2001, for instance, 46 percent of women were employed in executive, administrative, and managerial occupations compared to 32 percent in 1983 (U.S. Bureau of the Census 2002, Table 588). The number of female physicians increased from 16 percent to 30 percent between 1983 and 2003. During the same time, the proportion of female attorneys increased from 15 percent to 28 percent and that of female chemical engineers grew from 6 percent to 14 percent (U.S. Bureau of the Census 2002, Table 588; 2004, Table 597). We see a similar trend regarding women holding seats on the boards of Fortune 500 companies. According to Catalyst, a non-profit research & advocacy organization, women held 14.7 percent of all board seats in the Fortune 500 in 2005, an increase from 9.6 percent in 1995 when Catalyst began tracking these data (see Catalyst 2006).

Wage Gaps and Inter- and Intraoccupational Segregation

Increasing female labor-force participation has not eliminated the wage gap, nor has it brought to an end the practice of separating work along gender lines within the workplace (**occupational segregation**) or within occupations (**intraoccupational segregation**). Occupational segregation is reflected in data showing that 30 percent of all working women are found in just 10 occupations (Ruane and Cerulo 2004, 119), generally in some of the lowest-paid pink-collar jobs. Moreover, women tend to work in jobs filled largely by women; the typical woman works in an occupation that is 71 percent female (Cotter, Hermsen, and Vanneman 2004, 29).

Think for a moment. Which jobs would you consider typically female or male? For our purposes, we will consider "female" and "male" jobs those in which one sex accounts for a minimum of 96 percent of total employment in the occupation (data from the U.S. Bureau of the Census 2004/2005a); this idea comes from Newman 2002, 400).

Female: secretary, preschool teacher, child-care worker, dental assistant, and private house cleaner
Male: airplane pilot, firefighter, aircraft engine mechanic, construction worker, and miner

Next try to guess the average weekly salary for these jobs (U.S. Bureau of Labor Statistics 2005; data are for 2004).

Female: $439.00
Male: $939.00

What do these patterns suggest? First, gender ideology is alive and well; women dominate those jobs consistent with traditional roles in the home. Second, income is low; working for $439 per week for 52 weeks amounts to $22,828 a year *before* taxes and *with no* time off.

Gender ideology persists even as women enter traditionally male-dominated occupations in the form of intraoccupational segregation. In manufacturing, for instance, one-half of all assemblers in the United States are now women; unfortunately, women comprise 75 percent of the lower-paying electrical part–assembly jobs and only 17 percent of the higher-paying motor vehicle–assembly positions (Newman 2002, 398). In the high-wage service sector, such as management positions, women hold only 7 percent of the "line officer's jobs," those that lead to top CEO positions, making it difficult to advance to high-level management positions (cited in Lavelle 2001). Only 7.9 percent of Fortune 500 top earners and 1.4 percent of Fortune 500 CEOs are women,[7] and the majority of employees supervised by female managers are other women (Carrington and Troske 1998).

Similar patterns are evident in other fields, such as medicine and law. In medicine, women typically specialize in pediatrics and gynecology, while higher-paid specialties, such as neurosurgery and radiology, remain the preserve of male physicians (Ruane and Cerulo 2004, 120). In law, female lawyers are often given low-status projects that inhibit advancement; they are also underrepresented in private practice and in law-firm partnerships. Data show, for instance, that a man is three times more likely than a woman to make partner at a law firm (quoted in Newman 2004, 452).[8]

Gender, Educational Levels, and Earnings

Thus far, we have emphasized how globalization affects gender inequality through changes in the occupational structure. One final example that vividly illustrates these trends is a comparison of earnings by gender and educational levels. One of the most dramatic statistics from Figure 8.1 is that a woman with a bachelor's degree can expect to earn only slightly more income than a man with a high school diploma: mean annual earnings of $37,909 for college-educated women compared to $32,673 for high school–educated men. At the high end, women with doctoral degrees on average earn $66,426

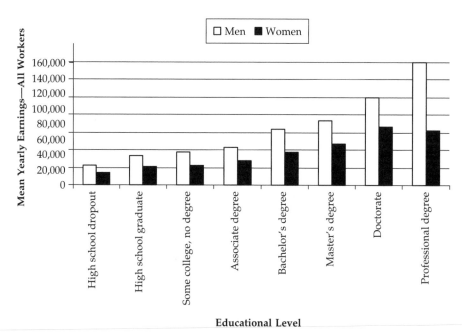

Figure 8.1 Earning gap between men and women by educational levels.
Source: U.S. Bureau of the Census 2004

annually while the average male with a bachelor's degree earns $63,505. At all levels, women earn less than men at the same level of education.

The Wage Gap Revisited

Before we leave this section, we need to address one last piece of the gender –wage issue. Recall that the male–female gender–wage gap *declined* during the 1980s and 1990s (from 37.5 to 21 percent). What we have just discussed, however, should serve as a cautionary note as we assess the long-term prospects for gender inequality. In Chapter 6, we analyzed how globally driven structural changes have led to *declining* male wages since the 1980s. To compensate for falling real family incomes, more women entered the workforce and those already working outside the home began to increase their work hours. More work hours and the growing number of women in professional jobs translate into higher incomes for women at the same time that male income has declined. Thus, we have seen a closing of the gender–wage gap. These results hardly offer cause for celebration; these data suggest that while there is growing wage equality between educated (mainly white) middle-class women and men, the gap is increasing among women of different classes, races, and ethnic backgrounds (Young 2000, 315).

Gender, Race, and Ethnicity

If we look more closely at the backgrounds of women making inroads into male-dominated professions, we can see two patterns emerging. As white women have entered "male" professions, such as medicine, law, and academics, women of color have been moving into the female-dominated positions that have been vacated by white women, such as social worker and teacher's aide. Many of these jobs comprise the low end of the U.S. hourglass economy. Data show that 35.8 percent of African American women and 46.6 percent of Latinas are employed in low-wage work compared to 26.2 percent of white women (Mishel, Bernstein, and Boushey 2003). As with sex in general, we find occupational segregation driven by racial and ethnic status; African American women and Latinas hold jobs in workplaces in which nearly one-quarter of the other workers are people of color (Dill, Cannon, and Vanneman 1987). These trends largely account for the growing income gap between white women, African American women, and Latinas since 1979 (U.S. Department of Labor 2004, 30). Today, for instance, African American women in the United States earn 86 percent and Latinas earn 72 percent of what white women earn (U.S. Department of Labor 2004).

The context is significant here. Because African American and Latino men earn less than white men (U.S. Department of Labor 2004), women's income is especially vital to African American and Latino families. According to data from the AFL-CIO's fact sheet "equal Pay for Women of Color" (AFL-CIO

Table 8.1 Major Occupations by Race and Ethnicity

RACIAL/ETHNIC GROUP	OCCUPATIONS
White	Physical therapists, dental hygienists, secretaries, bookkeepers, and accountants
African American	Social workers, postal clerks, child-care workers, nurses' aides, and teachers' aides
Latinas	Private household cleaners and servants, child-care workers, garment workers, and machine operators
Asian	Electrical assemblers, dressmakers, and launderers
Native American	Welfare aides, child-care workers, and teachers' aides

Source: Newman (2004, 408).

2005), 77 percent of African American women and 68 percent of Latinas contribute one-half or more to their household income. As globalization increases the importance to families of second incomes, the occupational location of women is crucial; yet, as we just saw, Latinas and African American women typically work in some of the lowest-paying jobs (sees also Andersen 1997). As the data in Table 8.1 show, these jobs include various "aides," dental hygienists, child-care workers, private housecleaners, and garment workers —occupations that represent some of the lowest-paid and fastest-growing sectors in the U.S economy (Alpert and Auyer 2003).[9]

The broader point is that different occupational and geographical locations mean that globalization and economic restructuring will not have the same effects on each group. As Browne and Misra (2003) argue, studies which show that a decline in manufacturing has affected men more than women mistakenly assume the concentration of female workers in services protects them from economic restructuring. While this generalization holds for white women and African American women in some regions, young African American women in other regions, such as the Midwest, experienced a drop in wages when manufacturing jobs left the central cities. Moreover, Puerto Rican women in New York and New Jersey lost jobs and wages with economic restructuring, whereas recently arrived female Mexican immigrants in California were incorporated into low-wage factory jobs (Scott 1996, Zentgraf 2001, Browne and Misra 2003). In the Los Angeles region, for example, Latina immigrant women are concentrated in labor-intensive craft industries, especially in small establishments focusing on clothing, textiles, and leather production that together form the backbone of the Los Angeles garment industry (Bonacich 2000). As we showed in Chapter 7, relatively inexpensive immigrant labor (in this case women) benefits both global capitalists and consumers who are able to purchase a diverse range of quality fashion at a reasonable cost.

Why is this important? As Browne and Misra (2003) argue, there is a dominant view held by neoliberals that group power and privilege in society is based on variations in human capital, *not* social location, race, gender, class, and sexual orientation. Globalization, as we have seen, is highly compatible with—indeed, has been based upon—a gender ideology that legitimizes how women from different racial and ethnic backgrounds are incorporated into labor markets; it may in fact reinforce existing patterns of domination and subordination. By ignoring this issue, we will likely find inequalities deepening over time.

Conclusion

More so than any other variable, gender allows us to tease out the complexities of globalization. One conclusion we can draw from this chapter is that gender is vital to understanding how neoliberal globalization has unfolded; women are increasingly producing the products circulating in global markets. It is also clear that we need to incorporate culture—the gender ideology— into any analysis of inequalities.

Global processes interact in multiple ways with ascribed (e.g., gender, race, ethnicity, age) and achieved (class) statuses to create different patterns of domination and subordination, or what Patricia Hill Collins (1991) calls the "matrix of domination." Location in the social structure and the underlying economic conditions dictate the experience of the matrix. Typically, globalization advantages those who are the most economically, culturally, and politically powerful. For others, the intersection of status and class is less beneficial. We saw this with transnational companies relocating to Mexico, Central America, the Caribbean, or South and East Asia to take advantage of young poor women of color; middle- and upper-class professionals hiring poor women of color to care for their homes and families; or wealthy tourists traveling to South Asia on "sex tours" to take advantage of young, poor women of color.

Still, despite everything, globalization is creating jobs that often provide a degree of autonomy and even empowerment for women. Work as part of the global assembly or care lines creates the possibility for women to acquire income, often while working at home and caring for children. Yes, the exploitation of women across the globe is undeniable, but we need to avoid a one-dimensional view of women as victims. As Fernandez-Kelly and Wolf (2001, 1248) point out, "exploitation, at least, entails a connection with the world of employment and, therefore, possible mobilization, resistance, and negotiation." With the deepening of globalization and the increasing incorporation of women into the global system, existing social and economic structures will be altered in a way that may create the possibility for women to transform their unequal status. Part of this involves the twin processes whereby the same conditions that gave rise to the global assembly line allow women to connect with each other and to tap into resources and information that were previously unavailable. We have seen these transnational linkages historically in terms of women's suffrage movements as well as struggles to overthrow the dictatorships in South America in the 1970s and 1980s. Today, globalization is potentially creating even greater opportunities for women to build transnational networks that are crucial to nurturing self-esteem and empowerment and to possibly reducing gender inequalities.

As in other parts of the world, we found that globalization increases the financial burden on families in the United States. To be sure, globalization did not create the need for women to work—here or elsewhere—though neo-liberal globalization has aggravated the situation for a growing number of families. As women increasingly move into the labor force, long-standing gender (and racial) ideologies continue to drive occupational gender segregation. At the same time, as women increase their participation in the paid labor force, their primary identity as homemaker may be transformed into that of wage earner. As global processes alter the role of women in our society, the "traditional" model of the sole male breadwinner is becoming outmoded. As a result, more women are able to challenge traditional family authority patterns, which in turn encourages the emergence of family structures that are more egalitarian (Safa 1990, Rubin 1996, Carnoy 2000).

Still, greater gender equality will not come easily. Employment may boost self-esteem, but this does not automatically translate into more equality. Moreover, a sense of empowerment will vary by sector; sex workers may be employed, but this employment is unlikely to have a positive effect on self-esteem or equality. Finally, many men and women continue to resist any change that alters the gender status quo. Think about this in the United States, where working women are blamed for "abandoning" their children and families, for creating the "crisis of the family," for exacerbating problems in our schools, and for the violence among our children. There are cries that we need to return to "traditional family values" and "traditional marriages" as a means to solve these problems. Yet, as we have argued in this chapter, those who take this position miss how these changes (and hence these problems) are being driven by larger structural transformations, not solely by individual choices. How these struggles play will determine the future of globalization. This is the focus of Part III.

Constructing Change

CHAPTER 9

Globalization

Countermovements and Community

> Progress is more plausibly judged by the reduction of deprivation than by the further enrichment of the opulent. We cannot really have an adequate understanding of the future without some view about how well the lives of the poor can be expected to go. Is there, then, hope for the poor (Sen 2000)?

Amartya Sen's belief that the gains of economic growth should be directly applied to reducing inequality challenges one of the core assumptions of neoliberal globalization. In the orthodox view, free markets may concentrate wealth in the hands of the few but the few in turn invest in ways that benefit the many. Neoliberal globalists see this model as the best hope for the poor; others, however, believe that the unfettered market model of neoliberal globalization actually deepens poverty and misery.

Intense political struggles have been waged over these ideas, but as we have seen, globalization seldom produces the kinds of tidy outcomes described above. In the heat of the battle, we often lose sight of the fact that globalization is a human construction, a product of the *actions* and *inactions* of people. Hence, the condition of the poor rests on the outcome of the struggles among various factions to conceptualize, define, and realize their contending visions of the future. In this chapter, we examine some of the movements that are attempting to exert democratic control over global processes and ensure that the needs of individuals and communities are not lost in the quest for greater profits.

Globalization, the State, Society, and Markets: Karl Polanyi

The changing relationship among the state, markets, and society is a central issue within the globalization debate. Since the 1970s, state autonomy has been compromised by the increasing power of global actors—transnational corporations and multinational political institutions. Questions of what causes shifts in the distribution of power among states and between the state and society are not new ones for social scientists. In the classic work *The Great Transformation*, Karl Polanyi addressed this problem in his analysis of the rise and demise of classical liberalism, or what he calls the "self-regulating market" of laissez-faire capitalism. According to Polanyi (1944, 141), the philosophy of economic liberals in the late eighteenth and early nineteenth centuries derived from the idea that laissez-faire was a natural system. For these theorists, only markets could ensure the optimal allocation of scarce resources; therefore, society should be subordinated to the self-regulating market. The quest then was to "dis-embed" the economy from society, or to uproot the market from social and political institutions, by removing all barriers to the free operation of markets.

Polanyi's critique convincingly demonstrates that the emergence of a self-regulating market was neither inevitable nor sustainable. Far from a "natural" process, he argued that the self-regulating market system was a creation of middle-class merchants and their political allies, who used the state to produce the laissez-faire system by removing state and business intrusions into the economy. By dis-embedding the market from society, the classical liberals engendered an industrial revolution that produced "an almost miraculous development of the tools of production," as well as an equally "catastrophic dislocation of the lives of common people" (Polanyi 1944, 33).

The problem, as Polanyi saw it, is the need for the market to commodify everything; and if left unchecked, the self-regulating market would lead to the very "destruction of humanity and transform the environment into a vast wilderness" (Polanyi 1944, 3). While this was a distinct possibility, Polanyi also believed that society contained a self-protection mechanism—the countermovement—that would be triggered by the dislocations caused by market forces.

The countermovement consists of those most "immediately affected by the deleterious action of the market . . . the working class . . . using protective legislation, restrictive associations" (Polanyi 1944, 132), such as trade unions and state intervention, to resubordinate market forces to society—to re-embed the market into the institutional structure of society. Quite unlike the conscious effort of creating laissez-faire capitalism, then, the countermovement arises spontaneously to defend society from the dislocations caused by the expansion of the free market. Thus, in Polanyi's theory, the relationship among the state, markets, and society is continually shaped by a double movement of forces: one consciously favoring self-regulating free markets and a spontaneous countermovement that checks its expansion.

Corpocracy and Civil Society

In the post-1980 period, neoliberals have replaced the classical liberals as the force doggedly pursuing the institutionalization of the self-regulating market system. The globalization of markets for goods and services pushed by neoliberals would not have surprised Polanyi; in fact, Polanyi argued that "nothing less than a self-regulating market on a world scale could ensure the functioning of" the laissez-faire system (Polanyi 1944, 138). Current policies have not only spread markets throughout the world but created the basis for a dramatic increase in the power of private corporations. As governments privatize and deregulate their previous social functions (e.g., social services, social welfare, job creation), the state becomes increasingly dependent upon corporations to carry out basic public services. The result, according to Charles Derber (2002), is a fusing of the interest among transnational corporations, national governments, and global institutions, or what Derber calls **corpocracy**. A defining feature of a corpocracy is the disappearance of a "firewall" between the state and large corporations; although the state and society remain independent, it is "one world under business" as corporations increasingly exercise decisive power over the course of national and global economic development (Derber 2002, see also Strange 1997).

Corpocracy is part of the second "great (global) transformation"—the industrial revolution that Polanyi analyzed is the first great transformation—as neoliberal globalization creates an almost miraculous development of capitalism and profound dislocations in the lives of ordinary people across the globe (Munck 2002, 3). What do corpocracy and the ability of corporations to produce anything anywhere mean for Polanyi's double-movement? As we have argued throughout this book, globalization has weakened nationally based movements such as labor unions, which have in the past served as a central force in the countermovement pushing for social legislation. Furthermore, globalization has frayed (or even broken) the social bonds between people and undermined their sense of community and their belief in the power of citizens to effect change (see Putnam 1996, 2000; Hertz 2001; Brecher, Costello, and Smith 2002). National governments are less and less fulfilling the basic role of providing public services such as trash collection, for instance. So what are the implications of these changes for the countermovement that has traditionally targeted national policy as a means to resolve social problems?

Although the state has become one of many global actors, we are not arguing that the state has *no* role in resolving local problems. To be sure, sovereign power has been transformed by globalization, but federal (national) and local (subnational) governments can still make a difference; thus, influence over government policy remains an important focus of struggle. Ultimately, control over corporations involves re-embedding the market through regulation and decommodification, as Polanyi argued; today, however, this must occur at the national and the global levels.

Almost as it heeds the call to fulfill its appointed mission, the information infrastructure is being used by activists to take advantage of declining costs of transportation and to organize and strengthen transborder movements in opposition to dislocations caused by neoliberal globalization. The World

Social Forum and the International Forum on Globalization are only two examples of the nascent global countermovement, which is not only challenging neoliberal globalization but, in the process, constructing a global civil society.[1]

What constitutes a global civil society? A civil society exists whenever people mobilize social movements and/or voluntary associations to initiate change in the *national or local* social order. In a global civil society, people mobilize social movements and/or form voluntary associations to initiate change in the *global* social order (Scholte 2000a, 177). Specifically, a global civil society encompasses civic activity that (1) addresses transworld issues, (2) involves transborder communication, (3) has a global organization, and (4) works on the premise of supraterritorial solidarity (Scholte 2000a, 180–181). While the four characteristics often go hand-in-hand, many global civic associations do not have all of them (see Scholte 2000a, 180).

Why is civil society important? At the national level, civil society provides the basis for the development and maintenance of democratic and social-welfare institutions. If we reflect for a moment on how the democratic states of Europe were built, we find that rulers never willingly extended civil, political, or social rights to subjects; only through demands did the masses transform Europe's oligarchies into democracies and eventually into social welfare states. As the countermovement expands and a global civil society develops, pressure from below may transform the neoliberal global system and create a set of democratic global institutions capable of controlling transnational corporations and providing social support for the least powerful. In other words, just as nineteenth-century and early twentieth-century women and men had to mobilize through voluntary associations in protest at the national level to achieve voting rights, better working conditions, and social policies to improve their lives, people at the turn of the millennium are engaged in a similar effort on a global scale.

Globalization and Its Countermovement

In the remainder of the chapter, we focus on a selection of organizations and groups that can be considered part of a budding global civil society—the global countermovement—and some of the diverse new tactics and strategies they are using to resolve local problems associated with globalization. Among these are *Agir pour les Femmes en Situation Pécaire* ("Acting for Women in Distressing Situations," AFESIP), which combats the global sex industry; living-wage campaigns in the United States, which are addressing wage and other community problems; consumer-advocacy campaigns in the United States, which are attempting to control the behavior of global corporations; and the Southeast Georgia Community Projects, which addresses the needs of Latinos in Georgia.

Asian Sex Trafficking[2]

AFESIP is a French global nongovernmental, nonpartisan, and nonreligious grassroots organization founded in 1996 and headquartered in Cambodia. It is devoted to "humanly correct development" and the "fight against the trafficking of women and children for sex slavery" (AFESIP 2004a, 3). Since its founding, AFESIP has developed an extensive anti-trafficking research-and-support network spanning the world from Spain to France to the United States to Cambodia, Thailand, and Vietnam. Working with governments, universities, institutes, and other nongovernmental organizations, AFESIP is creating social and legal structures that enhance official efforts to combat sex trafficking and slavery (AFESIP 2004c).

The activities of AFESIP cover all consequences of sex trafficking (AFESIP 2004a, 2004b). Specific programs in Southeast Asia include the legal and practical—such as rescue operations and safe houses—to support victims wishing to leave the sex industry; HIV/AIDS outreach; counseling and psychological treatment; family reunification, if viable; employment placement; and support for family income-generating opportunities. The philosophical underpinnings of the organization are similar to the entrepreneurial literacy theory of the Brazilian Clodomir Santos de Morais (2000), which emphasizes a "learning-by-doing" strategy to help individuals develop the capabilities necessary to more fully participate in society (see also Sobrado and Rojas 2004).[3]

Perhaps the most important aspect of AFESIP's work is its reintegration program. With limited opportunities to acquire entrepreneurial skills and productive and economic resources, women often fall victim to sexual slavery through poverty and vulnerability. As AFESIP's Research unit's former Director Pierre Le Roux points out, the realities of rural Southeast Asia have transformed daughters into an important commodity for poor families (Aguilar 2005). Years of war and armed conflict, and more recently dislocations caused by free market policies, have caused severe social and economic devastation in this region. These circumstances have conspired to make the sex-trafficking industry a significant part of the region's economy.

In view of these conditions—and the possibility of victims being retrafficked unless they develop skills to become self-sufficient—AFESIP emphasizes basic education, entrepreneurial literacy, and human and worker rights. Achieving sustainable financial independence begins with training in one of AFESIP's rehabilitation centers and a "business starting kit" that contains either in-kind or cash assistance that can be used to create income-generating activities. AFESIP also networks women with organizations that can provide additional support when needed.

AFESIP's fair trade business—called Fair Fashion—is one of its more ambitious programs. The idea behind Fair Fashion is to take advantage of globalization by creating links with global markets as a means to achieve greater autonomy and control for women and communities. Partnering with the global fair-frade movement (the Fair Trade Federation and the International Federation for Alternative Trade), the Fair Fashion program is a skill-building and income-generating project that helps victims return to a "normal" life.[4] Women trained in AFESIP rehabilitation centers work in Fair Fashion garment-production facilities that produce high-quality products under the principles of fair trade (e.g., living wages, safe and hygienic working conditions, no child or forced labor, nondiscrimination policies, and so on). Currently, there are two programs. One, founded in February 2003, is located in rural Tloc Tchroeu (Kompong Cham Province), Cambodia. Currently, 16 women work in this center. A second center, started in June 2004 with five women, is in Saigon.

How successful has AFESIP been in combating sex slavery? Its Fair Fashion program provides on-the-job training in basic sewing skills and design, while AFESIP training seminars cover an array of issues from human rights to globalization, fair-trade, and gender issues to managing microbusinesses. Victims also have access to counselors and psychologists. Together, these programs create opportunities for self-development that lead to improved living standards and reduced dependence and vulnerability. Globally, AFESIP's research and information programs are raising awareness about the problem of trafficking and forging networks capable of combating trafficking.

Still, AFESIP faces many challenges, including the disparity between the region's poverty and the wealth and power of those running the sex industry as well as the inability or unwillingness of government officials to stop sex trafficking (this is often due to a lack of resources).[5] Equally problematic, in January 2005, the U.S. government began phasing out all quotas on textiles, which means that foreign exporters and U.S. importers will be free to export or import any textile products into the United States without having to worry about quantitative limitations, import licenses, or other special requirements. In addition, with its entrance into the World Trade Organization (WTO), China is dramatically increasing its share of total global textile exports. These two factors mean increasing competition for Fair Fashion products and an uncertain future for this project.

Challenging Corporate Power

Incredible as it may sound, under U.S. law corporations have the legal status of "personhood," meaning that they enjoy the same protections as human beings under the U.S. Constitution.[6] With the reach of corporations spreading beyond the control of any one government and with the growing material inequities between corporations and most individuals, this legal definition takes on new meaning in the political process. As corporations increasingly pursue a global agenda and the ties between business and communities are severed (Rubin 1996, 53), enormous problems are created for communities. As we noted earlier, corpocracy creates a pattern of control in which the federal government responds to the demands of big business and county and city governments are increasingly responsible for those functions abdicated by the federal government. In this section, we look at forms of activism targeting the growth of corporate power and the challenge of bringing democratic control over corporations.

Living-Wage Campaigns

Living-wage campaigns address the immediate local problems of declining wages and benefits and increased need for higher-paying jobs with the expansion of welfare-to-work programs. With the emergence of the neoliberal state, the traditional functions of the federal government are increasingly the responsibility of state and local governments. Less federal support for local governments, both fiscally and in terms of social programs, places immense political pressures on local officials (state, county, and city) to generate new sources of revenue and employment. Often, local elected officials resort to a policy of creating "jobs at any cost." It is not uncommon to see states or cities bid against each other to attract investment. Strategies include tax holidays, or the elimination of certain taxes for a set amount of time; "guarantees" of union-free workplaces; and the "temporary" suspension of workplace and environmental regulation, such as minimum wages. Unfortunately, these inducements do little to resolve the fiscal crisis of the local areas and generally create nonunion employment (which pays less and has fewer benefits) or low-wage service sector jobs that do little to resolve the problems of low incomes and poverty.

The ongoing battle against poverty and the growing ranks of the working poor have been intensified by the declining real value of the minimum wage. In 1969, if one member of a family of four held a full-time minimum-wage job, the family would subsist at approximately 10 percent below the poverty line; today, a family of four supported by a single minimum-wage job would fall into an income category 39 percent below the poverty line (Clawson 2003, 168). In constant 2000 dollars, the 1968 minimum wage would equal $7.92 per hour and, if adjusted for inflation and productivity, it would equate to $13.80 per hour (Clawson 2003, 168; Pollin and Luce 1998, 40). By the beginning of the twenty-first century, the average worker toiling at the federal minimum wage would have to work 66 hours a week and pay *no taxes* to bring his or her family of four up to the poverty line (Clawson 2003, 168–169).

The obvious and traditional remedy for this problem is for the federal government to raise the federal minimum wage. The level of the minimum wage, however, reflects the distribution of political power and not some neutral set of forces (see Clawson 2003). Not surprisingly, business people and their political allies respond to attempts to raise the floor under the lowest-paid workers with claims that increasing the minimum wage will inevitably augment inflationary pressures and job losses and cause grave damage to global competitiveness.

To combat these arguments, proponents of a "living wage" make the simple point that anyone working full time should earn enough to support a family at least at the poverty line. Indeed, recent survey data show that over 90 percent of those polled in the United States support this idea, agreeing with the statement that "people who work full time should be able to earn enough to keep their families out of poverty" (Ehrenreich 2001). The novelty of the living-wage approach makes these some of "the most interesting and underreported grassroots enterprise[s] to emerge since the Civil Rights Movement," according to the editor of *The American Prospect*, Robert Kuttner (quoted in Unitarian Universalistic Service Committee 2005).

Living-wage campaigns arrived on the scene in 1994 and are innovative in two important respects. First, they target communities rather than minimum-wage or even low-wage workers in specific workplaces. A typical campaign will focus on enacting a city or county ordinance that covers city or county employees or employees of any company doing business within that city or county. Between 1994 and 2005, living-wage ordinances were enacted in over 130 cities or counties (Labor Studies Center 2003). These ordinances have established wage levels from $6.25 to $13.00 per hour, with wages generally indexed to inflation or the poverty level. Moreover, employers are often required to pay health benefits as part of a compensation package (Levi, Olson, and Steinman 2003). Second, these campaigns are forging networks and alliances among labor organizations, community-based organizations, clergy, and students that can pursue campaigns beyond wages to other quality-of-life issues. The broad spectrum of local groups that form living-wage coalitions is a significant change from past mobilizations. As David Reynolds (1999, 69–70) points out, groups in the past tended to focus on concerns unique to each one; consequently, they acted alone on specific issues or in smaller coalitions. Unions, for instance, fend off the latest concession demands from management; community groups for the poor battle against the harsh aspects of welfare reform; churches struggle to find resources to feed the hungry and house the homeless; students fight against the rising cost of education. Today, however, there is a growing awareness among these groups that they cannot go it alone. While not every campaign involves all of these groups, broader coalitions typically enjoy greater access to resources and a better chance of achieving their goal of "capacitating" individuals, or capacity building by empowering people to have greater control over their own destinies. By forging broader coalitions, the movement is establishing a basis for these movements to address more general community problems that are created by "jobs-at-any-cost" strategies.

Labor: Unions are often central players in these local campaigns for several reasons. Organized labor has long been involved in the struggle to raise wages and improve the working conditions of workers; yet, since the 1960s, unionization in the United States has declined from over 35 percent of private-sector workers to less than 8 percent today.

Many of the changes described in this book are responsible for the weakening of organized labor. Unions, however, remain relevant in today's globalized world, and living-wage campaigns provide an opportunity for labor to develop new organizing strategies and coalitions that may attract new members. The United Food and Commercial Workers Union (UFCW), for instance, has forged ties with community and environmental groups in its struggle against Wal-Mart (Iritani 2005b). A second example of extensive labor–community ties is the Justice for Janitors movement (Clawson 2003).

Religion: Faith-based organizations are active in living-wage campaigns for many of the same reasons as labor. These campaigns offer opportunities for recruiting and retaining members by showing the relevance of the church to people's daily struggles. Equally important, living-wage campaigns directly engage the moral claims of adequate wages and benefits (Kazin 1999). Rabbinical students, Muslims, and born-again Christians alike express concerns that workers "made in the image of God" are not being treated that way or are "pushed so hard" that they do not have the time to "lead an abundant life" (Simon 2005). The role of churches and synagogues in addressing labor and community issues is neither new nor unusual. Bishop Bernard J. Sheil, for instance, offered support to John L. Lewis's attempts to organize steelworkers in 1938. In the 1960s and 1970s, Cesar Chavez drew moral and practical support from the Catholic Church while organizing the United Farm Workers in California, and Reverend Martin Luther King was working with sanitation workers and poor people before he was killed in 1968 (Simon 2005, Levy 1975).

Community Organizations: Margaret Levi, David Olson, and Erich Steinman (2003) argue that community organizations bring vital resources, strategies, and energy to a coalition. At the same time, they lack the legitimacy and institutionalized structure of churches or the legal claim of unions to represent workers. Community organizations are often created by residents who have few other avenues for seeking redress to their problems, and their legitimacy stems from successfully mobilizing the community to achieve desired changes. Although the early history of the living-wage campaigns of the Industrial Areas Foundation (IAF) and the Association of Community Organization for Reform Now (ACORN) did not involve unions, there is recognition that better working and living conditions and prospects for long-term change can only be accomplished through joint partnerships and a mutual commitment of resources (Levi, Olson, and Steinman 2003). Thus, community organizations forge alliances with other organizations to address basic quality-of-life issues. For instance, the IAF and Valley Interfaith came together in the Rio Grande Valley of south Texas to bring running water, sewers, electricity, and paved roads to *colonias*.[7]

The coalition's philosophy of capacity building, leadership develop-ment, and "learning by doing" not only accomplished its immediate goals but has helped to give these communities an ongoing voice in local politics (Putman, Feldstein, and Cohen 2003, Chapter 1).

Students: Since the 1990s, students have served as a key force in the move-ment focused on confronting corporate power, most visibly the student **anti-sweatshop movement** that grew out of the public disclosures in the mid-1990s that Gap apparel, Kathie Lee Gifford's Wal-Mart clothing line, and Nike shoes were being produced by girls as young as 13 in Asia and Latin America.

From the beginning, the anti-sweatshop movement has been a student-labor coalition. Groups such as the Union of Needletrades, Industrial, and Textile Employees, or UNITE, provide organizational, strategic, and financial resources to local student groups. The movement's origins date from the years 1997–1998 when students from Duke, Harvard, Illinois, and Georgetown spent the summer at the AFL-CIO's Summer Labor Organizing Program. Students traveled to Central America to witness the conditions under which apparel was produced for the U.S. market and, over the next few years, organized the United Students Against Sweatshops (USAS). By 2001, USAS had mounted campaigns on over 200 U.S. university and college campuses.

More recently, students associated with the anti-sweatshop campaigns have initiated actions focusing on the wages and working conditions of service workers on their campuses. Similar to the USAS strategy of directly connecting activists with workers, the American Federation of State, County, and Municipal Employees union (AFSCME) began pair-ing students with janitors to work side-by-side on night shifts at several universities. As students began to experience firsthand what it means to be a low-wage worker on their campuses, living-wage campaigns sprung up on over 30 campuses, including the largest private employer in Baltimore, Johns Hopkins, as well as Harvard, Fairfield, and Wesleyan Universities (Clawson 2003, 180–181).

Similar to the living-wage movement, these are limited campaigns that focus on service workers—janitors and food-service workers—at universities. The story is by now a familiar one: to cut costs, univer-sities use private companies that subcontract workers who receive lower pay and fewer benefits than if the university had directly hired the workers. The idea driving the university-based living-wage cam-paigns, then, is to win an agreement (in some cases, a union with a contract) with the university that any worker hired directly or indirectly through a subcontractor would receive a certain level of benefits. Generally, these include a living wage, safe working conditions, mini-mal job security, among other benefits negotiated directly with univer-sity officials or indirectly on the part of the union (see Clawson 2003, 180–187).

Still, if ordinances narrowly target cities, communities, or universities, are they simply symbolic victories in the battle against corporate power? The answer to this question is not so simple. To be sure, these campaigns are limited in the number of workers they cover; however, social change is often about *perception*, and small—even symbolic—victories are important to placing new ideas on the table for discussion. Living-wage victories also begin to raise the bar for companies and industries not covered that may create opportunities for more extensive organizing attempts (see Clawson 2003, Chapter 6). By raising the wages of the lowest-paid workers, for instance, these campaigns put pressure on higher wage levels and counter the existing jobs-at-any-cost strategy that is central to the present form of globalization.

Furthermore, living-wage campaigns do not reflect politics as usual. They are intended to supplement or replace the supervision and control of employer–employee relations by the federal, state, and court system with one that emphasizes community activism, community control, and mass mobilization (see Clawson 2003, 170–171). These coalitions are targeting local government officials to respond to the problem of employment and poverty in ways that previous movements pressured the federal government. This requires the creation and deepening of social networks among residents within and across different organizations and groups, as well as with local government officials and agencies, to ensure the ongoing monitoring and enforcement of ordinances. In effect, these groups are building community from the bottom up by creating social networks that can be utilized for community projects beyond the workplace.

If these campaigns fail to reach out and mobilize low-wage workers and community residents, however, they will likely suffer from the same limitations as other movements that drive change "from above." Clawson (2003) identifies some of these pitfalls in a recent justice-for-janitors living-wage campaign at Wesleyan University that, while successfully winning a contract, tended to reproduce patterns of dependence on the part of the university's workers. In this case, the organizing strategy did not fully or adequately integrate the workers into the process. Students often took action on behalf of the workers; the workers in turn tended to look toward the students for guidance on priorities and strategies. Because they were not fully incorporated into the organizing process, workers were never empowered to effectively carry on the struggle without the organizers. The case is suggestive. If movements are to successfully challenge neoliberal globalization, people need to be empowered to take control of their lives and circumstances over the long run. Yet, without concrete short-term results, the organizational effort may never get off the ground. The fundamental lesson, and one echoed in the experiences of the above IAF and Valley Interfaith campaigns in south Texas, is to empower people in the process of devising solutions to their immediate problems so that they develop the capacity to "defend themselves and exercise power tomorrow and the day after" (Clawson 2003, 166–167; also Carmen and Sobrado 2000).

Consumer-Advocacy Movements

Consumer advocacy is another movement addressing growing corporate power. Here, the strategy is to harness market forces as a mechanism to reward or punish global corporations and thereby alter corporate behavior. Consumer movements and consumer activism have a long history, and the contemporary form continues in the spirit of protecting consumers from big business. Today, however, the challenge is broader—consumer groups also attempt to protect workers by compelling companies to adopt corporate codes of conduct. *Codes of conduct* are formal statements of the values and business practices of a corporation that may include sections on wages and working conditions, child labor, the environment, and so on.[8] The idea is to use codes to establish and protect the basic rights of workers in situations where unions and state regulations are either weak or nonexistent.

Codes, however, only specify appropriate behavior, and there are no formal mechanisms through which codes can be enforced. How then can the consumer-advocacy movement ensure that company behavior is consistent with codes of conduct? The key, according to Naomi Klein (2000a, 2000b, 2001), lay in the significance of corporate brands. The notion of brands came about during the industrial revolution as an attempt to create individuality within a production process of sameness (Klein 2000a)—sugar is sugar, but only C&H is "pure cane sugar." In other words, identical products had to be differentiated from each other, and brands became the mechanism to identify the superiority of one product over another.

With globalization, brands as a means of differentiating products evolved into a process through which *individuals* differentiate themselves. This is the notion of **branding** (Klein 2000a, 2000b, 2001; Quart 2004). Although branding often refers to advertising, Klein (2000a) argues that branding is in reality more ominous. It is a process through which individuals—even public spaces—become linked to corporations as a way of defining themselves (or the space). Branding goes beyond advertising to the selling of a lifestyle; with branding, brands are no longer an add-on to a company's existence but *the* reason for its existence. Today, corporations are locked in a struggle to achieve a greater market share in highly competitive global markets where goods are produced not by them but by the same nameless subcontractors. In other words, with globalization, fewer companies are producing things and more are producing images. Nike, for instance, does not produce shoes and Dell does not make computers; their work lay not in manufacturing but in marketing a lifestyle, a look, a culture.

Branding is ubiquitous, and in this age of lower taxes and shrinking social programs, where communities and schools are ever more pressed to find sufficient resources, branding is insidious. We have 3Com Park in San Francisco, Staple's Center in Los Angeles, Quest Field in Seattle, Coors Field in Colorado, and FedEx Field for the Washington Redskins. Increasingly, school districts are looking to the private sector for funds, which results in the branding of schools. Pepsi, Coke, McDonalds, Nike, Procter & Gamble, Toyota, and Microsoft are only a few corporations that provide advice, funds, and managerial support to help children develop basic skills and education (Hertz 2001, 173). This is what Klein (2000a) calls "the branding of learning." The question few are asking in this new age of public–private partnering is to what extent are these genuine public service programs or innovative ways to "brand" children in the quest for a greater market share; moreover, if the needs of a democratic society clash with those of corporations, whose interests will prevail?

Branding is not only about what happens "out there." Individuals are branded as they increasingly define themselves by their possessions (Quart 2004, 43–45). Stop for a moment and think about what you wear and why: Are you branded by Nike, Reebok, or Payless; do you drive a Mercedes Benz, a BMW, or a Hyundai? Consumption of the "right" brands no longer reflects the quality of the company or product but the "quality" and "value" of the individual. Even a person's identity (or quality as a human being) is determined by the brands she or he consumes; sure, brands have long signified one's social position, but this has taken on a completely new meaning in today's world. Thus, buying Nike or a BMW is not about a shoe or a car but the image we wish to project to the public about our attitude, philosophy, quality, and values.

The importance of corporate brands and logos in the highly competitive global system creates social and psychological problems, but enormous potential as well (Klein 2000a, 2001). Brand reputation is paramount for corporations. Advocacy groups can use brand supremacy to enforce codes by monitoring corporate adherence and by exposing violators through print, radio and visual media, and the Internet, as well as through protests and leafleting (see Mandle 2000, Alpert 2002, Conroy 2002, Ross 2004). The threat of a consumer backlash is real, and rebuilding a damaged brand is costly; thus, companies will go to great lengths to avoid negative publicity (Hertz 2001, 118–129).

Have these campaigns proved successful? Again, there is no easy answer. Data, for instance, show an increase in consumer activism and value-influenced buying behavior throughout the world since 1995 (Hertz 2001, 210).[9] By the 1990s, images of "children bowed over workbenches, or adults crammed thirty at a time into squalid dormitories . . . stitching sneakers, footballs, and sweatshirts that we wear and play with" troubled many consumers (Hertz 2001, 117–118). This has meant, according to Noreena Hertz (2001, 127), "a substantial increase not only in the number of multinationals that now have codes of conduct (*all* Fortune 500 companies in the U.S. do), but also in those now willing to undergo an audit of their environmental, and to a lesser extent social, policies."

Along with the effects of student anti-sweatshop campaigns on college and university campuses,[10] public protests against Nike produced a significant and well–publicized change in the company's policies. Today, Nike allows independent monitoring of its factories and, as of spring 2005, has made public the location of the factories producing its products. This is an important victory for the consumer-advocacy movement; as long as factory locations remain secret, it is nearly impossible to monitor corporate behavior.

Other consumer actions in the 1990s caused manufacturers of soccer balls to change policy and to add labels certifying the product as "child labor-free." In 2000, Starbucks executives signed a letter of intent with TransFair USA, a "fair-trade" certification organization, to certify that its fair-trade coffee would be produced under fair-trade conditions (e.g., long-term contracts offering higher wages than the going global market rate). Consumer-advocacy groups have successfully convinced the major do-it-yourself lumberyards, as well as Kinkos', The Gap, and other companies, to stop buying products from "old growth" forests and to give preference to products produced through sustainable forest practices (Conroy 2002). Greenpeace International has persuaded refrigerator maker Whirlpool Corporation to use environmentally friendly insulation, and The Gap and Nike have collaborated with labor advocates to clean up sweatshops in Cambodia (Iritani 2005a). Sister Ruth Rosenbaum, founder of the Center for Reflection, Education, and Action, an antipoverty group based in Hartford, Connecticut, summed up the consumer-advocacy movement this way: "When we first started working on codes of conduct back in the 1990s, this was kind of like way out there, now, it is absolutely normal for a company to have a code of conduct" (Iritani 2005a).

Still, it is not clear whether these examples illustrate fundamental change or if they are corporate marketing ploys equivalent to "window dressing." If these campaigns are to create long-term change, several conditions need to be present: *transparency* on the part of the company, *monitoring* of corporate behavior on the part of an independent advocacy group, and *informed* consumers with access to a variety of merchandise. This is a *demand-driven market* process requiring that advocacy groups have reasonably free access to company factories and the capability to expose violations to a large number of consumers. Moreover, consumers must care enough to change their buying habits. Absent these conditions, violators will be unlikely to suffer in the marketplace and the strategy will fail.

In the end, however, these movements *are not* substitutes for unions or community-level participation in the countries where factories are located. Consumer-advocacy groups can harness the market power of consumers to create codes as a means to halt abuses against workers—and to support fair-trade products—but it is difficult for an organization in one country to effectively monitor and enforce company behavior in another. Furthermore, subcontracting makes it exceedingly difficult to monitor compliance by rendering producers invisible to outside observers. This means that consumer-advocacy groups need to work on "globalizing" trade union rights that can support the growth of local unions that can serve as allies in the quest for higher wages and better working conditions in producing countries (see Mandle 2000).[11]

Immigration and Empowerment in the Deep South

Southeast Georgia Community Project

The Southeast Georgia Community Project (SEGCP), in Lyons, Georgia, is one of the local grass-roots organizations that form part of an emerging global civil society. Unlike states with a long history of Latino immigration, such as California or Texas, Georgia has few organizations capable of meeting the needs of a burgeoning Spanish-speaking population. The absence of bilingual and bicultural resources and organizations committed to meeting the needs of the Latino community effectively renders Latinos invisible to the mainstream society. Examples abound of mothers being told in Spanish by *telephone* that their baby did not survive childbirth or of minor traffic violations that resulted in overnight jail time—or longer—because no one could explain the problem (or the person's rights) in Spanish.

These problems are compounded by the more general issues of stratification. According to the report "America's Children: Key National Indicators of Well-Being 2005," Latino children are less likely than other children to have health insurance or to receive recommended vaccinations. The report also found that Latino children are more likely to live in poverty. Another study showed that Latinos in Georgia have the lowest graduation rates in the country—a rate of 32 percent compared with 54 percent nationwide (Greene 2002). These data provide a partial picture of the challenges SEGCP faces.

Andrea Cruz founded the community-based SEGCP in 1994 to meet the health, social, legal, and economic needs of the Latino farmworker community in southeast Georgia. Based on a philosophy of empowerment similar to that of the Brazilians Paolo Freire and Clodomir Santos de Morais, the organization emphasizes dialogue and "learning-by-doing." The goal is to promote human dignity through self-empowerment in order to reduce dependence and create the basis for active community participation. By building bridges among immigrant farmworkers, farmers, local citizens, local service providers, and legal advocates, SEGCP is educating the Anglo, Latino, and black communities about each other.[12]

SEGCP is run by an 11-member board of directors, of whom six are migrant farmworkers, while the remaining five are community leaders and clergy. Funding comes from local, state, and national grants and community-support efforts. Since farmworker board members are nonprofessional, the SEGCP offers training that introduces new members to basic board-member responsibilities, such as how to be effective in decision-making processes. Farmworkers serving on the board learn the basic skills that enable them to later serve on other community boards, such as Migrant Head Start and Migrant Health.

Decisions on how SEGCP should prioritize the range of social problems confronting the Latino community emerge from an ongoing dialogue among the various communities. These discussions have produced an array of programs and projects that include cultural-sensitivity workshops for local (non-Latino) health personnel, English classes, health and HIV/AIDS education, assistance in filling out citizenship applications, as well as programs that provide emergency food and clothing assistance. SEGCP has also developed a network of interpreters and health-care workers for its prenatal education program and to conduct follow-up home visits to new migrant farmworker mothers. Youth projects include antitobacco and antigang projects and domestic violence–prevention programs. By cultivating networks between health providers and the Latino community, SEGCP serves a vital role in bringing health care to the Latino community. Finally, as a means to maintain contact with the mobile farmworker community, SEGCP produces a Spanish-language radio program with a public-service emphasis.

As with many community-based organizations, SEGCP reflects a trend of citizens organizing themselves to take on problems government officials cannot or will not confront. The emergence and growth of SEGCP is a positive example of what can be accomplished by community activists possessed of conviction and creativity even when the odds are stacked against them.[13] The emphasis on promoting English and computer literacy, leadership skills, and health provides the basic enabling (capacity building) conditions for empowering residents to become more active in their communities. Through dialogue and community participation in local churches, schools, and businesses, Latinos can devise germane, applicable solutions to community problems consistent with their needs and create opportunities for upward social mobility for themselves and their children.[14]

Building Community Through Creating Social Capital

The effects of stratification and the importance of social networks are two recurring themes in all these cases. As we discussed in Chapter 5, class and status stratification matter because of the *consequences* of unequal distributions of wealth, income, and power. We have touched on some of these throughout the book, including access to health, education, and good jobs. The scope of these problems means that transforming our communities into livable spaces will require cooperation among members of disparate communities and between these communities and government agencies. Yet, as we noted in Chapter 4, globalization and global processes are undermining a sense of community by atomizing individuals and reducing the role of government in people's lives. Given these conditions, any solution will require that we rebuild our communities *from below*, that we recreate—or, in many cases, create—community-level social bonds between people through the kinds of efforts we have discussed in this chapter.

The groups described here are actively forging networks and coalitions to address the immediate problems created by globalization. By networks and coalitions, we are really talking about social capital, or the trust and social norms that govern reciprocity, sharing of resources, and other features of social organization—that is, networks, coalitions, and mutual assistance— and even social norms which set boundaries on the levels of inequality that a society tolerates (see Coleman 1988; Putnam 1993, 1996, 2000; Putnam, Feldstein, and Cohen 2003; Portes 1998; Light and Gold 2000; Santos de Morais 2000; Hytrek and Sobrado 2002; Krugman 2002; Sobrado and Rojas 2004). Social capital is something distinct from physical capital (tools) and human capital (education); unlike these forms of capital, social capital *increases*, rather than *decreases*, through use. In other words, the supply of social capital will be depleted if not used (Hirschman cited in Putman 1993, 169). Illustrations of social capital include the social networks and coalitions developed to pass living-wage ordinances, to monitor and enforce corporate codes of conduct, and to promote Latino health and literacy in Georgia.

Putnam (1996) and Putnam, Feldstein, and Cohen (2003) argue that communities with greater social capital also tend to be more livable. In these communities, residents have access to more resources and a capacity for self-organization and participation that enhances the chances for upward social mobility. We saw this in Georgia, where SEGCP's networks are connecting Latino and Anglo communities and improving the Latino population's access to resources. In many ways, SEGCP has made existing governmental organizations more effective by serving as a bridge between the Spanish- and English-speaking communities and public agencies. The construction of social networks is also critical to the operation of AFESIP, which is collaborating with nongovernmental organizations, activists, and scholars to share resources and information and to develop solutions to the global problem of sex trafficking. Similarly, living-wage campaigns and consumer-advocacy groups address the unequal distribution of power between communities and big business by forging community-based coalitions. In each case, activists are creating bonding social capital by tightening the links among members of the immediate (e.g., Latino) group as well as bridging social capital across different groups (e.g., religious, labor, student, environmental, class, and ethnic and racial groups). The latter, as you might expect, is the more difficult to build and the most important for creating livable and democratic communities.

While these networks are essential to the long-term health of our communities, the aforementioned groups did not set out to build social capital. Their immediate intent was to address a lack of jobs and opportunities, to provide access to health care, and to bring to individuals some control over the direction of change. Nonetheless, the result has been to create bonds between people within and across groups and, with them, the possibility for healthier communities. The lesson we can derive from these examples is that creating communities with greater opportunities for upward social mobility does not rest exclusively on the individual assets of community members, nor is the unequal distribution of physical and human capital an insurmountable obstacle; the success of these communities depends on the quantity and distribution of social capital networks.

Conclusion

With globalization altering the traditional role of the nation-state, we are left with a vision of globalization as a set of inevitable global forces wreaking havoc on the lives of ordinary and defenseless people and communities (Sklair 1999, 158). While the role of the nation-state has indeed changed, we explored in this chapter how "ordinary and defenseless people" are organizing themselves, building community as part of Polanyi's countermovement, and challenging governments to address basic community needs. What we have seen are groups pressuring *different levels* of government to resolve local problems, from AFESIP's targeting national governments to halt sex-based trafficking to living-wage campaigns focusing on city and county governments to SEGCP's pressuring community professionals and officials to address local ethnic-based inequality.

Often labeled "antiglobalization," they cannot be reduced to such a simplistic phrase; these groups do not romanticize a mythical preglobalization "good old days" but employ creative strategies in the active pursuit of solutions to local problems within the context of globalization. Furthermore, globalization is not the primary concern of these groups; rather, their goals are to bring better-paying jobs to neighborhoods and to ensure that people have access to health care, education, and clean communities in the United States and abroad. Even though globalization is not the target, their efforts are transforming the very nature of globalization.

Like Polanyi, many within these groups see laissez-faire free-market globalization as destructive to humanity and nature. Neoliberal globalization has produced incredible wealth and brought jobs to communities sorely lacking employment opportunities. Still, we need to ask under what conditions and at what cost? We have seen wealth rapidly and obscenely concentrated in the hands of a few, ecological devastation, families thrown into poverty because of low-paying jobs, and communities reduced to the places they merely occupy. These are the predictable results of elite-driven change and the idolization of free markets. Markets are not infallible and the failure of neoliberal globalization to widely deliver benefits to those on the bottom of the stratification hierarchy, and increasingly to those in the middle, has engendered a diverse countermovement.

In the end, we might ask ourselves what these groups have achieved. While we have discussed some of their accomplishments in this chapter, perhaps the most significant aspect is the forging of a global network that may be capable of confronting the global reach of powerful individuals and corporations. Above all, the groups that are part of the countermovement attest to the widespread belief in, and moreover the *possibility* of, making positive social change. There are thousands of individuals across the United States and the world who are educating us, informing us, and infecting us with their optimism for a better world. So is there any hope for the poor? As the groups described in this chapter continue their struggles consciously and even unintentionally against neoliberal globalization, there may yet be hope, not only for the poor, but for all of humanity.

CHAPTER 10

Conclusion

How Globalization Is Transforming America

> Globalization . . . is not simply about how governments, business, and people communicate, not just about how organizations interact, but is about the emergence of completely new social, political, and business models. It's about things that impact some of the deepest, most ingrained aspects of society right down to the nature of the social contract. . . . There are certain pivotal points or watersheds in history that are greater than others because the changes they produce were so sweeping, multifaceted, and hard to predict at the time (David Rothkoph, quoted in Friedman 2005, 45).

David Rothkoph, a former senior Department of Commerce official in the Clinton administration, captures the essence of our argument in this book. Globalization reflects deep-seated changes in human social relations. Long gone are the social structures and social norms that provided predictability and stability in the Fordist era; consumerism, flexibility, and risk rule the day. People are increasingly connected, and their lives have been radically transformed. No one is beyond the direct or indirect reach of globalization that has generated great prosperity and enormous misery; helped to spread democracy and disillusionment with democratic processes; and increased the fortunes of some while exacerbating already wide gaps in political, social, and economic opportunities and power (Sen 2002, Giddens 2003).

Globalization

Globalists and skeptics disagree on whether *globalization* is an accurate term to describe the nature of these changes over the past 30 years. Our position is that globalization is more than an ideological or mythical construction with marginal explanatory value, as the skeptics claim. As we argue in Chapter 4, contemporary globalization is a real and significant historical development with unprecedented effects even in comparison with the belle époque. While globalization is not a new process, it exhibits characteristics that differentiate it from earlier phases. Vital in this respect are the emergent conditions—advances in communication technologies, improvements in transportation, and political ideology—through which the basic economic forces of competition and the pursuit of profits operate. An understanding of the current structure of globalization is impossible without reference to these conditions.

From the end of World War II until the 1970s, the United States and much of the world enjoyed what is often called the "Thirty Glorious Years," a time of rapid growth, rising material prosperity, and declining inequality. Throughout this period, competition was moderated by state intervention, which regulated and supported the business sector and protected ordinary men and women from the hazards of the market. The creation of the Bretton Woods system after World War II brought global stability within which societies managed their economies. This was the heyday of the Keynesian social-welfare strategy. Over time, however, tensions emerged within the Keynesian model, generated by growing competition from a reconstructed Europe and Japan, the growth of Euro-currency markets, and technological advances. By the 1970s, Keynesianism was viewed as an obsolete approach to economic policy.

The stagflation of the 1970s created a political crisis in the United States and England that brought Ronald Reagan and Margaret Thatcher to power. Reagan and Thatcher (and their respective political parties) embraced the neoliberalism of Friedrich von Hayek and embarked on a course to deregulate and privatize their governments as a solution to the economic malaise. Globally, the World Bank and International Monetary Fund (IMF) became their missionary institutions, through which the neoliberal policies of deregulation and privatization were pushed on reluctant poor countries in need of their loans and grants (see Stiglitz 2002). By the 1980s, the spread of the neoliberal ideology combined with the global information infrastructure and improvements in transportation set the stage for a new phase of globalization. The unfolding of globalization is built, however, upon one additional factor: existing patterns of global inequality.

Class has been a fundamental factor in shaping the most recent phase of globalization, where unequal distributions of power and material resources create unequal opportunities to effect change. We saw this in the shaping of political policies in the 1980s as well as in the location of production and service jobs. Class is also a factor in accounting for the patterns of immigration into the United States. Still, one of the most essential ingredients for contemporary neoliberal globalization has been the universal subordination of women and girls. By the beginning of the twenty-first century, women and girls were producing the majority of goods circulating in global markets. Equally important, as economic restructuring reduces family resources in developed and developing countries alike, the incomes of women and girls are often the difference between survival and death for many households. The intersection of class and status reveals how globalization shapes and is shaped by inequality, specifically in the emergence and growth of the global assembly lines, the global care lines, and the global sex lines.

Globalization: Diversity Within Homogeneity

While it is true that globalization creates pressure toward homogeneity consistent with the interests of the major economic and political actors, we must not mistake what *appears* to be a process of convergence for *reality*. Globalization is a homogenizing and diversifying set of processes. We can see this along several lines:

- While the neoliberal strategy emerged as the new orthodoxy after 1980, social welfare polices remain in place in many parts of the world.

- Neoliberal policies accelerate the concentration of economic resources into the hands of a few, as well as the dispersion of production throughout the globe.

- Power has been concentrated in the hands of a few major trans-national corporations, which has undermined the ability of citizens to democratically influence the policies of their federal governments. At the same time, globalization made it possible for a transnational countermovement to emerge and reinvigorate political participation and increase people's control over their destiny.

- Even as the world's most powerful economic and political actors con-solidate their hegemony and set the rules of the game, the diffusion of power throughout the global system creates the basis for groups to challenge these actors in historically unprecedented ways.

- English is increasingly the global lingua franca, and the process of "McDonaldization" is standardizing local cultures; however, a com-plex process of borrowing and sharing is creating a hybridization of culture.

- The dominance of Asian and Latin American immigrants in the global flow of people involves a diverse array of immigrants, including those with high levels of education and ample resources and those with little formal education and few resources.

These examples illustrate the complex, contradictory, and contested nature of the globalization process in the twenty-first century.

Globalization and the United States

Importantly, the globalization debate has focused our attention on the most pressing issues of the twenty-first century. To understand these—health and environmental risks, security, peace, inequality, democracy, and justice—we must think beyond the individual micro- (or even the societal) level and situate local events and problems within broader (in this case global) social structures. This perspective, as C. Wright Mills shows, gives context to our problems and to our lives. Our concern in this book has been to put the changing patterns of work, inequality, and life chances in the United States into the broader global, institutional, and historical context.

Globalization has not unfolded in a haphazard fashion, as we noted. This is equally true in the United States, where the crisis of the 1970s emboldened the neoliberals to institutionalize their vision of the "good society." Global changes that contributed to stagflation and corporate uncompetitiveness in the United States triggered an ideological and policy shift away from the social welfare state of John Maynard Keynes. As Hayek's policies of deregulation and privatization were institutionalized after the 1980s, the New Deal was replaced by Reaganomics, the U.S. version of neoliberalism.

This transformation radically altered the basic institutional structure of society and the cultural norms that govern social life and shape individual life chances. The mildly socialistic managerial world (i.e., welfare capitalism) run once by "the man in the gray flannel suit"[1] (Krugman 2002) driving a Ford automobile has been replaced by investor capitalism run by "the man in the Armani suit" who is whisked to work by helicopter or limousine. In contrast to the previous period's understanding that markets can and do fail, the investor capitalism of twenty-first century U.S. society is founded on the unabashed belief in market infallibility. The New Deal era social compact based on mutual loyalty between employers and employees has been discarded in the dustbin of history; no longer do employers feel some obligation to workers, and increasingly workers feel little dedication to the company (Rubin 1996, Krugman 2002, Munck 2002, Selvin 2006). The new breed of CEOs is devoted not to employees or even the company but to the bottom line. Throughout the 1990s, managers were inundated with the message that all worker-related expenditures are bad and bombarded with the idea that greed is good, that greed works.

"Greed" is inherent in a system based on profit. The often neglected issue, however, is how norms shape behavior, or even what is viewed as "greedy." An important corollary to the growing power of capital was the ability of political and economic neoliberals to set the parameters of debate and, hence, to define the norms that once limited excess (i.e., greed) as quaint but ill-suited for the new era. A new attitude spread quickly throughout the business world during the post-1980 period, best exemplified by the "show me the money" chants of Microsoft employees at their annual conventions and the obscene salaries of executive officers. No longer were multimillion-dollar annual salaries for top executives the exception as CEO compensation soared to unprecedented heights (see Chapter 6). A slew of management books appearing on the market in the 1990s further legitimized this new "greed is good" corporate philosophy. Best sellers included *Only the Paranoid Survive: How to Exploit the Crisis Points that Challenge Every Company* by Andrew S. Grove (Former CEO of Intel) and *Mean Business: How I Save Bad Companies and Make Good Companies Great* by Bob Andelman and Albert J. Dunlap (Dunlap was former CEO of Scott Paper; to "dunlap" came to mean eliminate everything that is not the best). Designed to enhance the competitiveness of U.S. corporations, these books helped to institutionalize the lean-and-mean corporate strategy in which massive layoffs were rewarded with equally massive incentive packages for CEOs. The new corporate culture was no longer concerned with building companies; guided by the principle "if it feels good, do it," the new corporate leaders focused on making as much money as quickly as possible (Krugman 2002, also Fraser 2001).

Patterns of Work and Life

For most men and women in the United States, the "trickle-down" effects of these changes were evident in the increasing flexibility and insecurity in the home, workplace, and community. By the twenty-first century, the basic institutions of society were no longer functioning as they used to, nor were they organized in the same way, according the Martin Carnoy (2000). The disappearance of the Keynesian–Fordist-era two adult–one breadwinner family has increased conflicts in relationships over child care, housework, and finances. Moreover, flexibility means that friends, like our work lives, are more temporary and the friends we do have are, like us, absorbed by the demands of work.

Today, most workers can no longer count on long-term employment at the same firm or even the same position within the same firm. Concerns over the future of our jobs mean that we have less time to spend with our children, friends, and neighbors. Instead of participating in community- and neighborhood-oriented social capital networks to create quality neighborhood environments, we are consumed with work-related networking or skill upgrading in anticipation of the next wave of downsizing. Where we might have relied on government support in the past, new social programs are improbable, existing programs are smaller, and many others have been eliminated. Herein lies the contradiction: at the very time we need *more* supportive communities, community networks (i.e., social capital), and social programs, we are living and raising children in a *less* secure and *less* supportive environment in which we are forced to rely on our own resources. Thus, as a society, we may be materially richer but there is less social community and greater isolation.

Class and Status

How these processes evolve is further structured by social class, gender, race, and ethnicity. This is particularly visible when we look at the workplace. Those most affected by globalization are older workers, middle-management workers, those with few skills, those with little education, and those coming off welfare. Many who experience downward social mobility have historically been denied access to quality education and overrepresented in production jobs currently on the verge of disappearing as they are reengineered by technology or reorganized by CEOs.

In the hourglass economy, women and racial and ethnic minorities are most likely to be located in the lowest-paid jobs. At the other end, white males—those who have long enjoyed advantages in education and opportunities—typically monopolize the highly paid positions requiring high levels of training, education, and skill. Yet, white middle-class professional men are not immune to the changes. Nor are women and racial and ethic minorities entirely absent from higher-paying jobs; U.S. society has always been able to "accept" a few exceptional women, and racial or ethnic minorities. Henry Louis Gates, Jr. (1998), talks about the "two nations of black America" that reflect an emerging sector of middle-class blacks alongside the black underclass that William Julius Wilson (1996) suggests is directly connected to the economic restructuring of the post-1980 period. Similarly, "two nations" can be identified in the Latino and Asian communities, which have been structured along existing patterns of inequality that intersect with economic and political changes.

For women, the changes are equally mixed. White women in particular have experienced a process of upward social mobility as they enter the traditional male professions of medicine, law, and academics. At the same time, women of color have been moving into the female-dominated positions that have been vacated by white women that inhibit upward social mobility. These changes are reflected in complex patterns of income and wealth inequality, patterns that since the 1970s have become more *unequal*, reversing the trend toward greater equality during the 1950–1970 period. Today, U.S. society is simultaneously producing an appalling number of billionaires and children in poverty.

Economic restructuring associated with globalization has also shaped patterns of immigration. Throughout the post-1970s period, growing numbers of workers have immigrated to the United States to work, including low-wage workers from Mexico and Central America and highly educated workers from India, China, Hong Kong, and Taiwan. As competitive pressures reverberated throughout the economy, low-wage immigrant workers began to appear in non-traditional states of the Midwest and the deep South. While immigrants contribute to the economic dynamism of the U.S. economy, immigrants bring their entire culture with them, which not only exerts influence on the existing culture but also has economic, social, and political effects. These new patterns have been institutionalized, as we saw in Chapter 7, by employer decisions and the creation of social capital networks that provide access to information and resources necessary to survive in unfamiliar environments.

The State

The effects of global forces on the state have been similarly complex. Political policies and market forces have transferred power *upward* and *outward* and compromised—but have not eliminated—the ability of the nation-state to pursue locally (i.e., nationally) determined goals. While nation-states have lost some of their sovereignty in this regard, internal social and economic policies remain diverse across the globe. This suggests, as the skeptics point out, that the state (and government policy) still matters. We need to be careful, however, not to overestimate the degree of autonomy of national governments. Clearly, the most powerful nation-states enjoy the greatest autonomy in the global system, but global actors (transnational corporations), global institutions (World Trade Organization, WTO), and regional and global rules (North American Free Trade Agreement [NAFTA] Chapter 11) are compromising the authority and independence of even these states.

What is happening under the onslaught of neoliberal free-market attacks on governments is not that state intervention disappears but, rather, that the government's priorities shift. The neoliberal strategy is not so much about the elimination of state intervention as about reducing the *social* intervention of the state. Neoliberals continue to insist that government programs are necessary to support the business sector and ensure economic growth, but social programs are superfluous. What has emerged, according to Charles Derber (2002), is a new alliance between big business (i.e., capital) and the state, or what he calls "corpocracy." Increasingly, the state's new role is to meet the needs of big business and the demands of the new dominant global elites (Perrons 2004, 253; also Strange 1997; Robinson and Harris 2000; Derber 2002). As this new neoliberal elite consolidates its hegemony within global institutions (e.g., IMF, World Bank, WTO), the power of the state may be further compromised, its policies further constrained by the global rules these institutions establish, and its role in protecting ordinary women and men further diminished.

While we have limited our discussion of the federal (national) government, this is not the only level of government that affects the lives of citizens. Our emphasis on the state (and federal government) reflects the tendency of neoliberal globalization primarily to affect this level. As local governments experience the fallout of the shift from the welfare state to the neoliberal state, they are de facto assuming many of the social and economic responsibilities once reserved for the federal government. As federal programs are eliminated or scaled back, governors and mayors are increasingly responsible for social welfare and for enhancing competitiveness through job training and infrastructural development that will attract investment and lead to gains in employment and increased tax revenue.

The increased local responsibilities for the social and economic welfare of citizens may afford new opportunities for local groups to engage local governments and force public officials to address the needs of the communities. We can see this in the growing number of local politicians and officials who are filling the void created by the shrinking federal state by directly engaging with the global economy and establishing transnational linkages among regions and cities. Some talk about the new entrepreneurial cities or regions as cities form alliances with other regions or cities (see Perrons 2004, also Harvey 2000). Catalonia, Spain, for instance, has formed alliances with other regions in southern Europe, and the mayor of Barcelona has become active on the global stage (Perrons 2004, 296), as have many U.S. mayors and governors.

In the United States, shrinking federal budgets for redistributive projects have created a sense of urgency, reflected in the development of new entrepreneurial regions and redevelopment projects designed to transform areas that were abandoned in the transition to the service economy (see Perrons 2004, 265–270; Harvey 2000). As the federal government loses is ability or will to address local issues relating to the quality and quantity of jobs and well-being, local movements are springing up to pressure city and county governments. Often, these are joint projects funded by private capital and federal and local governments, but the initiative comes from local activists.

The Countermovement

As the emergence of the neoliberal state lays bare the local contradictions of globalization, people are losing faith in the possibility (indeed, the ability) of the federal government solving their problems. Citizens seem to be giving up on traditional politics (voting) as a mechanism for change. As they do, many resign themselves to inaction or, worse, to new destructive ways of achieving the American Dream. Others, however, are becoming more active. Living-wage campaigns, consumer-advocacy groups, and other grass-roots organizations (e.g., South East Georgia Community Project) are focusing on the problems falling below the federal government's radar screen or that proponents of neoliberalism assume will be solved as benefits trickle down from economic growth. In each of the cases we examined in Chapter 9, links were forged with various levels of government as a means to achieve the group's goals.

The countermovement is also responding to the challenges created by corporate branding we discussed in the last chapter. The phenomenon of corporate branding raises two concerns. First, branding reflects the growing power of corporations to shape our cultural worlds: our values, beliefs, perceptions; who we are and what we feel is important. Second, declining public resources often translate into growing dependence on corporate funding for local projects. As corporations increasingly brand places and transform public areas into quasi-private ones, what goes on in these spaces comes under the control of big business. Why is this problematic? The exercise of certain basic rights is the principle of any democracy, and corporate control over public space can easily limit these rights. For instance, a Georgia high school student was reprimanded for wearing a Pepsi T-shirt in violation of "Coke Day" at the school; and New Hampshire anti-sweatshop activists were barred from leafleting at a local mall. In an increasingly privatized world that places restrictions on what local and national governments can legislate, even how individuals think and behave, the countermovement we discussed in Chapter 9 "may be the *only* alternative to the competitive downgrading of social, [political] and environmental practices of firms worldwide" (Conroy 2002, 215).

We need to be careful, however, and not overstate the ability of these groups to usher in a new alternative form of globalization. We are not arguing that even well-organized transnational groups can easily change government policy at the federal level, as exemplified by the failure to prevent the invasion of Iraq. What we are suggesting is that globalization is creating new space for the countermovement to challenge these decisions and to shape the debates. For instance, we might entertain the counterfactual scenario of what the U.S.-led "coalition" in Iraq would have looked like in the absence of the massive worldwide demonstrations. The coalition may well have been larger without these demonstrations throughout the world, and the speed at which the antiwar movement materialized is illustrative of the sophistication of groups within the countermovement.

The global justice movement illustrates the potential of the countermovement. At the 1999 WTO meeting in Seattle, the global justice movement burst on the scene as 40,000–60,000 people protested the refusal of the leading economic and political elites to discuss labor and environment issues. The demonstrations were both violent and peaceful and may be best remembered for unifying the often opposing forces of organized labor and environmentalists (the "Teamsters and the Turtles") and for sparking widespread global protest.

The world has witnessed tremendous changes since the protest in Seattle. The U.S. labor movement is more "global" in its strategy and working with unions throughout the world to challenge the global reach of corporations (Iritani 2005b). Elites are more attuned to local concerns over the cultural, economic, social, and political ramifications of neoliberal globalization. In January 2005, activists from groups critical of neoliberal globalization were given the opportunity to question the three candidates for the WTO's position of director general—for the first time in the WTO's 10-year history. Even the proceedings of the corporate-dominated World Economic Forum in Davos, Switzerland, have been somewhat opened to the public with former pariah groups like Amnesty International invited to participate. To be sure, this does not mean that the economic and political elites have suddenly embraced the goals of their critics, but it is a sign of the countermovement's influence in the ongoing debate. By 2005, citizen-activist groups or nongovernmental organizations (NGOs) ranked as the most trusted institutions in the United States, Europe, Latin America, and much of Asia, with "trust ratings" of NGOs in the United States soaring to 55 percent from 36 percent in 2001 (Iritani 2005a). Mark Ritchie, president of the Institute for Agriculture and Trade Policy, summarizes the changes in this way: "In the old days . . . [t]here was a moat and a castle, and we were serfs. It is very different now.

We're not inside, but at least we're visiting from other realms of the kingdom" (Iritani 2005a C1).

Participatory Change: Empowerment or Façade?

One response on the part of global institutions (World Bank), governments, and NGOs to downward diffusion of power and the growing pressure from the countermovement has been to advocate increased local-level participation. Participation per se does not automatically or easily translate into empowerment or endow individuals and communities with greater control over their destinies. Much of what passes for participation are in fact attempts to legitimate existing decisions made by powerful actors far from where the impact of those decisions will be felt. The World Bank, for instance, has taken up the ideas of capacity building and wider participation in its programs as a means to counteract criticism of its top–down management style. In 1996, it produced its *Participation Source Book*, which provides guidelines and examples of "participatory development" (Perrons 2004, 298). The approach, however, involves "a rather simplistic assumption that wider participation would lead to the emergence of a singular community interest or general will" and hence more inclusive outcomes (Perrons 2004, 297–304). There are dangers, as Diane Perrons (2004) points out. Participation without empowerment will transform the participation project into a new tyranny that is imposed on people in order to create the appearance of an inclusive process as a means to legitimate a decision determined elsewhere.

As with other elite-driven (top–down) strategies, development and policy experts tend to distrust the judgment of the "masses," believing that ordinary men and women are incapable of devising solutions to their problems and that only the experts have adequate problem-solving capabilities. But experts and consultants typically follow set formulas rather than engaging in a dialectical process in which solutions emerge from a dialogue among residents and experts as they strive *together* to solve the problem. Too often, the experience reinforces dependence and pessimism, rather than empowerment. One project participant summarizes this tendency: "I've been capacity built under three different schemes and quite frankly, my view on capacity building is that if you employ a consultant, the money will go to the consultants" (quoted in Perrons 2004, 301). Yet, it need not be this way. We saw this in the ability of the South East Georgia Community Project among Latinos in south Georgia. Numerous other examples exist, such as the participatory budgeting in Porto Alegre, Brazil; neighborhood councils in Chicago (Fung and Wright 2001); the Dudley street neighborhood initiative in Boston; and the Valley Interfaith community development project in south Texas (Putnam, Feldstein, and Cohen 2003). Each of these capacity-building schemes serves as an important reminder that it is possible to devise successful projects that are based on the participation and empowerment of people.

Conclusion

So what does all of this mean? Globalization, as we have examined it throughout this book, is transforming the economic, cultural, social, and political boundaries of life in ways that are sweeping, multifaceted, and hard to predict. As class and status interact within the globalization process, some people are clearly better off, others less so, but no one is left untouched. This unevenness reflects the ability of global processes to crosscut geography, class, and status; to intersect with existing patterns of inequality; and to create new and complex patterns of inclusion and exclusion. Globalization has made work and life worse for many women and men in the United States but not for all; globalization has meant that women and men in developing countries toil under extreme hardships, but this may be preferable for some to working in the fields. Moreover, if we encourage boycotts of globally produced goods, those working in the global factory will likely lose their jobs and, with them, their only source of survival. Globalization too often means that traditional familial and kinship support networks have been broken; survival now depends on wage employment. As a result, the countermovement must bring with it respect and understanding for the situations of workers and their families in the developed and developing countries.

How globalization will continue to unfold is less than clear and will be determined by the countermovements it spawns and the unexpected events that are part of the process of change. The attacks on the World Trade Center buildings in New York and the Pentagon in Washington, D.C., for instance, have made the world more unstable. These tragic events have strengthened the position of the individuals Ronaldo Munck (2005, 165) calls the "regressive globalizers"—those who see the world as "a zero-sum game, in which they seek to maximize the benefit of the few, which they represent, at the expense of the welfare of the many, about which they are indifferent at best." Another major attack in the United States may well strengthen the position of the regressive globalizers, yet it is not so clear. As the countermovement becomes more organized and sophisticated in its strategies, the debate could be quite different: more reflective on the conditions for terrorism and more thoughtful in response.

Ultimately, the goal of the countermovement is to ensure that the needs of individuals and communities are not obliterated in the quest for greater profits or narrow definitions of security and to protect the rights of people and their right to control their future. As globalization alters the way power is organized and exercised in an increasingly linked system, our immediate task in the twenty-first century is to bring the exercise of power closer to those who are subject to its effects. To this end, currents within the countermovement are forging complex transnational- and national-level ties among different groups, elected politicians, government officials, and NGOs. It is a horizontal "network of networks" that extends outward like a spider web—much like the Internet itself (Klein 2000b)—to challenge the flexibility and mobility of capital locally as well as globally. As local governments assume greater responsibly for the social and economic welfare of communities, these changes may put the countermovement in a better position to ensure that people (not corporations) have control over public resources.

We began this chapter with a quote from former Commerce Department official David Rothkoph; it is perhaps fitting to end with a second quote from Rothkoph. In his most recent book *The World is Flat*, Thomas Friedman (2005, 45) cites Rothkoph as saying that, "What happens if the political entity in which you are located no longer corresponds to a job that takes place in cyberspace, or no longer really encompasses workers collaborating with other workers in different corners of the globe, or no longer really captures products produced in multiple places simultaneously? Who regulates the work? Who taxes it? Who should benefit from those taxes?" These are some of the basic issues we have examined in this book. The equally vital question is *who* or *what* will be involved in resolving these issues; what should be the role of the market; will change come from below or continue to be driven from above, or will there emerge some form of elite–popular coalition?

We offer no pat answers to these questions. Globalization is a deeply political and contested process, and no structural reform or change can make the world a more secure, peaceful, equitable, and just place without the active participation of those outraged by the absence of security, peace, equality, and justice. Globalization may work magic, as proponents argue, but like all magic, the outcomes are determined by the magician on stage, not by those in the audience. We are confronting social problems that are no longer limited by national boundaries as globalization erases the neat distinctions between a "developed" and a "developing" world. We face dangers and possibilities without parallel in human history, and we need a set of global–local democratic institutions that attend to the social, cultural, and material needs of ordinary women, men, and children, as well as the needs of the planet upon which we all depend. In response to these challenges, the countermovement has begun to move toward the stage. The question we leave you with is this: The magic show has already begun; where will you decide to be, in a seat watching the magician or on the stage taking part in creating the magic? How globalization unfolds and what this means for humanity and nature greatly depends on how each one of us answers this question.

NOTES

Preface

1. Full employment is not the same thing as zero unemployment. Paul Samuelson, for instance, defined full employment in 1960 as a figure less than 4 percent (*U.S. News and World Report*, Dec. 26, 1960). The Full Employment and Balanced Growth Act of 1978 (Humphrey-Hawkins Act) identifies the same 4 percent unemployment rate as a national goal. Although the rate has been adjusted upward at times, the 4 percent figure continues to be used as a benchmark of full employment and based on the assumption that at anytime approximately 4 percent of the U.S. population will be frictionally unemployed. Frictional unemployment includes those unemployed due to the seasonal nature of their jobs, others who are between jobs for various reasons, and those looking for their first jobs.

Chapter 1

1. To understand and make sense of these broad transformations, a new social-science literature sprang up revolving around the concept of "globalization." The number of articles and books on globalization in the sociological, economic, and political literature over time illustrates Waters's point. Between 1980 and 1985, for instance, the number of articles on globalization increased from 172 to 512; between 1985 and 1998 from 512 to 2,631: and the number of books increased from 48 to 92 and from 92 to 589, respectively (Guillen 2001).

2. In the last decades of the nineteenth century, Frederick Winslow Taylor developed a system of routinizing and standardizing work called "scientific management" based on the systematic study of jobs and the division of labor into separate tasks. Based on time-and-motion studies, he argued that management could calculate exactly how much time each part of a job would take. By minimizing any extra movement involved in each task, the job could be made more efficient (more production with less effort), an approach that fit perfectly with Ford's flow-line principle of the assembly line. Breaking down the process into smaller steps also reduced the skill necessary to produce products. The method, subsequently called "Taylorism," created the conditions for increased management control over employees (Braverman 1974, Chapter 4; Rubin 1996, 67). Simon Head (2003) has an excellent overview of the implementation of Taylor's ideas in the United States, the adaptation of them by the Japanese after World War II, and the readaptation of the Japanese modifications by the United States in the 1980s.

3. J. M. Keynes's theory of regulating capitalist markets to solve problems of unemployment served to legitimize Roosevelt's actions. A good overview of the changing priorities resulting from the shift to the post-Fordist period is in Chapter 4 of Joel Bakan's *The Corporation* (2004).

4. It is important to note that the formal social compact (actually negotiated union contracts) was largely limited to the core industries of the economy, such as the major unionized industries of automobiles and steel. The importance of the Fordist era and the compact was that employer–employee relations were regulated, class struggles were institutionalized, and workers were provided a stake in the system. As a result of the formal compact, the "bar was raised" for smaller nonunion enterprises, which tended to base wage and benefit negotiations on the standards set by the larger unionized enterprises. In the latter example, there existed an informal social compact. These informal and formal compacts created the basis for improvement in wages and such benefits as health care, paid vacations, and pensions. Additionally, the social compact involved a set of informal social norms that set boundaries on how much inequality was acceptable, as well as the need for state intervention to solve social problems. In this period, the debates were focused on how the government could best intervene in social problems, not on the issue of intervention itself. This being said, we agree with Robert Brenner's (1998) analysis that capital–labor relations continued to involve struggle and that not all employees in all advanced countries and in all industries equally enjoyed the benefits of a social compact. There remained a great deal of labor suppression in this period. Nonetheless, as Ronaldo Munck (2002) argues, during the period up to about 1980, labor did enjoy benefits and a degree of compromise was institutionalized in comparison to the previous liberal period and the present neoliberal period.

5. Whether measured by the share of the industrial sector to total output or labor force composition, high-income nations all experienced deindustrialization between 1980 and 1995 (see Firebaugh 2003, 190–193).

6. By "life chances," Max Weber (1978) refers to the extent to which an individual has access to important societal resources, such as food, clothing, shelter, education, and health care.

7. These data are further reflected in recent estimates by the International Labour Organization (ILO) that nearly one-third of the world's labor force of about 3 billion are either unemployed, underemployed in terms of seeking more work, or earning less than is needed to keep their families out of poverty. According to the ILO, open unemployment at the end of the year 2000 stood at approximately 160 million, 20 million higher than before the peak of the Asian financial crisis in 1998. Unfortunately, the ILO concludes, economic growth alone will not create the over 500 million new jobs needed by 2010 to accommodate new entrants to the workforce and to achieve the ILO's goal of reducing the current unemployment level by one-half.

Chapter 2

1. For a fascinating and prophetic look at the origins of the Second World War, see Keynes's *The Economic Consequences of the Peace*, written in 1919. Polanyi detailed his "double movement" argument in *The Great Transformation*, written in 1944.

2. See the two-part series in the *Los Angeles Times* on water privatization in the United States (Hudson 2006, Reiterman 2006).

3. A good summary account of Bretton Woods is in Ellwood (2002, Chapter 2).

4. Although 44 nations were involved in the negotiations, it was in reality a U.S.- and Britain-dominated process: essentially "three of four chaps got together and wrote a plan, and then took it up with forty-four other technicians stating that 'this is what the United States and Great Britain are willing to'" tolerate (quoted in Harris 1983, 14).

5. The United States, for instance, wields 17.5 percent of the total IMF voting power; Germany and Japan roughly 6 percent, England and France 5 percent, Italy 3.3 percent, Canada and The Netherlands 2.4 percent. Compare this to China's 3 percent, Brazil's and India's less than 2 percent, and Bangladesh's 0.2 percent; a host of smaller countries, like Somalia, hold only 0.02 percent of the total (Dawkins 2003, 27).

6. For the Soviets, there was fear that the U.S. government would sequestrate Soviet dollar holdings (if they were in U.S. banks) as a consequence of Cold War rivalry (see Held et al. 1999, section 4.6).

7. The rise in Euromarkets signaled a shift in global power toward Europe. For instance, if the United States pursued a policy with which Europe or a European country disagreed, the country (or countries) could dump excess dollars in the global economy. As U.S. dollars lost value, holders of U.S. dollars would demand gold in exchange (since the dollar was "as good as gold"), causing chaos in the U.S. economy.

8. We should mention that the public health law prohibited pictorial depictions of healthy babies aimed at inducing illiterate people to replace breast-feeding with formula which, when mixed with unsanitary water, was causing an epidemic of avoidable infant deaths. The ability of the law to reduce infant deaths had led UNICEF to tout Guatemala as a success story (see Wallach, Woodall, and Nader 2004).

Chapter 3

1. As Held et al. (1999, 3, note 1) point out, the approaches discussed in this chapter are general summaries of the different ways of thinking about globalization and do not fully represent the particular positions and differences among the individual theorists mentioned. What we aim to accomplish in this chapter is to provide a general overview of the main arguments dividing the literature.

2. An "ideal-type" was one of Max Weber's major contributions to sociology. Ideal-types are conceptual models of phenomena that are constructed from the direct observations of a number of specific cases that represent the essential qualities found in those cases. For instance, from his observations of bureaucracies, Weber created the ideal-type, arguing that "ideally" a bureaucracy has a specialized division of labor, a hierarchical structure, and a set of formal rules and is impersonal.

3. OECD countries include the world's major economies, such as the United States, Canada, Germany, England, France, Italy, the Scandinavian countries, Japan, Australia, etc.

Chapter 4

1. According to the *Economist* magazine, the cost of a 3-minute phone call between New York and London has fallen from $300 (in 1996 dollars) in 1930 to $1 in 1996. By 2002, the same call cost less than 50 cents (Clawson 2003, 131). The graph below illustrates the change since 1960 (ILO 2004, 53).

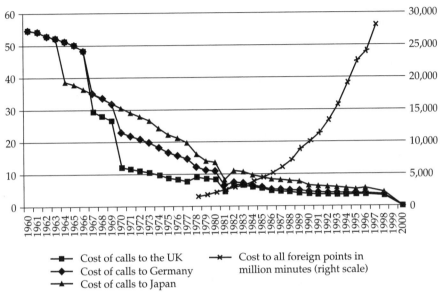

Figure 4.N1 Cost and Volume of International Telephone Calls from the United States: 1960–2000 (cost in constant 1995 US$ per 3-minute rate).

2. See note 5 for Chapter 1.

3. See note 4 for Chapter 4 for a definition of the terms *developing* and *developed* or *industrialized* countries.

4. The categories of countries are as follows:

   Industrialized countries: Australia, Austria, Belgium, Canada, Denmark, Finland, France, Germany, Greece, Iceland, Ireland, Italy, Japan, Luxembourg, The Netherlands, New Zealand, Norway, Portugal, Spain, Sweden, Switzerland, United Kingdom, United States (22).

   Manufactures-exporting developing countries: Argentina, Bangladesh, Brazil, China, Egypt, Hong Kong (China), India, Indonesia, Israel, Korea (Republic), Malaysia, Malta, Mauritius, Mexico, Morocco, Pakistan, Philippines, Singapore, South Africa, Sri Lanka, Taiwan (China), Thailand, Tunisia, Turkey (24).

   Petroleum-exporting developing countries: Algeria, Angola, Bahrain, Brunei, Cameroon, Ecuador, Gabon, Iran (Islamic Republic), Iraq, Kuwait, Libyan Arab Jamahiriya, Nigeria, Oman, Qatar, Saudi Arabia, United Arab Emirates, Venezuela (17).

Other developing countries: Afghanistan, Bahamas, Barbados, Belize, Benin, Bermuda, Bhutan, Bolivia, British Indian Ocean Territory, Burkina Faso, Burundi, Cambodia, Cayman Islands, Central African Republic, Chad, Chile, Colombia, Comoros, Congo (Republic), Congo (Democratic Republic), Costa Rica, Cote d'Ivoire, Cuba, Djibouti, Dominican Republic, El Salvador, Equatorial Guinea, Ethiopia, Falkland Islands, Fiji, French Guiana, Gambia, Ghana, Greenland, Guadeloupe, Guatemala, Guinea, Guinea-Bissau, Guyana, Haiti, Honduras, Jamaica, Jordan, Kenya, Kiribati, Korea (Democratic People's Republic), Lao (People's Democratic Republic), Lebanon, Liberia, Madagascar, Malawi, Maldives, Mali, Mauritania, Mongolia, Mozambique, Myanmar, Nepal, Netherlands Antilles, New Caledonia, Nicaragua, Niger, Panama, Papua New Guinea, Paraguay, Peru, Reunion, Rwanda, Senegal, Seychelles, Sierra Leone, Solomon Islands, Somalia, Saint Helena, Saint Kitts and Nevis, Saint Pierre and Miquelon, Sudan, Suriname, Syrian Arab Republic, Tanzania (United Republic), Togo, Trinidad and Tobago, Turks and Caicos Islands, Uganda, Uruguay, Vietnam, Western Sahara, Yemen, Zambia, Zimbabwe (90).

European transition countries: Albania, Bulgaria, former Czechoslovakia, Hungary, Poland, Romania, former Yugoslavia, former USSR (8).

5. In Botswana, for instance, manufactures comprised 91 percent of total merchandise trade in 2003, but total merchandise trade was only $2,886 million (U.S. dollars). Similarly, in Swaziland, manufactures were 76 percent of $905 million (World Bank 2005). Compare this to 58 percent of $36,482 million for South Africa. Nonetheless, trade in manufactures has increased dramatically since 2000 in both Botswana and Swaziland, which may foretell greater incorporation of Africa in the global economy.

6. Countries include Chile, Mexico, Brazil, China, Indonesia, and others; regions include those covered by APEC and NAFTA.

7. *Outsourcing* (or *subcontracting*) refers to a process whereby a company hires another to perform tasks that used to be done in-house. Say, an automaker used to make its own tires but now buys them from another company that specializes in the production of tires; it has outsourced the tire-producing portion of the business. The term *outsourcing*, however, does not necessarily indicate nationality —functions can be outsourced to either domestic or foreign workers. As global trade has grown in importance to the U.S. economy, however, more and more functions are provided by foreign workers.

8. Examples include *Cold Mountain* filmed in Romania and *Gangs of New York* filmed in Italy. Interestingly, *Cold Mountain* (a film about the U.S. South during the Civil War) was nominated for an Oscar for its cinematography!

9. Killer app, or killer application, refers to the use of a particular technology that makes that technology popular: electricity; killer app is lighting.

10. The process spills over to other occupations as well. For instance, electrical engineering: it used to be that the world's best electrical engineers graduated from U.S. universities and worked in the industrialized world earning $80,000 a year designing things to be made in factories that were probably overseas. But now an engineer from an Indian university is just as good as the U.S.-educated one, and he or she will work in New Delhi—for a U.S. or an Indian company—for $18,000 a year (see Colvin 2003).

11. We should also mention that the increasing power of TNCs potentially threatens employment opportunities as small companies find it difficult to compete.

12. On November 10, 2003, Reuters ran the following news story. "The World Trade Organization's highest court ruled Monday that U.S. steel import duties violated trade rules, increasing pressure on Washington to remove them. . . . The WTO's Appellate Body upheld the decision of a panel of trade judges that the tariffs were 'inconsistent' with trading regulations. President Bush must quickly remove the tariffs or face retaliation from the European Union, which is threatening to hit back with some $2.2 billion in duties on U.S. goods. [. . .] The steel conflict is just one of a number of high-profile disputes involving the United States and the EU and which threaten to further sour the mood at troubled WTO talks on lowering barriers to world trade. Already, the EU is preparing a raft of sanctions against U.S. exports after winning another WTO tussle with Washington over exporter tax breaks. The United States has taken aim at the WTO over its effective ban on genetically modified crops" (Cited in CATO Institute 2003).

13. In 2005, the Canadian firm lost its case, but the threat remains and is in fact increased with the passage of other regional pacts such as the Central American Free Trade Agreement, or CAFTA.

14. Equally important have been policies of privatization that move massive amounts of money and assets from the public sector to the private. In Latin America, for instance, between 1989 and 1997 $120,000,000 was transferred into private hands. Many of these assets result in private monopolies that are responsible for delivering formerly public goods, such as education, airports, telephones, water, and energy. The process of neoliberal privatization, which is one of the hallmarks of globalization, has not only widened the gap between the rich and poor in the region but jeopardized access to goods that many consider basic human rights (*Tiempos del Mundo*, 2004 A1).

15. An excellent example of the long-term process of globalization is HSBC. Named after its founding member, the Hong Kong and Shanghai Banking Corporation Limited, HSBC was established in 1865 to finance the growing trade between China and Europe. Information is available on its web site, http://www.hsbc.com/hsbc/about_hsbc.

16. Amartya Sen (2002) provides a brief but useful critique of the notion that globalization is Westernization or Americanization or that the world should become more "Americanized" as a vital step toward a more stable world (see the latter argument in Rothkoph 1997). As Sen points out, a millennium ago crossbows, gunpowder, the iron-chain suspension bridge, the wheelbarrow, among other forms of technology were used extensively in China—and practically unknown elsewhere. Similarly, mathematical ideas originated in the East, with globalization spreading them across the world, including Europe (Sen 2002). Sen's point is that globalization has always been a complex process of borrowing characterized by global–local linkages.

17. Glocalization comes from a Japanese term, *dochakuka*, which is a Japanese business practice involving the selling or making of products for particular markets or the simultaneous promotion of a standardized product for particular markets, in particular flavors, and so on. Robinson (1994) defines this as the creation and

incorporation of locality, processes which themselves largely shape, in turn, the compression of the world as a whole.

18. The term *genocide*, when talking about the Second World War, holds a specific global meaning and memory that the world shares; yet for sub-Saharan African communities that have lost the majority of the adult population to the AIDS virus and where "child-headed households" are now the norm, the term holds a more local-specific meaning and memory. Similarly, the date 9/11 has global meaning, but to a Chilean it has a local-specific meaning as well (Tuesday, September 11, 1973, was the day President Salvador Allende was overthrown and killed).

Chapter 5

1. The last three examples are from the AFL-CIO website. (AFL-CIO 2004a, n.d.c)

2. In class systems, the affluent have greater life chances, or opportunities, because they have greater access to safe neighborhoods, high-quality education and health care, higher-quality food, among other basic and not so basic goods.

3. We thank our colleague Jeff Davis for stimulating our thoughts on the direct and indirect linkages.

4. In 1999, for instance, the Rainforest Action Network succeeded in forcing Home Depot—through public demonstrations, advertising campaigns, and lobbying—to stop buying products produced from old growth forests.

5. See *Fortune*, http://money.cnn.com/magazines/fortune/fortune500_archive/full/1997/.

6. An excellent illustration of the latter is how the description of a secretary's job in the U.S. Department of Labor's *Occupational Outlook* has changed over time. Twenty-five years ago, secretaries "relieved their employers of routine duties . . . type, take shorthand, and deal with callers." Today, the core responsibilities of secretaries remain the same—to perform and coordinate an office's administration activities. In addition, secretaries have assumed "a wide range of new responsibilities once reserved for managerial and professional staff." Among these new duties are training and orientation of new staff, conducting research on the Internet, and operating new office technologies (quoted in Levy and Murnane 2004, 4).

7. In his *Capitalism, Socialism and Democracy*, Joseph Schumpeter ([1942] 1975, 82–85) argued that capitalism involves a "process of industrial mutation that incessantly revolutionizes the economic structure *from within*, incessantly destroying the old one, incessantly creating a new one. This process of Creative Destruction is the essential fact about capitalism. It is what capitalism consists in and what every capitalist concern has got to live in. . . ." One contemporary example is the personal computer industry, led by Intel and Microsoft, which destroyed many mainframe companies while creating one of the most important industries of the last century.

8. EPZs were initiated in Ireland in 1954. According to the World Bank (2005), there were over 3,000 EPZs in place throughout the world in 2002. By their nature, EPZs are linked closely to the global economy, with few linkages back to national economies.

9. Between 1950 and 2003, the percentage of the U.S. GDP accounted for by financial services increased from 10.9 to 20.4 percent, while the percentage share of manufacturing declined from 29.4 to 12.7 percent. This reflects what Kevin Philips (2006: 265–268) calls the financialization of the U.S. economy.

10. The remaining 10 percent includes middle-range/pay positions such as registered nurses and postsecondary teachers.

11. This is equally true in the blue-collar world. American Apparel©, for instance, located in Los Angeles, pays an average hourly wage of $12.50 to produce apparel (Hoffman 2006).

Chapter 6

1. According to Paul Kennedy, each robot "employed" replaces four jobs in the economy, and if in constant use 24 hours a day, it will pay for itself in just over 1 year (Kennedy 1993, 86; Winpisinger 1989, 149).

2. Technology also affects which occupations will likely expand and when. Sales, for example, is an occupation that has rapidly grown since 1969, due "in part from the way that an increased flow of new products—driven by computers—increases the need for selling, and in part from the inability of rules to describe the exchange of complex information that salesmanship requires" (Levy and Murnane 2004, 43).

3. Typically, they are based on the common law structure of the United Kingdom and United States.

4. We might note that this is an old debate, one largely initiated by Stephen Hymer in the early 1960s (see Hymer 1965, 1976).

5. Want to find out how long you would have to work at your present salary to earn what a CEO of a major corporation makes in 1 year? First, go to the AFL-CIO website (http://www.aflcio.org/corporateamerica/paywatch/). Second, scroll down to "The CEO and You" link. Click on this link and follow directions. For instance, Hytrek and Zentgraf would each have to work over 100 years to equal General Electric CEO Jeffrey R. Immelts's 2003 compensation. How long would you have to work?

6. The poverty line, developed in 1965 by the Social Security Administration, is based on what is called a "thrifty food plan." The plan is used to calculate the cost of a minimum level of nutrition for a family—note that this does not specify the items that would provide a *nutritious* diet. The market value of the goods in the plan is multiplied by 3 because the research indicated that an average family spent one-third of its income on food each year. In 1969, the idea was adopted by the U.S. government as the official poverty line.

7. We might also note that in 2000 80.9 percent of the working poor who usually worked full-time experienced at least one of the three major labor market problems that can impede a worker's ability to earn an income over the poverty threshold: low earnings, periods of unemployment, and involuntary part-time employment (U.S. Department of Labor 2004).

Chapter 7

1. Looking only at the United States, for instance, over one-third of all scientists and engineers emigrated from India or China.

2. In the early years of the twenty-first century, the same corporate and neo-liberal political and economic interests that promoted NAFTA pushed for the hemisphere-wide Free Trade Area of the Americas (FTAA) and the Central American Free Trade Agreement (CAFTA). Together these will incorporate 36 Latin American and Caribbean countries into a regional trade pact based on the NAFTA formula. When fully implemented, we can expect similar social and economic disruptions throughout Latin America that will increase pressures to emigrate to local urban centers or internationally.

3. Other examples include listservs such as Vietnet (linking the Vietnamese diaspora worldwide), which help to sustain collective identities among immigrants with a common national origin (cited in Scholte 2000a, 171).

4. According to the "new immigrant survey," the median number of years of education for legal immigrants is 13, which is one full year higher than that for native-borns (as cited in Anderson 2000).

5. A novel method has been the reported use of signs and billboards in Mexico advertising jobs in the United States.

6. This was the case until the passage of the 1986 Immigration Reform and Control Act.

7. Undocumented workers are most likely to be employed in low-wage jobs. The best estimates of undocumented immigrants in the United States are based on the March 2002 Current Population Survey and other data sources. According to these sources, there are 9.3 million undocumented immigrants in the country, or about 26 percent of the foreign-born population (Passel, Capps, and Fix 2004).

8. According to the *Los Angeles Times* (2005a, C1), U.S. imports of cotton trousers from China increased 1,519 percent during the first 3 months of 2005.

9. The U.S. industry lost 800,000 textile and apparel jobs between 1994 and 2004—350,000 of those jobs were lost since 2001. Data from the U.S. Department of Labor's Bureau of Labor Statistics show that total apparel-manufacturing employment declined 5.2 percent in April 2006 compared to April 2005 (see U.S. Bureau of Labor Statistics 2006).

10. As happened in the economy more generally during the 1980s and 1990s, many meatpacking firms closed plants that provided good wages and benefits and "outsourced" them to rural areas to save on costs. Of course, immigrant workers in food processing are nothing new, as Upton Sinclair's novel *The Jungle* shows; and today immigrants are once more providing the labor to drive these industries and working under conditions that Sinclair would recognize (see Human Rights Watch 2005).

11. Latinos are the largest nonwhite ethnic group in many rural Nebraskan communities, such as O'Neill, Scottsbluff, Norfolk, and Lexington. By the early twenty-first century, every county in Nebraska had a Latino presence.

12. Other important industries in the south, such as mobile home plants and construction, also heavily depend on Latino workers and bilingual Latino supervisors to manage the predominantly Spanish-speaking workforce.

13. H1-B visas allow employers to bring in skilled workers from overseas when there are no qualified U.S. workers to fill the jobs.

14. In April 2006, the *Los Angeles Times* published a series of articles on the local effects of remittances, or the "new foreign aid."

Chapter 8

1. An illustration of the social effects of racial theories is contained in Allan Brandt's essay "Racism and Research: The Case of the Tuskegee Syphilis Study." Scientific racism has a long history, where studies purport to "prove" that some races or ethnicities have "naturally" higher intelligence. A recent version of this is *The Bell Curve: Intelligence and Class Structure in American Life*, by Richard J. Herrnstein and Charles Murray. An excellent film focusing on Latino–Anglo relations is *Los Mineros* (PBS).

2. It is not unusual to find products in "formal" stores (and informal markets) produced from "leftover" pieces taken from maquiladora factories.

3. Debt bondage has become a conduit for young girls to the sex industry. The practice commonly develops as follows: a woman or a parent hears or reads about job opportunities abroad for young women. Typically, the jobs call for "nannies" or domestic workers, restaurant workers, dancers, or entertainers. The recruiter convinces the potential recruit (or parent of the recruit) that the job is legitimate and may even offer her a contract. She or he will also help get a passport or visa and take care of the rest of the recruit's travel arrangements. This practice occurs throughout the world. We see this in the United States, where girls and women from Latvia, Mexico, and China are sold into sex slavery. In one case, girls as young as 13 were trafficked from Mexico via Texas into Florida and forced into prostitution to "work off" a $2,000 debt bondage owed the smugglers (Coalition Against Trafficking in Women n.d.). Already by the mid-1990s, an estimated quarter of a million children worked as prostitutes in North America.

4. One important conclusion McCall draws from her analysis is that technological change and trade-related factors are of *minor* importance in explaining inequality. This is an interesting contrast with the technological effects on age. Recall that unemployment stints for older professional workers are increasing as a result of increased use of technology (see Chapter 6).

5. The *labor-force participation rate* refers to the proportion of the population that is either working or actively looking for work.

6. Title IX has been largely responsible for the increase in the number of women in postsecondary schools. By 2003, women were earning more associate's, bachelor's, and master's degrees than men, though men continued to earn more doctoral degrees (Catalyst 2006). In 2005, Caltech's entire chemical engineering class (six) was composed of women—chemical engineering has long been an exclusively male field; of the total Caltech graduates in 2005, 35 percent of the 217 were women, up from 25 percent in 1995 (Reitman 2005).

7. See www.catalystwomen.org/files/fact/Stereotype%20factsheet.pdf.

8. We should note that even in those positions typically assumed "female," pay differentials persist. For instance, among registered nurses, women earn 87 percent of the salary of men; among social workers, the pay gap is 7 percent, with women earning 93 percent of what men earn (U.S. Bureau of Labor Statistics 2005).

9. According to Alpert and Auyer (2003), the top three sectors with the greatest rates of expansion between 1988 and 2000 were social and human service assistants (141 percent), management analysts (140 percent), and personal and home-care aides (134 percent).

Chapter 9

1. The World Social Forum, founded in Brazil in 2001, is a network of groups that meet each year to discuss and formulate alternative models of globalization. The idea is to create a counterpoint to the elite-dominated World Economic Forum, where the major political and economic actors meet to develop strategies to further their agenda. In addition to the World Social Forum, there are other social forums, such as the European Social Forum and the Asian Social Forum (see Leite 2005).

   The International Forum on Globalization (IFG) is an alliance of 60 leading activists, scholars, economists, researchers, and writers formed to stimulate new thinking, joint activity, and public education in response to economic globalization. IFG members share the concern that the world's corporate and political elites are undertaking a restructuring of the global system with little public disclosure of the profound consequences to democracy, human welfare, local economies, and the natural world (see www.ifg.org).

2. AFESIP is only one of many NGOs that have emerged in response to the growing problem of human trafficking. See for instance the Polaris Project in the United States, and Japan, the Apne Aap in India, the Cambodian Women's Crisis Center in Cambodia, EPCAT International in Thailand, Friends International, among others.

3. Like Paulo Freire, Clodomir Santos de Morais emphasizes empowerment, though with reference to entrepreneurial literacy. One of his often-used examples is learning to ride a bicycle. Anyone can read a manual explaining how to ride a bike, but it is only through doing that one can actually master the art of riding a bicycle (see Carmen and Sobrado 2002, Sobrado and Rojas 2004).

4. See the AFESIP website, www.afesip.org/afesipfashion/fashion.php.

5. An example of what AFESIP and the local officials face is illustrated in the following story from *The Cambodian Times* (December 2004). Days after AFESIP and antitrafficking police rescued 83 women and girls from a Chinese-owned brothel, an armed group stormed the AFESIP women's center in Phnom Penh where the women were staying and abducted 80 of them. The armed group of about 30 men and women forced the rescued women into luxury sport-utility vehicles and drove off (see Soenthrith and Neubauer 2004).

6. The doctrine of "corporate personhood" arose out of the 1886 Supreme Court case of Santa Clara County v. Southern Pacific Railroad, through which corporations became defined as a "natural person." From that point on, the Fourteenth Amendment, enacted to protect the rights of freed slaves, was used routinely to grant corporations constitutional "personhood." Justices have since struck down hundreds of local, state, and federal laws enacted to protect people from corporate harm based on this premise. Armed with these "rights," corporations

increased control over resources, jobs, commerce, politicians, and even judges and the law (see ReclaimDemocracy.org).

7. *Colonias* are low-income, substandard housing that are predominantly occupied by Latino citizens in the U.S. border regions of Texas, Arizona, New Mexico, and California. Typically, they were constructed lacking paved roads, sidewalks, storm drainage systems, sewers, electricity, portable water, telephones, as well as other basic normal urban facilities.

8. For an excellent overview of the history of codes as well as the different kinds of codes, see codesofconduct.org.

9. There is even an ethical consumer magazine that indicates that it is the "UK's only alternative consumer organization looking at the social and environmental records of the companies behind the brand names" (see http://www.ethicalconsumer.org/magazine/news/newspages.htm). Using Corporate Watch's site at www.corpwatch.org, you can research corporations; NetAction provides information to fight Microsoft and Walmart.watch.com, to research the local impact of Wal-Mart. The list goes on and on.

10. As with the student-led anti-sweatshop movement, the consumer-advocacy movement is often a transnational movement that attempts to alter company behavior through pressure from the consumer. The USAS, often in alliance with unions and the National Labor Council, for instance, funds summer internships called the Collegiate Apparel Research Initiative (CARI) to send students to communities near factories in countries such as Honduras, Mexico, and Indonesia. The intent is to construct close ties between the movement in consuming countries and workers in the producing countries that serve as a basis to create new, or build upon existing, cross-border organizing efforts (see Armbruster-Sandoval 2005).

11. For instance, the International Labour Organization (ILO) is part of the United Nations and charged with the promotion of social justice and internationally recognized human and labor rights. It formulates minimum standards of basic rights: freedom of association, the right to organize, collective bargaining, abolition of forced labor, equality of opportunity and treatment, and other standards regulating conditions across the entire spectrum of work-related issues (see About the ILO, www.ilo/public/english/about/index.htm). Unfortunately, the two core conventions of the ILO, one addressing the right to organize (accepted in 1947) and one dealing with collective bargaining and the right to organize (passed in 1949), have never been adopted by the United States. By not ratifying these conventions, the United States can claim exemption. If the United States would endorse these, it would send a powerful message worldwide (Mandle 2000, 100–101). Consumer-advocacy groups could pressure the United States to adopt these measures as a step toward globalizing workers' rights.

12. This section is based largely on Hytrek's work with SEGCP during the 2000–2002 period. Additional information on the organization can be found on the following websites: http://leadershipforchange.org/awardees/awardee.php3?ID=109 and http://leadershipforchange.org/talks/cruz/.

13. One example of this creativity is their condom program. Activists working with SEGCP went into local bars to distribute condoms to men and into "red light"

districts to provide condoms to sex workers. While the organization has been heavily criticized, the program has been extremely effective at educating the community about sexually transmitted diseases.

14. By the turn of the century, Latino entrepreneurs had established a growing network of businesses catering to the Latino community, as well as other residents, throughout southeast Georgia.

Chapter 10

1. This quote refers to Sloane Wilson's book *The Man in the Gray Flannel Suit*. Rakesh Khurana of the Harvard Business School argues in his book *Searching for a Corporate Savior* "that during the 1980s and 1990s 'managerial capitalism'—the world of the man in the gray flannel suit—was replaced by 'investor capitalism'" (quoted in Krugman 2002).

GLOSSARY

Absolute poverty: A condition that exists when people cannot afford the minimum basic requirements for sustaining a reasonably healthy life (basic resources such as food, shelter, and clothing).

Achieved status: Meritocracy or placement in the stratification system based on attributes a person can control, such as effort and ability.

Anti-sweatshop movement: Part of the anti-globalization movement (or alternative to neoliberal globalization movement). A loosely coordinated network of groups, including trade unionists, interfaith organizations, college and high school students, human rights groups, socially responsible investors, and small non-governmental organizations involved in raising public awareness of substandard workplace conditions in the global apparel and needle-trade industries.

Ascribed status: Placement in the stratification system that is based on hereditary attributes which are beyond a person's control, such as race and sex.

Balance of trade: A summary record of all imports and exports for a country over a specific period of time, normally a month or a year.

Belle époque: Or the "beautiful era." Refers to the period from roughly the 1880s until 1914 or the First World War, which was characterized by classical liberalism; growing international economic integration; and the movement of goods, services, financial capital, and people across borders. For skeptics of globalization, the 1880–1914 period is considered the belle époque of globalization.

Branding: A process through which individuals become linked to corporations as a way of defining themselves by consuming certain products and services and, in so doing, conveying to others a particular image. Public spaces are also branded through corporate sponsorship of the space and, as a result, become de facto privatized.

Bretton Woods Trio: The set of global institutions founded at Bretton Woods, New Hampshire, after the Second World War that includes the International Monetary Fund, the World Bank, and the General Agreement on Trade and Tariffs (the latter was reorganized as the World Trade Organization).

Business processing outsourcing: The growing trend whereby companies outsource a variety of internal processes, from finance to accounting to human resource functions, which include payroll management and transaction processing.

Capital: Refers to business, financial, and investment resources (e.g., money, property) owned or used in business by a corporation or a person. Such financial resources are used or are capable of being used to produce more wealth. Our definition differs from economic definitions that emphasize the machines, tools, infrastructure, etc. used by labor to transform raw materials into goods. *Capital* as used here refers both to individuals such as Rupert Murdoch and George Soros (so-called capitalists) and to corporations such as Goldman Sachs and Nike. Small independent commercial enterprises, such as Owens Market or the Book Worm, are not considered part of capital, but large chain-store establishments, such as Kroger and Borders, are.

Civil society: The third sector distinct from the state and the market that comprises social movements, transnational coalitions, nongovernmental and noncommercial groups, and organizations and their activities which attempt to shape policies, norms, rules, and deeper structures.

Class: A group of people sharing a similar economic position based on income and wealth.

Class segments: The idea that the dominant class is a combination of potentially conflicting intraclass segments created by different locations in the productive process.

Closed stratification systems: Stratification systems that do not permit movement of individuals between strata, e.g., slave and caste systems.

Codes of conduct: Formal statements of a corporation's values and business practices that may include sections on wages and working conditions, child labor, and the environment.

Cognitive-intensive jobs: Jobs that are heavily based on generating and using information. Examples include engineering and programming, which emphasize perception, reasoning, remembering, and problem-solving skills. Workers in these industries face continued pressure to upgrade their skills, learn new information, and integrate new knowledge into their work practices.

Contingent labor: Part-time, temporary, and subcontracted work that increases the flexibility of employers but is often detrimental to workers' welfare.

Corpocracy: Charles Derber's term for the growing convergence of interest among transnational corporations, national governments, and global institutions. Comes from the words *corporation* and *democracy*, to mean a corporate-driven system.

Deindustrialization: Transition from an industrial economy to a service-based one. Investment is shifted from basic industry to other business practices, such as services, mergers and acquisitions, and foreign investment.

Democratic deficit: The idea that globalization has undermined accountability and transparency by shifting power to corporations and global institutions (e.g., the World Trade Organization). The lack of accountability and public discussion over decisions means that citizens are increasingly unable to shape public policy consistent with their needs.

Deskilling: Refers to the use of technological innovations to subdivide jobs into smaller, highly specific tasks requiring less skilled workers. With lower skill requirements, wages are lower and jobs can be more easily outsourced.

Deterritorialization: The idea that territoriality is declining in importance in favor of the movement of ideas, goods, services, capital, and increasingly labor. Also referred to as "supraterritoriality."

Dispute settlement body: The World Trade Organization's (WTO) system of resolving disputes in international trade. It consists of the WTO's General Council and has broad authority to establish panels, render binding decisions, oversee the implementation of rulings and recommendations, and authorize suspension of concessions and other obligations. Regional trade agreements, such as the North American Free Trade Agreement, have similar dispute settlement mechanisms.

Economic restructuring: The transforming of an economy through technological innovation, human resource development, privatization, and deregulation.

Ethnicity: The cultural heritage shared by a group of people.

Ethnoscape: The landscape of people who constitute the shifting world in which we live and profoundly affect the politics of and between nations. The term comes from Arjun Appadurai, who argues that we need to include an ethnic dimension to the study of globalization.

Eurocurrency: A currency that is deposited in a commercial bank outside the country of origin.

Eurocurrency markets: National currencies traded and deposited in banks outside the home country, generally but not always in Europe. Eurocurrency markets emerged in the 1950s and 1960s as a way for international firms and governments to avoid the regulations of national governments.

Export processing zones: Labor-intensive manufacturing sites with special incentives to attract foreign investors; workers in these zones assemble imported components (or raw materials) into finished goods for export. With advances in information technology, these zones have evolved from basic assembly and simple processing centers to include high-tech and science parks, finance zones, logistics centers, and even tourist resorts.

Feminization of the labor force: The trend whereby female labor-force participation has dramatically increased over the last 30 years.

Feminization of migration: The idea that females comprise an increasing proportion of migration flows, in contrast to the long-held assumption of male-dominated migration flows.

Feminization of poverty: The trend whereby women are disproportionately represented among those living in poverty.

Flexible market strategy: The unregulated, individualized, and market-based post-fordist model of development. The strategy emphasizes private capital and markets, as opposed to regulation and government intervention. The flexible model began around 1980.

Fordism: The strategy of development based on integrated production and assembly that emerged after the Second World War. The strategy was based on Keynesian regulation, mass production, mass consumption, and government social welfare programs.

Foreign direct investment: Investment involving the ownership and control of assets in one country by residents (generally transnational corporations) of another country. Generally, transnational corporations have managerial rights and control over a branch operation or subsidiary.

G-7 group: A global policy-making body composed of representatives from the world's seven richest nations: the United States, Germany, France, England, Japan, Italy, and Canada. The G-7 is now called the G-8 with the inclusion of Russia.

Gender: Culturally and socially constructed differences between females and males; based on attitudes, beliefs, and practices that a group or a society associates with femininity and masculinity.

Gender ideology: A system of ideas and beliefs that upholds and justifies an existing or desired gender-based arrangement of power, authority, wealth, and status in a society.

Gender stereotypes: An idea that men and women are naturally endowed with certain intellectual and physiological abilities that predispose them to specific tasks and professions.

Gender stratification: Hierarchical distribution, by gender, of economic and social resources in a society.

Global civil society: The third sector that is distinct from nation-states and global markets. The global civil society comprises nongovernmental and noncommercial transborder groups and organizations that are attempting to change the global social order, including global rules, by focusing on issues that transcend territorial boundaries.

Globalists: A group of scholars who consider contemporary globalization a real and significant historical development and that current processes of social change are being driven by global forces and are fundamentally different from earlier phases. Globalists include neoliberals and social democrats.

Gold standard: A monetary system in which central banks peg the value of the national currency in terms of gold and hold official international reserves of gold. This system was in place during the classical liberal period (1870–1914) and was replaced by the "flexible" gold standard of the Bretton Woods system. In the latter system, banks held international reserves in two forms—gold and foreign exchange, generally the U.S. dollar—in any proportion they chose.

Government: Refers to an established system of administration by which a nation, state, county, city, etc. is governed, ruled, and managed. Governments include a distinct set of personnel or agencies that are elected, employed, appointed, or created to carry out the functions of the state apparatuses.

Gross domestic product: Refers to the total value of goods and services produced by individuals, businesses, and the government inside a country in a given year. A similar measure, the gross national product, is the total value of goods and services that accrues to a nation whether or not it was produced in that country.

Imperialism: The territorial expansion and the economic and political domination of one people over another, generally in the form of conquest. In the globalization debate, imperialism means the dominance of the powerful core countries (and their corporations) over the world's markets and resources.

Income: The amount of money an individual or household receives in the form of wages, salary, investment, and transfers (government payments such as Aid for Dependent Families).

Inequality: The unequal distribution of valued goods, services, and positions in a society.

Informal sector: Refers to those economic activities carried on outside the formal institutionalized structures of the economy that are not reported; transactions are often based on reciprocity, payment in-kind, or cash. The informal sector is also called the "underground economy" or the "hidden economy."

Intraoccupational segregation: Refers to the segregation of workers or groups of workers into a particular job (or jobs) within an occupational category. Segregation patterns are often visible along gender, racial, and ethnic lines.

Job spill: The blurring of the line between job demands and personal time as job tasks spill over from the office to the home.

Just-in-time labor force: A labor force that is comprised largely of contract or temporary workers whereby employers quickly take on and let go workers as dictated by the market.

Just-in-time production: Entails having the parts delivered as they are needed, thereby avoiding costs for buying, storing, and protecting from theft.

Labor-force participation: Anyone employed or unemployed and looking for a job.

Life chances: Weber's notion referring to the probability that an individual will obtain good health, education, autonomy, and a long life. Reflects individual access to important societal resources, including food, shelter, clothing, health, and school.

Marketing companies: Companies that do not produce products but, rather, produce images; these images are bundled into a product the company designs and sells but are produced by subcontractors.

Mass layoffs: When at least 50 workers have been separated from jobs for more than 30 days. An *extended* mass layoff occurs when at least 50 initial claims are filed against an establishment during a consecutive 5-week period.

Matrix of domination: The idea formulated by Patricia Hill Collins to describe how the interaction between status and class creates different patterns of domination and subordination in a society.

Nation-state: A political system containing a group of people sharing a common culture and the centralization of political authority with a monopoly over the means of violence within a specified territory.

Neoliberal state: A society in which there is limited government intervention in economic and social matters. Private capital and unfettered markets are the primary engines of economic growth; few or no social programs.

New poor: Those individuals displaced by new technologies or mass layoffs and plant closings that have difficulty moving out of poverty.

Nongovernmental organizations (NGOs): The nonprofit sector or independent sector. Organizations that generally represent interests that are not part of the government and are often referred to as "civil society" or the "third sector" of governance representing the people. Global NGOs are often termed international nongovernmental organizations, or INGOs.

Nonstandard work arrangements: Part-time, contract, and temporary work; work that is not "standard" or permanent and full-time.

North Atlantic Treaty Organization (NATO): An organization established by the North Atlantic Treaty of 1949 to create a single unified defense force to safeguard the security of the North Atlantic area.

Occupational segregation: Segregating individuals or groups into different occupations based solely on one's ascribed status. Examples include women as secretaries and men as CEOs.

Offshore: Refers to the movement of economic or financial activities outside the country where the firm is located. Offshore assembly is the arrangement whereby firms based in advanced industrial countries provide design specifications to producers in developing countries, purchase the final goods, and then market the products throughout the world. Offshore services include banking and other financial operations that are located in countries or regions with lax regulations governing financial transactions (e.g., the Cayman Islands).

Open stratification systems: Stratification systems that permit movement of individuals between social strata, e.g., classes.

Organization for Economic Cooperation and Development (OECD): An organization of 30 mainly developed nations located in Paris, France. Member countries engage in policy studies on economic and social issues. The OECD also serves as a forum for member countries to discuss economic policy and promote cooperation and policy coordination.

Outsourcing: Subcontracting and shifting of work to other firms and locations outside the principal firm and geographical location.

Patriarchy: A hierarchical system of social organization in which the cultural, political, and economic institutions are controlled by men.

Poverty: A standard of living below the minimum needed to maintain a healthy existence.

Poverty line: The amount of annual income a family requires to meet its basic needs as established by the U.S. Bureau of the Census.

Poverty rate: The percentage of people who have incomes below the official poverty line.

Power: According to Weber, the ability to accomplish one's goal despite opposition and resistance from others.

Quota: A form of trade restriction that sets a quantitative limit on the amount of a good that can be imported.

Race: A group of people who share similar biological characteristics.

Relative poverty: A measure of one's economic position compared to the living standards of the majority in a given society.

Sex: The biological identity of an individual as male or female.

Sexual division of labor: The process whereby work tasks either in the private household or in the public economy are separated on the basis of one's sex.

Skeptics: A group of scholars who consider social change as consistent with internationalization or imperialism; they view "globalization" as an ideological or mythical construction that has marginal explanatory value. Skeptics include Marxists and realists.

Social capital: The trust and social norms that govern reciprocity, the sharing of resources, and other features of social organization, such as networks, coalitions, and mutual assistance. Unlike other forms of capital, social capital is depleted unless used.

Social capital networks: Friendship or kinship networks that provide access to resources. These can be transnational as well as national connections.

Social compact: The explicit and implicit set of understandings that govern social life and structure cooperation among self-interested people possessing unequal resources. Often called the "accord" or a compromise between labor and capital, the social compact in the United States endured from roughly the end of the Second World War until the late 1970s.

Social differentiation: The natural distinct qualities and social roles people have in terms of sex, skills, and occupations that are not ranked relative to each other in terms of importance.

Social mobility: The upward or downward movement in a class system that occurs in a person's lifetime and between generations.

Social movement: Part of civil society that involves a sustained public effort based on a common collective identity among people of different classes and statuses making collective claims on national and/or transnational target authorities using old and new strategies based on local, national, and global contexts.

Social reproductive labor: The myriad of activities, tasks, and resources expended in the daily upkeep of homes and people; the social re-creation of human life.

Social status: A ranking that, according to Weber, involves a style of life based on honor or prestige.

Social stratification: The hierarchical arrangement of groups of people based on their control over basic resources. The form of stratification (caste, estate, class) both determines the distribution of resources and legitimizes that distribution.

Stagflation: The simultaneous emergence of low rates of economic growth, high unemployment, and inflation. Stagflation emerged in the 1970s.

State: Weber defined the state as a rational institution characterized by a system of law, a rational economy, and a bureaucratic means of administration. Characteristic of the modern state institution is the monopoly over the legitimate use of violence within a given territory. Thus, the state is a collection or organizations vested with the authority to make and implement binding collective decisions, if necessary by force.

Structural adjustment programs (SAPs): Programs mostly associated with the International Monetary Fund (IMF) but also with the World Bank after the 1980s. SAPs are sometimes described as "conditional" because loans from the IMF or World Bank are conditioned on the borrower's agreement to follow a prescribed set of policies. These policies include decreased governmental spending on social programs, increased government revenues, and greater openness to the global economy through deregulation and privatization of the economy.

Subcontracting: The strategy of contracting out the production of goods and services to workers not part of that firm.

Tariffs: Taxes levied on products that pass through a customs border. These can be on imports or exports and are often used as a means to protect national industries but also serve as a means to raise revenue. Although tariffs are obstacles to trade, unlike quotas, there is no quantitative restriction on the amount of the good that can be imported.

Thirty Glorious Years: The heyday of the Keynesian strategy lasting from roughly 1945 to 1973, when much of North America and Western Europe enjoyed dramatic improvements in the standard of living.

Transborder civic associations: Organizations that transcend national borders, focus on global problems, and are motivated by transborder solidarity.

Transnational corporation: A firm that is headquartered in one country and locates its design, production, marketing, service, and distribution divisions in other countries.

Washington Consensus: Often used synonymously with *neoliberalism*, it refers to a consensus between the International Monetary Fund, World Bank, and the U.S. Treasury on the correct economic policies—the so-called conventional wisdom. Others included in the Washington Consensus are neoliberal business people and politicians throughout the world, sort of a global power elite or ruling class typically drawn from the G-8 countries (the United States, England, France, Germany, Japan, Italy, Canada, and now Russia).

Wealth: Accumulated assets in the form of various types of valued goods, including income, personal property, and income-producing property.

Welfare state: A society in which the government takes on broad responsibility for solving social problems through intervention in economic and social matters. Governments regulate private capital and provide for the general welfare of the population through "womb to tomb" social programs.

Working poor: Refers to anyone who works a minimum of 27 weeks per year and remains below the official poverty line.

REFERENCES

AECF (Annie E. Casey Foundation). 2004. Working hard, falling short: America's working families and the pursuit of economic security. http://www.aecf.org/publications/data/working_hard_new.pdf.

AFESIP (Agir pour les Femmes en Situation Précaire) 2004a. *Humanly Correct Development.* Phnom Penh: AFESIP Internacional. http://www.afesip.org.

AFESIP (Agir pour les Femmes en Situation Précaire). 2004b. *AFESIP Database and Research Unit Program.* Phnom Penh: AFESIP Internacional. http://www.afesip.org.

AFESIP (Agir pour les Femmes en Situation Précaire). 2004c. *Draft Cambodian Law on Commercial Sexual Exploitation of Children.* Phnom Penh: AFESIP Internacional. http://www.afesip.org.

AFL-CIO (American Federation of Labor and Congress of Industrial Organizations). 2004a. Working America: Job tracker exposes companies that export jobs. http://www.aflcio.org/yourjobeconomy/jobs/ns09162004.cfm.

AFL-CIO. 2004b. Fact sheet: Women in the global economy. http://www.aflcio.org/issuespolitics/globaleconomy/women.cfm.

AFL-CIO. 2004c. Statement by AFL-CIO Secretary-Treasurer Richard Trumka on new working America and AFL-CIO job tracker (September 16). http://www.aflcio.org/mediacenter/prsptm/pr09162004a.cfm.

AFL-CIO. 2005. Fact sheet: Equal pay for women of color. www.aflcio.org/issues/jobseconomy/women/equalpay/.

AFL-CIO. n.d.a. America's heartland reeling from broken economic policies. http://www.aflcio.org/mediacenter/resources/upload/policies.pdf.

AFL-CIO. n.d.b. Work & families. http://www.aflcio.org/issues/jobseconomy/women/global/.

AFL-CIO. n.d.a. Corporate myths about shipping jobs overseas. http://www.aflcio.org/issues/jobseconomy/jobs/outsourcing_myths.cfm.

Aguilar, DeeAnn. 2005. Trafficking Cambodia. Undergrad. research paper, Dept. Sociology, California State Univ., Long Beach.

Alarcón, Rafael. 2000. Skilled immigrants and cerebreros: Foreign-born engineers and scientists in the high technology industry of Silicon Valley. In *Immigration Research for a New Century,* ed. Nancy Foner, Rubén G. Rumbaut, and Steven J. Gold, 301–321. New York: Russell Sage Foundation.

Alpert, Andrew, and Jill Auyer. 2003. The 1988–2000 employment projections: How accurate were they? *Occupational Outlook Quarterly* (Spring):3–21.

Alpert, Arnie. 2002. Bringing globalization home is no sweat. In *Living in Hope,* ed. John Feffer, 37–52. London: Zed Books.

Andersen, Margaret. 1997. *Thinking About Women: Sociological Perspectives on Sex and Gender*, 4th ed. Boston: Allyn and Bacon.

Anderson, Benedict. 1991. *Imagined Communities*, rev. ed. London: Verso Press.

Anderson, Sarah, and John Cavanagh. 2000. The rise of corporate global power. Institute for Policy Studies. http://www.ips-dc.org/reports/top200.htm.

Anderson, Stuart. 2000. Muddled masses. *Reason Magazine* (February), http://reason.com/0002/bk.sa.muddled.shtml.

Appadurai, Arjun. 1990. Disjuncture and difference in the global cultural economy. *Public Culture* vol. 2, no. 2 (Spring):1–24.

Appadurai, Arjun. 1996. *Modernity at Large: Cultural Dimensions of Globalization*. Minneapolis: University of Minnesota Press.

Appelbaum, Eileen, Annette Bernhardt, and Richard J. Murnane. 2003. *Low Wage America*. New York: Russell Sage Foundation.

Appiah, Kwame Anthony. 2006. *Cosmopolitanism: Ethics in a World of Strangers*. New York: W. W. Norton and Company.

Armbruster-Sandoval, Ralph. 2005. *Globalization and Cross-Border Labor Solidarity: The Anti-Sweatshop Movement and the Struggle for Social Justice*. New York: Routledge.

Athreya, Bama. 2003. Trade is a women's issue. *Global Policy Forum* (February 20), http://www.globalpolicy.org/socecon/inequal/labor/2003/0220women.htm.

Bakan, Joel. 2004. *The Corporation: The Pathological Pursuit of Profit and Power*. New York: Free Press.

Barber, Benjamin. 1996. *McWorld vs. McJihad*. New York: Times Books.

Barber, Benjamin. 2003. How globalization is changing the world's cultures. Cato Institute. http://www.cato.org/events/030304bf.html.

Bardhan, Ashok Deo, and Cynthia A. Kroll. 2003. The new wave of outsourcing. Research Report. Berkeley: Fisher Center for Real Estate and Urban Economics.

Barretos, Matt A., and Jose Muñoz. 2003. Reexamining the "politics of in-between": Political participation among Mexican immigrants in the United States. *Hispanic Journal of Behavioral Sciences* 25, no. 4:427–448.

Barrington, Linda. 2000. *Does a rising tide lift all boats?: America's full-time working poor reap limited gains in the new economy*. Conference Report 1271-00-RR. New York: Conference Board. http://www.conference-board.org.

Beck, Urich. 1992. *Risk Society: Toward a New Modernity*. London: Sage.

Belman, Dale, and John S. Heywood. 1991. Direct and indirect effects of unionization and government employment on fringe benefit provision. *Journal of Labor Research* 12, no. 2 (Spring):111–122.

Belous, Richard. 1997. The rise of the contingent workforce: Growth of temporary, part-time and subcontracted employment, National Policy Institute, *Looking Ahead*, vol. 19, no. 1.

Bergensen, Albert J., and Michelle Bata, ed. 2002. Global Inequality: Part I. Special issue, *Journal of World-Systems Research* 8, no. 1 (Winter). http://jwsr.ucr.edu/archive/vol8/number1/index.shtml.

Bernstein, Jared, Heather Boushey, Elizabeth McNichol, and Robert Zahradnik. 2002. *A State-by-State Analysis of Income Trends*. Washington, D.C.: Center of Budget and Policy Priorities and the Economic Policy Institute. http://www.epinet.org/briefingpapers/pulling_bp_2002.pdf.

Bernstein, Jared, and Karen Kornbluh. 2004. *Running Faster to Stay in Place: The Growth of Family Work Hours and Incomes*. Washington, D.C.: Economic Policy Institute and the New America Foundation.

Bivens, Josh. 2004. Lack of domestic demand is not the cause of manufacturing's woes. (March 10) *Economic Policy Institute.* http://www.epinet.org/content.cfm/webfeatures_snapshots_archive_03102004.

Board of Governors of the Federal Reserve System. 2003. Consumer credit outstanding. (December). http://www.federalreserve.gov/Releases/G19/20031205/g19.htm.

Boli, John, and George Thomas, 1997. World culture in the world polity: A century of international non-governmental organization. *American Sociological Review* (April): 171–190.

Bonacich, Edna. 2000. Intense challenges, tentative possibilities: Organizing immigrant garment workers in Los Angeles. In *Organizing Immigrants: The Challenge for Unions in Contemporary California*, ed. Ruth Milkman, 130–149. Ithaca, NY: Cornell University Press.

Boudreaux, Richard. 2006. The New Foreign Aid: Mexico. Los Angeles Times, April 16. A.1.

Bradshaw, York, and Michael Wallace. 1996. *Global Inequalities.* Thousand Oaks, CA: Pine Forge Press.

Brandt, Allan. 1978. Racism and research: The case of the Tuskegee Syphilis Study. *Hastings Center Report* 8, no. 6:21–29.

Braverman, Harry. 1974. *Labor and Monopoly Capital.* New York: Monthly Review Press.

Brecher, Jeremy, Tim Costello, and Brendan Smith. 2002. *Globalization from Below.* Cambridge, MA: South End Press.

Brenner, Robert. 1998. The economics of global turbulence. *New Left Review* I, no. 229 (May–June): 1–265.

Brown, Sharon P. 2004. Mass layoff statistics data in the United States and domestic and overseas relocation. Bureau of Labor Statistics, U.S. Department of Labor. http://www.bls.gov/mls/mlsrelocation.pdf.

Browne, Irene, and Joya Misra. 2003. The intersection of gender and race in the labor market. *Annual Review of Sociology* 29:487–513.

Brysk, Alison. 2000. Globalization: The double-edged sword. *NACLA Report on the Americas* 34, no. 1 (July/August): 29–31.

Budd, John W., and Brian P. McCall. 1994. The effect of unions on the receipt of unemployment insurance benefits. Industrial Relations Center. Working Paper Series, 94-08 (August).

Budd, John W., and Brian P. McCall. 2004. Unions and unemployment insurance benefits receipt: Evidence from the CPS, *Industrial Relations* 43, no. 2 (April), pp. 339–355.

Burbach, Roger, Orlando Nunez, and Boris Kagarlitsky. 1997. *Globalization and Its Discontents.* London: Pluto Press.

Burn, Shawn Meghan. 2000. *Women Across Cultures: A Global Perspective.* Mountain View, CA: Mayfield Press.

Business Week. 2004a. 54th Annual executive compensation scoreboard. (April 19). http://www.businessweek.com.

Business Week. 2004b. The China price: Special report. (December 6). http://www.businessweek.com/magazine/content/04_49/b3911401.htm.

Callinicos, Alex. 1994. *Marxism and the New Imperialism.* London: Bookmarks.

Capelouto, Susan. 2000. Georgia Hispanics. *All Things Considered.* National Public Radio (February 2). http://www.npr.org/ramfiles/atc/20000202.atc.07.

Capps, Randolph, Michael E. Fix, Jeffrey S. Passel, Jason Ost, and Dan Perez-Lopez. 2003. A profile of the low-wage immigrant workforce. Brief 4 in series *Immigrant*

Families and Workers: Facts and Perspectives. Washington, D.C.: Urban Institute. http://www.urban.org/url.cfm?ID=310880.

Card, David. 1998. Falling union membership and rising wage inequality: What's the connection? Working Paper 6520. National Bureau of Economic Research. http://www.nber.org/papers/W6520.

Carmen, Raff, and Miguel Sobrado. 2000. *A Future for the Excluded.* London: Zed Press.

Carnoy, Martin. 2000. *Sustaining the New Economy: Work, Family, and Community in the Information Age.* New York: Russell Sage Foundation.

Carrington, William J., and Kenneth R. Troske. 1998. Sex segregation in U.S. manufacturing. *Industrial Labor Relations Review* 51, no. 3 (April): 445–464.

Castells, Manuel. 1997. *The Power of Identity.* Oxford: Blackwell Press.

Castells, Manuel. 2000. *The Rise of the Network Society,* 2nd ed. Oxford: Blackwell Press.

Castles, Stephen, and Mark Miller. 1998. *The Age of Migration,* 2nd ed. New York: Guilford.

Catalyst. 2006. http://www.Catalystwomen.org.

Catalyst. 2006. 2005 Catalyst census of women board directors of the fortune 500 shows 10-year trend of slow progress and persistent challenges. http://www.catalyst.org/pressroom/press_releases/3_29_06.

CATO Institute. 2003. Daily dispatch. (November 10). http://cato.org/dispatch/11-10-03d.html.

Center for Immigration Studies. 2002. Census releases immigrant numbers for year 2000. http://www.cis.org/articles/2002/censuspr.html.

Center on Budget and Policy Priorities and the Economic Policy Institute. 2002. Pulling apart: A state-by-state analysis of income trends. http://www.cbpp.org/4-23-02SFP-PR.htm.

Chang, Grace. 2000. *Disposable Domestic: Immigrant Women Workers in the Global Economy.* Cambridge, MA: South End Press.

Children's Defense Fund. 2004. Child poverty. http://www.childrensdefense.org/familyincome/childpoverty/default.aspx.

Children's Defense Fund. 2005. Child abuse and neglect fact sheet. http://www.childrensdefense.org.

Christie, Les. 2005. Number of millionaires hits record. *CNN Money* (May 25). http://money.cnn.com/2005/05/25/pf/record_millionaires/.

Clawson, Dan. 2003. *The Next Upsurge.* Ithaca, NY: Cornell University Press.

CNN Money. 2006. Number of billionaires surges. (March 9). http://money.cnn.com/2006/03/09/news/newsmakers/billionaires_forbes/index.htm?cnn=yes.

Coalition Against Trafficking in Women. n.d. http://www.catwinternational.org/factbook/usa1.php.

Cockburn, Alexander, Jeffrey St. Clair, and Allan Sekula. 2000. *5 Days that Shook the World.* London: Verso Press.

Cohn, Theodore H. 2003. *Global Political Economy: Theory and Practice,* 2nd ed. Boston: Allyn and Bacon.

Coleman, James. 1988. Social capital in the creation of human capital. *American Journal of Sociology* Suppl. no. 94:S95–S120.

Collins, Patricia Hill. 1991. *Black Feminist Thought.* New York: Routledge.

Colvin, Geoffrey. 2003. The U.S. is falling asleep on the job. *Fortune Magazine.* http://money.cnn.com/magazines/fortune/fortune_archive/2003/09/01/348203/index.htm.

Connor, Timothy. 2002. We are not machines: Indonesian Nike and Adidas workers. Clean clothes campaign and others. http://www.cleanclothes.org/companies/nike_machines.htm.

Conroy, Michael E. 2002. Can advocacy-led certification systems transform global corporate practices? In *Global Backlash*, ed. Robin Broad, 210–215. Lanham, MD: Rowman and Littlefield.

Cotter, David A., Joan M. Hermsen, and Reeve Vanneman. 2004. *Gender Inequality at Work*. New York: Russell Sage Foundation and Population Reference Bureau.

Cowen, Tyler. 2002. *Creative Destruction: How Globalization Is Changing the World's Cultures*. Princeton: Princeton University Press.

Craypo, Charles, and Bruce Nissen. 1993. *Grand Designs*. Ithaca, NY: ILR Press.

Crossette, B. 1998. Kofi Annan's astonishing facts! *New York Times*, September 27. Section 4:16.

Dawkins, Kristin. 2003. *Global Governance*. New York: Seven Stories Press.

de la Luz Ibarra, Maria. 2000. Mexican immigrant women and the new domestic labor. *Human Organizations* 59, no. 4:452–464.

DeNavas-Walt, Carmen, Dernadette D. Proctor, and Robert J. Mills. *Income, Poverty, and Health Insurance Coverage in the United States: 2005*. Washington D.C.: U.S. Government Printing Office.

Derber, Charles. 2002. *People Before Profit*. New York: St. Martin's Press.

Dicken, Peter. 1998. *Global Shift: Transforming the World Economy*, 3rd ed. New York: Guilford Press.

Dickey, Fred. 2002. Levi Strauss and the price we pay. *Los Angeles Times Magazine* (December 1): 14–17.

Dill, Bonnie Thornton, Lynn Weber Cannon, and Reeve Vanneman. 1987. Race and gender in occupational segregation. In *Pay Equity: An Issue of Race, Ethnicity and Sex* 11–70. Washington, D.C.: National Committee on Pay Equity.

Dobbs, Lou. 2004a. *Exporting America*. New York: Time Warner Book Group.

Dobbs, Lou. 2004b. Lou Dobbs Tonight. *CNN* (September 19).

Dollar, David, and Aart Kraay. 2002. Spreading the wealth. *Foreign Affairs* 18, no. 1 (January/February): 120–133.

Domhoff, William. 1998. *Who Rules America? Power and Politics in the Year 2000*. Mountain View, CA: Mayfield.

Domhoff, William. 2002. *Who Rules America? Power and Politics*, 4th ed. New York: McGraw-Hill.

Drori, Isreal. 2000. *The Seam Line: Arab Workers and Jewish Managers in the Israeli Textile Industry*. Stanford, CA: Stanford University Press.

Duran, Jorge, Douglas S. Massey, and Ferdando Charvet. 2000. The changing geography of Mexican immigration to the United States. *Social Science Quarterly* 81, no. 1:1–15.

Economic Policy Institute. 2003. Offshoring. EPI Issue Guide. http://www.epinet.org.

Economic Report to the President. 2001. Washington, D.C.: United States Government Printing Office. (January). http://www.gpoaccess.gov/eop/download/html

Economist. 1997. Thinking about globalization: Popular myths and economic facts. (October 17): 4–19.

Ehrenreich, Barbara. 2001. *Nickel and Dimed*. New York: Metropolitan Books.

Ehrenreich, Barbara, and Arlie Russell Hochschild. 2002. *Global Woman: Nannies, Maids, and Sex Workers in the New Economy*. New York: Metropolitan Books.

Eitzen, D. Stanley, and Maxine Baca Zinn. 2003. *Social Problems*, 9th ed. Boston: Allyn and Bacon.

Eitzen, D. Stanley, and Maxine Baca Zinn. 2004. *Conflict and Order*, 11th ed. Boston: Allyn and Bacon.

Ellwoood, Wayne. 2002. *The No-Nonsense Guide to Globalization*. London: Verso Press.

Elson, Diane, ed. 1995. *Male Bias in the Development Process*, 2nd ed. Manchester, UK: Manchester University Press.

Engstrom, James D. 1999. Industry and immigration in Dalton, Georgia. In *Latino Workers in the Contemporary South*, ed. Arthur D. Murphy, Colleen Blanchard, and Jennifer A. Hill, 44–56. Athens: University of Georgia Press.

Enloe, Cynthia. 1989. *Bananas, Beaches and Bases: Making Feminist Sense of International Politics*. Berkeley: University of California Press.

Enloe, Cynthia. 1995. The globetrotting sneaker. *Ms. Magazine* 6:10–15.

Ettinger, Michael, and Jeff Chapman. 2004. Jobs shift from higher-paying to lower-paying industries. Economic Snapshots. Economic Policy Institute (January 21). http://www.epinet.org/content.cfm/webfeatures_snapshots_archive_01212004.

Evans, Peter. 2000. Counter-hegemonic globalization: Transnational networks as political tools for fighting marginalization. *Contemporary Sociology* 29 (January): 230–241.

Farr, Kathryn. 2005. *Sex Trafficking*. New York: Worth Publishers.

Faux, Jeff. 1999. Slouching toward Seattle. *American Prospect* 11, no. 2 (December 6): 36–39.

Faux, Jeff. 2001. The global alternative. *American Prospect* 12, no. 12 (July 2): 15–18.

Faux, Jeff. 2006. *The Global Class War: How America's Bipartisan Elite Lost Our Future— and What It Will Take to Win It Back*. Hoboken, NJ: Wiley.

Featherstone, Mike. 1995. *Undoing Culture*. Thousand Oaks, CA: Sage Press.

Fernandez-Kelly, Maria Patricia. 1983. *For We Are Sold, I and My People*. Albany, NY: SUNY Press.

Fernandez-Kelly, Maria Patricia, and Saskia Sassen. 1995. Recasting women in the global economy: Internationalization and changing definitions of gender. In *Women in the Latin American Development Process*, ed. Christine E. Bose and Edna Acosta-Belén, 99–124. Philadelphia: Temple University Press.

Fernandez-Kelly, Maria Patricia, and Diane Wolf. 2001. A dialogue on globalization. *Signs: Journal of Women in Culture and Society* 26, no. 4: 1243–1249.

Ferraro, Gayle. 2003. *Anonymously Yours*. DVD. Berkeley: Berkeley Media.

Firebaugh, Glenn. 2003. *The New Geography of Global Income Inequality*. Boston: Harvard University Press.

Fix, Michael, and Jeffrey S. Passel. 1994. *Immigration and Immigrants: Setting the Record Straight*. Washington, D.C.: Urban Institute Press.

Foner, Nancy, Rubén Rumbaut, and Steven J. Gold. 2000. Immigration and immigration research in the United States. In *Immigration Research for a New Century*, ed. Nancy Foner, Rubén G. Rumbaut, and Steven J. Gold, 1–43. New York: Russell Sage Foundation.

Forbes. 1999–2006. The world's billionaires. http://www.forbes.com/billionaires.

Forbes. 1996–1997. The world's largest public companies. http://www.forbes.com.

Fortune. 2003–2006. http://money.cnn.com/magazines/fortune.

Fosu, Augustin Kwasi. 1993. Non-wage benefits as a limited-dependent variable: Implications for the impact of unions. *Journal of Labor Research* 14, no. 1 (Winter): 29–43.

Fox, Justin. 2003. Where your job is going. *Fortune Magazine*. http://www.fortune.com/fortune/subs/article/0,15114,538786,00.html.

Fraser, Jill. 2001. *White-Collar Sweatshop: The Deterioration of Work and Its Rewards in Corporate America*. New York: W. W. Norton and Company.

Freeman, Carla. 2000. *High Tech and High Heels in the Global Economy: Women, Work and Pink-Collar Identities in the Caribbean*. Durham, NC: Duke University Press.

Freeman, Richard B. 1980. The effect of unionism on worker attachment to firms. *Journal of Labor of Labor Research* 1, no. 1 (Spring): 29–61.

Freeman, Richard B. 1996/1997. Solving the new inequality. *Boston Review* 21, no. 6 (Dec/Jan): 3–10.

Friedman, Thomas L. 2000. *The Lexus and the Olive Tree*. New York: Knoph Publishing Group.

Friedman, Thomas L. 2005. *The World Is Flat*. New York: Farrar, Straus and Giroux.

Freire, Paolo. 1972. *Pedagogy of the Oppressed*. Harmundsworth: Penguin.

Fuentes, Annette, and Barbara Ehrenreich. 1983. *Women in the Global Factory*. Boston: South End Press.

Fung, Archon, and Eric Olin Wright. 2001. Deepening democracy: Innovations in empowered participatory governance. *Politics & Society* 29, no. 1 (March): 5–41.

Gabel, Medard, and Henry Bruner. 2003. *Global Inc*. New York: New Press.

Gailbraith, James K. 1999. The crisis of globalization. *Dissent* 46, no. 3 (Summer): 12–16.

Galinsky, Ellen, and James T. Bond. Forthcoming. Helping families with young children navigate work and family life. In *Research into Practice in Infant/Toddler Care*, ed. Debby Cryer and Thelma Harms. Baltimore: Brookes Publishing.

Gallagher, Kevin, and Timothy A. Wise. 2002. NAFTA: A cautionary tale. Testimony on the Free Trade Area of the Americas to the Office of the United States Trade Representative, Washington, D.C., September 20. http://ase.tufts.edu/gdae/publications/articles_reports/FTAATestimonySept02.PDF.

Gates, Henry Louis, Jr. 1998. The two nations of black America. *Frontline*. Public Broadcasting Service (Feb 10).

George, Susan. 1999. A short history of neo-liberalism: Twenty years of elite economics and the emerging opportunities for structural change. Presented at the Conference on Economic Sovereignty in a Globalizing World, Bangkok, Thailand, March 24–26.

Georgia State University. 2000. 1998–1999 Georgia education report card. Georgia Department of Education. http://accountability.doe.k12.ga.us/Report99.

Gerson, Kathleen, and Jerry A. Jacobs. 2004. The work–home crunch. *Context* 3, no. 4 (Fall): 29–37.

Ghose, Ajit K. 2003. *Jobs and Incomes in a Globalizing World*. Geneva: International Labour Office.

Gibson, Campbell J., and Emily Lennon. 1999. *Historical Census Statistics on the Foreign-Born Population of the United States: 1850 to 1990*. Working Paper 29, Washington, D.C.: U.S. Government Printing Office.

Giddens, Anthony. 1990. *The Consequences of Modernity*. Cambridge: Polity Press.

Giddens, Anthony. 1999. *The Third Way*. Cambridge: Polity Press.

Giddens, Anthony. 2003. *Runaway World*, 2nd ed. London: Profile Books.

Gill, Jennifer. 2001. We're back to serfs and royalty. *Business Week* (April 9), http://www.businessweek.com/careers/content/apr2001/ca2001049_100.htm.

Gilpin, Robert. 1981. *War and Change in World Politics*. Cambridge: Cambridge University Press.

Gilpin, Robert. 1987. *The Political Economy of International Relations*. Princeton: University of Princeton Press.

Girvan, Norman. 1999. Globalisation and counterglobalisation: The Caribbean in the context of the south. Paper presented at a seminar at the University of the West Indies, Mona, entitled Globalisation: A strategic response from the south, February 1–2. http://www.acs-aec.org/About/SG/Girvan/speeches/G15.htm.

Glenn, Evelyn Nakano. 1992. From servitude to service work: Historical continuities in the racial division of paid reproductive labor. *Signs: Journal of Women in Culture and Society* 18, no. 1:1–43.

Gothoskar, Sujata. 1995. Computerization and women's employment in India's banking sector. In *Women Encounter Technology: Changing Patterns of Employment in the Third World*, ed. Swasti Mitter and Sheila Rowbotham, 150–178. New York: Routledge.

Gouveia, Lourdes. 2000. From aliens to neighbors: The incorporation of Latino families into the rural midwest. *Catholic Rural Life Magazine* 43, no. 1 (Fall). http://www.ncrlc.com/crl-magazine-articles/vol43no1/Gouveia.pdf.

Gouveia, Lourdes, and Donald D. Stull. 1995. Dances with cows: Beefpacking's impact on Garden City, Kansas, and Lexington, Nebraska. In *Any Way You Cut It: Meat Processing and Small-Town America*, ed. Donald D. Stull, Michael J. Broadway, and David Griffith, 85–107. Lawrence: University Press of Kansas.

Gouveia, Lourdes, and David D. Stull. 1997. Latino immigrants, meatpacking, and rural communities: A case study of Lexington, Nebraska. *East Lansing, MI Julian Samora Institute of Research*, Michigan State University. Research Report 26.

Greene, Jay P. 2002. High school graduation rates in the United States. Manhattan Institute for Policy Research. http://www.manhattan-institute.org/html/cr_baeo.htm.

Greenhouse, Steven. 2005. An $8 billion restaurant industry, a study finds mostly "Bad Jobs." *New York Times*, January 25. B:7.

Grieco, Elizabeth. 2002. Characteristics of the foreign-born in the United States: Results from census 2000. Migration Policy Institute. Migration Information Source. http://www.migrationinformation.org/issue_dec02.cfm.

Griffith, David. 1995. Hay trabajo: Poultry processing, rural industrialization, and the Latinization of low-wage labor. In *Any Way You Cut It: Meat Processing and Small-Town America*, ed. Donald D. Stull, Michael J. Broadway, and David Griffith, 129–152. Lawrence: University Press of Kansas.

Guadalupe, Maria 1999. *The Maquila Reader*. Philadelphia: American Friends Service Committee.

Guillén, Mauro F. 2001. Is globalization civilizing, destructive or feeble? A critique of five key debates in the social science literature. *Annual Review of Sociology* 27:235–260.

Guthery, Greir. 2001. Mexican places in southern spaces: Globalization, work, and daily life in and around the north Georgia poultry industry. In *Latin Workers in the Contemporary South*, ed. Arthur D. Murphy, Colleen Blanchard, and Jennifer A. Hill, 57–67. Athens: University of Georgia Press.

Gwynne, Robert, Thomas Klak, and Denis J. B. Shaw. 2003. *Alternative Capitalism*. London: Arnold.

Halford, Susan, and Mike Savage. 1997. Rethinking restructuring: Embodiment, agency and identity in organizational change. In *Geographies of Economics*, ed. Roger Lee and Jane Willis, 108–117. London: Arnold.

Halliday, Fred. 2000. Global governance: Prospects and problems. In *The Global Transformations Reader: An Introduction to the Globalization Debate*, ed. David Held and Anthony McGrew, 431–441. Cambridge: Polity Press.

Han, Wen-Jui. 2005. Maternal nonstandard work schedules and child cognitive outcomes. *Child Development* 76, no. 1:137–155.

Harris, Laurence. 1983. *Banking on the Fund—The IMF*. Milton Keynes: Open University Press.

Harrison, Bennett, and Barry Bluestone. 1988. *The Great U-Turn: Corporate Restructuring and the Polarizing of America*. New York: Basic Books.

Harvey, David. 2000. *Spaces of Hope: Towards a Critical Geography*. Edinburgh: Edinburgh University Press.

Hayek, F. A., von. 1944. *The Road to Serfdom*. Chicago: University of Chicago Press.

Head, Simon. 2003. *The Ruthless Economy: Work and Power in the Digital Age*. New York: Oxford University Press.

Healey, Joseph F. 2001. Assimilation and pluralism. In *Sociology for a New Century*, ed. York W. Bradshaw, Joseph F. Healey, and Rebecca Smith, 205–238. Thousand Oaks, CA: Pine Forge Press.

Healy, Melissa. 2005. Leaving a job that's just too stressful. *Los Angeles Times*, February 14. F:1.

Held, David. 1997. Cosmopolitan democracy. *Peace Review* 9, no. 3 (September): 309–315.

Held, David. 2004. *Global Covenant: The Social Democratic Alternative to the Washington Consensus*. Cambridge: Polity Press.

Held, David, and Anthony McGrew, ed. 2000. *The Global Transformations Reader*. Cambridge: Polity Press.

Held, David, and Andrew McGrew. 2002. *Globalization/Anti-Globalization*. Oxford: Polity Press.

Held, David, Andrew McGrew, David Goldblatt, and Jonathan Perraton. 1999. *Global Transformations: Politics, Economics and Culture*. Stanford, CA: Stanford University Press.

Helyar, John. 2005. 50 and fired. *Fortune* 151, no. 10 (May 16): 78–90.

Henslin, James M. 2004. *Essentials of Sociology*, 5th ed. New York: Allyn and Bacon.

Henwood, Doug. 1999. Booming, borrowing, and consuming: The U.S. economy in 1999. *Monthly Review* 51, no. 3 (July–August): 122–126.

Hernández-Léon, R., and Víctor Zúñiga. 2000. Making carpet by the mile: The emergence of a Mexican immigrant community in an industrial region of the U.S. historical south. *Social Science Quarterly* 81:49–66.

Herrnstein, Richard J., and Charles Murray. 1994. *The Bell Curve: Intelligence and Class Structure in American Life*. New York: Free Press.

Hertz, Noreena. 2001. *The Silent Takeover: Global Capitalism and the Death of Democracy*. New York: Free Press.

Hetherington-Gore, Jeremy, Mike Godfrey, Lisa Ugur, and Mandy Robinson. 2000. The future of offshore as a business location following the EU/OECD/FATF/FSF initiatives. http://www.tax-news.com/asp/res/st_offshorefuturecontents.html.

Hiltzik, Michael. 2006. Employer is for open U.S. door. *Los Angeles Times*. (April 20). C:1.

Hirst, Paul, and Grahame Thompson. 1999. *Globalization in Question*, 2nd ed. Cambridge: Polity Press.

Hochberg, Adam. 2003. Pillowtex goes bankrupt, putting thousands out of work in Kannapolis, North Carolina. Morning Edition National Public Radio (August 21).

Hochschild, Arlie Russell. 2001. Global care chains and emotional surplus value. In *Global Capitalism*, ed. Will Hutton and Anthony Giddens, 130–146. New York: New Press.

Hoffman, Claire. 2006. Apparel factory chief gives day off. *Los Angeles Times*, May 2. A:11.

Hondagneu-Sotelo, Pierrette. 2001. *Domestica: Immigrant Workers Cleaning and Caring in the Shadows of Affluence*. Berkeley: University of California Press.

Houstoun, Marion F., Roger G., Kramer, and Joan Mackin Barrett. 1984. Female predominance in immigration to the United States since 1930: A first look. *International Migration Review* 18, no. 4:908–963.

Huber, Joan. 1990. Macro-micro links in gender stratification. *American Sociological Review* 55, no. 1 (February): 1–10.

Hudson, Mike. 2006. Misconduct taints the water in some privatized systems. *Los Angeles Times*, May 29. A:1.

Human Rights Watch. 2005. Blood, sweat, and fear: Workers' rights in U.S. meat and poultry plants. http://www.hrw.org/reports/2005/usa0105.

Huntington, Samuel. 1996. *Clash of Civilization*. New York: Simon and Schuster.

Hurst, Charles E. 2004. *Social Inequality: Forms, Causes, and Consequences*. New York: Allyn and Bacon.

Huws, Ursula. 2003. *The Making of a Cybertariat: Virtual Work in a Real World*. London: Merlin Press.

Hymer, Stephen H. 1965. *Direct Foreign Investment and International Oligopoly*. New Haven, CT: Yale University Press.

Hymer, Stephen H. 1976. *The International Operations of National Firms: A Study of Direct Foreign Investment*. MIT Monographs in Economics. Cambridge, MA: MIT Press.

Hytrek, Gary. 2001. Subordinate class struggles and institutional formation: Explaining the social development trajectories in Costa Rica, the Dominican Republic and South Korea. *International Journal of Contemporary Sociology* 38, no. 2 (October): 119–145.

Hytrek, Gary, and Jeff Davis. 2002. Poverty, globalization and welfare reform. *University Magazine* 7, no. 3 (Fall): 6.

Hytrek, Gary, and Miguel Sobrado, eds. 2002. Clientelism and empowerment in Latin America. Special issue, *Latin American Perspectives* 29, no. 5 (September).

ILO (International Labour Organization). 2001. U.S. leads industrialized world in hours worked, productivity. http://www.us.ilo.org/archive/ilofocus/2001/fall/0110focus_6.cfm.

ILO (International Labour Organization). 2004. A fair globalization: Creating opportunities for all. http://www-ilo-mirror.cornell.edu/public/english/wcsdgdoes/report.pdf.

Instituto Nacional de Estadistica: *Geografia e Informatica*. 2000.XII Censo General De Población y Vivienda 2000. http://www.inegi.gob.mx/est/default.asp?c=701.

International Monetary Fund. 2006. World economic outlook: Globalization and inflation. http://www.imf.org/external/pubs/ft/weo/2006/01/index.htm

Iritani, Evelyn. 2005a. From the streets to the inner sanctum. *Los Angeles Times,* February 20. C:1.

Iritani, Evelyn. 2005b. Unions go abroad in fight with Wal-Mart. *Los Angeles Times,* August 24. A:1.

ITEP (Institute on Tax and Economic Policy). 2000. Corporate income taxes in the 1990s. http://www.ctj.org/itep/corp00pr.htm.

Jacobe, Dennis. 2005. Many consumers lack a "rainy day" fund. *Gallup Organization* (June 2). http://www.gallup.com/poll/content/?ci=16564&pg=1.

Jacobe, Dennis. 2005. Many consumers lack a "rainy day" fund. *The Gallup Organization.* (June 2). http://www.galluppoll.com/content/?ci=16564&pg=1.

Jones, R. J. Barry. 1995. *Globalization and Interdependence in the International Political Economy.* Cambridge, MA: Harvard University Press.

Jordan, Mary. 2003. Workers falling behind in Mexico. *Washington Post,* July 15. A:15.

Kahn, Joseph. 2003. Chinese girls: Toil brings pain, not riches. *New York Times,* October 2. A:1.

Kazin, Michael. 1999. Faith in labor. *Nation* (October 11).

Kendall, Diana. 2003. *Sociology in Our Times,* 4th ed. New York: Allyn and Bacon.

Kennedy, Paul. 1993. *Preparing for the 21st Century.* New York: Random House.

Keohane, Robert O., and Joesph S. Nye, ed. 2001. *Power and Interdependence: World Politics in Transition,* rev. ed. New York: Addison-Wesley.

Kerbo, Harold R. 2003. *Social Stratification and Inequality: Class Conflict in Historical Comparative and Global Perspectives,* 5th ed. Boston: McGraw-Hill.

Kernaghan, Charles. 2001. Exposed: The truth behind the label. In *Global Uprising: Confronting the Tyrannies of the 21st Century: Stories from a New Generation of Activists,* ed. Neva Welton and Linda Wolf, 189–193. New York: New Society.

Keynes, Jonn Maynard. 1995. *The Economic Consequences of the Peace.* New York: Peguin Classics.

Keynes, Jonn Maynard. 1997. *The General Theory on Employment Interest, and Money.* New York: Promethus Books.

Klein, Naomi. 2000a. *No Logo.* New York: Picador Press.

Klein, Naomi. 2000b. The vision thing. *Nation* (July 10), 270:23, p. 12–16.

Klein, Naomi. 2001. Branded: Breaking out of the corporate corral. In *Global Uprisings: Confronting the Tyrannies of the 21st Century: Stories from a New Generation of Activists,* ed. Neva Welton and Linda Wolf, 194–199. New York: New Society.

Koenig-Archibugi, Mathias. 2003. Introduction: Globalization and the challenge to government. In *Taming Globalization: Frontiers of Governance,* ed. David Held and Matias Koenig-Archibugi, 1–17. Cambridge, MA: Polity Press.

Koretz, Gene. 1999. Solving a labor–market puzzle. *Business Week* (April 26): 26.

Krasner, Stephan D. 1985. *Structural Conflict: The Third World Against Global Liberation.* Berkeley: University of California Press.

Krasner, Stephan D. 1993. Economic interdependence and independent statehood. In *States in a Changing World,* ed. Robert H. Jackson and Alan James, 301–321. Oxford: Oxford University Press.

Krugman, Paul. 2002. For richer. *New York Times,* Magazine October 20: 62.

Labor Studies Center. 2003. *Living Wage Campaigns: An Activist's Guide to Organizing a Movement for Economic Justice.* Wayne State University. http://www.laborstudies. wayne.edu/research/LivingWage.html.

LaFeber, Walter. 2002. *Michael Jordan and the New Global Capitalism*. New York: W. W. Norton & Company.

Larsen, Luke J. 2004. *The Foreign-born Population in the United States: 2003*. Washington, D.C.: U.S. Census Bureau.

Lavelle, Louis. 2001. For female CEOs, it's stingy at the top. *BusinessWeek Online* (April 23). http://www.businessweek.com/magazine/content/01_17/b3729116.htm.

Lee, Ching Kwan. 1998. *Gender and the South China Miracle: Two Worlds of Factory Women*. Berkeley: University of California Press.

Leicht, Kevin T. 2001. The future of work. In *Sociology for a New Century*, ed. W. Bradshaw, Joseph F. Healey, and Rebecca Smith, 421–439. Thousand Oaks, CA: Pine Forge Press.

Leite, Jose Correa. 2005. *The World Social Forum: Strategies of Resistance*. Chicago: Haymarket Books.

Levi, Margaret, and David Olson. 2000. The battles in Seattle. *Politics & Society* 28, no. 3:217–237.

Levi, Margaret, David J. Olson, and Erich Steinman. 2003. Living wage campaigns and laws. *Working USA* 3, no. 3 (January 31): 111–127.

Levy, Frank, and Richard J. Murnane. 2004. *The New Division of Labor*. New York: Russell Sage Foundation.

Levy, Jacques. 1975. *Cesar Chavez*. New York: W. W. Norton & Company.

Light, Ivan, Richard Bernard, and Rebecca Kim. 1999. Immigrant incorporation in the garment industry of Los Angeles. *International Migration Review* 33, no. 1:5–25.

Light, Ivan, and Parminder Bhachu, eds. 1993. *Immigration and Entrepreneurship: Culture, Capital, and Ethnic Networks*. New York: Transaction Publishers.

Light, Ivan, and Stephan Gold. 2000. *Ethnic Economies*. San Diego: Academic Press.

Lim, Lin Lean. 1998. *The Sex Sector: The Economic and Social Bases of Prostitution in Southeast Asia*. Geneva: International Labour Office.

Lopez-Garza, Marta, and David F. Diaz, eds. 2001. *Asian and Latino Immigrants in a Restructuring Economy: The Metamorphosis of Southern California*. Stanford, CA: Stanford University Press.

Los Angeles Times. 2005a. U.S. to limit some textiles from China. May 14. C1.

Los Angeles Times. 2005b. When cash crosses over. May 21. B:18.

Los Angeles Times. 2005c. Sending home a house. May 21. B:18.

Los Angeles Times. 2005d. Migrant dollars: Thinking out loud. May 21. B:18.

Lusane, Clarence. 1997. *Race in the Global Era: African Americans at the Millennium*. Boston: South End Press.

Lynch Capgemini Consulting. 2000. *World Wealth Report 2000*. New York: Merrill.

Lynch Capgemini Consulting. 2001. *World Wealth Report 2001*. New York: Merrill.

Mandle, Jay R. 2000. The student anti-sweatshop movement: Limits and potential. *Annals of the American Academy of Political and Social Science* 570:92–103.

Mann, Michael. 1986. *Sources of Social Power*, Vol. 1. New York: Cambridge University Press.

Manning, Susan, ed. 1999. Globalization. Special issue, *Journal of World-Systems Research* 5, no. 2 (Summer). http://jwsr.ucr.edu/archive/vol5/number2/idex.shtml.

Maquila Health and Safety Support Network. n.d. http://mhssn.igc.org/.

Marchand, Marianne H., and Anne Sisson Runyon. 2000. *Gender and Global Restructuring: Sightings, Sites, and Resistances*. New York: Routledge.

Marx, Karl. [1848] 1955. *The Communist Manifesto*, 38th printing, ed. Samuel H. Beer. Arlington Heights, IL: AHM Publishing.

Martinez, Elizabeth, and Arnoldo Garcia. n.d. What is neoliberalism. http://www.corpwatch.org/article.php?id=376.

Massey, Douglas S., Rafael Alarcón, Jorge Duran, and Humberto González. 1987. *Return to Aztlan: The Social Process of International Migration from Western Mexico*. Berkeley: University of California Press.

Massey, Douglas S., and Kristin E. Espinoza. 1997. What's driving Mexico–U.S. migration? A theoretical, empirical, and policy analysis. *American Journal of Sociology* 102, no. 4:939–999.

Massey, Douglas S., Luin P. Goldring, and Jorge Durand. 1994. Continuities in transnational migration: An analysis of nineteen Mexican communities. *American Journal of Sociology* 99:1492–1533.

Mathews T. J., and M. F. MacDorman. 2006. Infant mortality statistics from the 2003 period linked birth/infant death data set. *National Vital Statistics Reports* 54 (May 3): 16.

McCall, Leslie. 2001. *Complex Inequalities*. New York: Routledge.

McGrew, Anthony, ed. 1997. *The Transformation of Democracy? Globalization and Territorial Democracy*. Cambridge: Polity Press.

McIntyre, Robert S., Robert Kenk, Norton Francis, Matther Gardner, Hill Gomaa, Fiona Hsu, and Richard Sims. 2003. Who Pays?: A distributional analysis of the tax systems in all 50 states, 2nd ed. Washington, D.C.: The Institute on Taxation & Economic Policy. http://www.itepnet.org/wp2000/text.pdf.

McKendrick, David G. 2004. Leveraging location: Hard disk drive producers in international comparison. In *Locating Global Advantage: Industry Dynamics in the International Economy*, ed. Martin Kenney and Richard Florida, 142–174. Stanford, CA: Stanford University Press.

McMichael, Philip. 2000. *Development and Social Change: A Global Perspective*. Thousand Oaks, CA: Pine Forge Press.

Meyers, Deborah, and Jennifer Yau. 2004. U.S. immigration statistics in 2003. *Migration Policy Institute*. Migration Information Source (November 1). http://www.migrationinformation.org/USfocus/display.cfm?ID=263.

Meyerson, Harold. 1999. Liberalism with an accent. *Nation* (October 11), 269:11, p. 15–20.

Michalak, Wieslaw. 1994. The political economy of trading blocs. In *Continental Trading Blocs: The Growth of Regionalism in the World Economy*, ed. Richard Gibb and Wieslaw Michalak, 34–74. Chichester: John Wiley.

Mies, Maria. 1986. *Patriarchy and Accumulation on a World Scale: Women in the International Division of Labor*. London: Zed Publishing.

Migration Policy Institute. 2004. *What Kind of Work Do Immigrants Do?* http://www.migrationpolicy.org/foreignborn/.

Mills, C. Wright. 1959. *The Sociological Imagination*. New York: Oxford University Press.

Mills, Mary Beth. 2003. Gender and inequality in the global labor force. *Annual Review of Anthropology* 32:41–62.

Mishel, Lawrence, and Jared Bernstein. 1993. *The State of Working America, 1992–1993*. Armonk, NY: M. E. Sharpe/Economic Policy Institute.

Mishel, Lawrence, Jared Bernstein, and Sylvia Allegreto. 2005. *The State of Working America, 2004–2005*. Ithaca, NY: ILR Press.

Mishel, Lawrence, Jared Bernstein, and Heather Boushey. 2003. *The State of Working America, 2002–2003.* Ithaca, NY: ILR Press.

Mishel, Lawrence, Jared Bernstein, and John Schmitt. 2001. *The State of Working America, 2000/2001.* Ithaca, NY: Cornell University Press.

Mohl, Raymond, and Eric Knudsen. 2000. Latinization in the heart of Dixie: Hispanics in late-twentieth century Alabama. Presented in the panel *New Patterns of Migration: Hispanic Labor in the Deep South,* Social Science History Association Meeting, Pittsburgh, PA, October 27.

Mooney, Chris. 2001. Localizing globalization. *American Prospect* 12, no. 12 (July 2): 23–26.

Morin, Monte, and Carla Hall. 2005. Laborers, leaders mourn "the real Miguel Contreras." *Los Angeles Times,* May 13. B:1.

Morse, David. 2002. Striking the golden arches: French farmers protest the McD's globalization. In *McDonaldization: The Reader,* ed. George Ritzer, 245–249. Thousand Oaks, CA: Pine Forge Press.

Moyers, Bill. 2002. Trading democracy. *Frontline.* Public Broadcasting Service (February 1).

Moyers, Bill. 2003. Rich world, poor women. *Now.* Public Broadcasting Service (September 5).

Munck, Ronaldo. 2002. *Globalisation and Labor.* London: Zed Press.

Munck, Ronaldo. 2005. *Globalization and Social Exclusion.* Bloomfield, CT: Kumarian Press.

Muñoz, Carolina Banks. 2004. Mobile capital, immobile labor: Inequality and opportunity in the tortilla industry. *Social Justice* 31, no. 3:21–39.

Murphy, Arthur D., Colleen Blanchard, and Jennifer A. Hill. 2001. *Latin Workers in the Contemporary South.* Athens: University of Georgia Press.

Nagel, Joane. 2003. *Race, Ethnicity, and Sexuality.* New York: Oxford University Press.

Naím, Moisés. 2000. Washington Consensus or Washington confusion? *Foreign Policy* (Spring): no. 118, 86–103.

National Center for Health Statistics. 2004. Health, United States, 2004. Centers for Disease Control and Prevention. http://www.cdc.gov/nchs/data/hus/hus04trend.pdf#topic.

National Intelligence Council. 2001. *Growing Global Migration and Its Implications for the United States.* Washington, D.C.: National Foreign Intelligence Board, NIE 2001-02D (March). http://www.dni.gov/nic/NIC_home.html.

Nebraska Department of Economic Development. 1999. *Nebraska Profit Opportunities.* Lincoln: Nebraska Department of Economic Development. http://sites.nppd.com/studypdfs/foodstudy.pdf.

Newman, David M. 2002. *Sociology: Exploring the Architecture of Everyday Life,* 4th ed. Thousand Oaks, CA: Pine Forge Press.

Newman, David M. 2004. *Sociology: Exploring the Architecture of Everyday Life,* 5th ed. Thousand Oaks, CA: Pine Forge Press.

Ng, Cecilia, and Carol Yong. 1995. A case study of the telecommunications industry in Malaysia. In *Women Encounter Technology: Changing Patterns of Employment in the Third World,* ed. Swasti Mitter and Sheila Rowbotham, 177–204. New York: Routledge.

Ni, Ching-Ching. 2005. China's use of child labor emerges from the shadows: The deaths of five girls draw attention to the practice, common in struggling rural areas. *Los Angeles Times,* May 13. A:1.

Nichols, John. 2000. What now?: Seattle is just a start. *Progressive* 64, no. 1 (January): 16–19.

Ohmae, Kenichi. 1990. *The Borderless World*. London: Collins.

O'Neil, Kevin. 2003. Remittances from the United States in context. Migration Policy Institute. Migration Information Source (June 1). http://www.migrationinformation.org/USfocus/display.cfm?ID=138.

Ong, Aihwa. 1987. *Spirits of Resistance and Capitalist Discipline: Factory Women in Malaysia*. Albany, NY: SUNY Press.

Ong, Aihwa. 1991. The gender and labor politics of post modernity. *Annual Review of Anthropology* 20:279–309.

Paddock, Richard C. 2006. The New Foreign Aid: Philippines. Los Angeles Times, April A.1.

Paral, Rob, and Benjamin Johnson. 2004. Maintaining a competitive edge: The role of the foreign-born and U.S. immigration policies in science and engineering. *Immigration Policy in Focus* 3 (August): 3. http://www.ailf.org/ipc/ipf081804.asp.

Parenti, Michael. 1978. *Power and the Powerless*. New York: St. Martin's Press.

Parrenas, Rhacel Salazar. 2001. *Servants of Globalization: Women, Migration and Domestic Work*. Stanford, CA: Stanford University Press.

Passel, Jeffrey S., Randy Capps, and Michael Fix. 2004. Undocumented immigrants: Facts and figures. *Urban Institute Immigration Studies Program* (January 12). http://www.urban.org/url.cfm?ID=1000587.

Perraton, Jonathan, David Goldblatt, David Held, and Anthony McGrew. 1997. The globalization of economic activity. *New Political Economy* 2, no. 2:257–277.

Perraton, Jonathan, David Goldblatt, David Held, and Anthony McGrew. 2000. Economic activity in a globalizing world. In *The Global Transformation Reader*, ed. David Held and Anthony McGrew, 287–300. Cambridge UK: Polity Press.

Perrons, Diane. 2004. *Globalization and Social Change: People and Places in a Divided World*. London: Routledge.

Petruno, Tom. 2006. Emerging nations powering the global economic boom. *Los Angeles Times*, May 14. A:1.

Philips, Kevin. 2006. *American Theocracy*. New York: Viking Press.

Polanyi, Karl. 1944. *The Great Transformation*. Boston: Beacon Press.

Pollin, Robert, and Stephanie Luce. 1998. *The Living Wage*. New York: Free Press.

Porter, Keith. n.d. Poverty or prosperity: Is either caused by globalization? *Globalization Issues*. http://globalization.about.com/cs/whatisit/a/gzpoverty.htm.

Portes, Alejandro. 1998. Social capital: Its origins and applications in modern sociology. *American Review of Sociology* 24:1–24.

Portes, Alejandro, and Robert Bach. 1985. *Latin Journey: Cuban and Mexican Immigrants in the United States*. Berkeley: University of California Press.

Portes, Alejandro, and Rubén G. Rumbaut. 1996. *Immigrant America: A Portrait*. Berkeley: University of California Press.

Powell, John A., and S. P. Udayakumar. 2000. Race, poverty & globalization. *Global Exchange* (May/June). http://www.globalexchange.org/campaigns/econ101/globalization072000.html.

Presser, Harriet B. 2003. *Working in a 24/7 Economy: Challenges for American Families*. New York: Russell Sage Foundation.

Public Citizen. 2004. *The ten-year track record on the North American Free Trade Agreement*. http://www.citizen.org/documents/NAFTA_10_mexico.pdf.

Putnam, Robert. 1993. *Making Democracy Work: Civic Traditions in Modern Italy.* Princeton: Princeton University Press.

Putnam, Robert. 1996. The strange disappearance of civic America. *American Prospect* 7, no. 24 (Winter): 34–48.

Putnam, Robert. 2000. *Bowling Alone.* New York: Simon and Schuster.

Putnam, Robert, Lewis Feldstein, and Donald J. Cohen. 2003. *Better Together.* New York: Simon and Schuster.

Pyle, Jean L. 2001. Sex, maids, and export processing: Risks and reasons for gendered global production networks. *International Journal of Politics, Culture, and Society* 15:55–76.

Pyle, Jean L., and Kathryn Ward. 2003. Recasting our understanding of gender and work during global restructuring. *International Sociology* 18:461–489.

Quart, Alissa. 2004. *Branding: The Buying and Selling of Teenagers.* New York: Basic Books.

Rayman-Reed, Alyssa. 2001. Is the new economy family-friendly? *American Prospect* 12, no. 1 (January 1–15): 29–32.

Redmond, Karen. 2003. Personal bankruptcy filings continue to rise in fiscal year 2003. Administrative Office of the U.S. Courts, News Release, November 14. http://www.uscourts.gov/Press_Releases/fy03bk.pdf.

Rees, Kathleen, and Jan Hathcote. 2004. The U.S. textile and apparel industry in the age of globalization. *Global Economy Journal.* 4, no. 1. http://www.bepress.com/gej/vol4/iss1/4.

Reiterman, Tim. 2006. Small towns tell a cautionary tale about the private control of water. *Los Angeles Times*, May 30. A:1.

Reitman, Valerie. 2005. Caltech to Harvard: Redo the math. *Los Angeles Times*, June 20. B:1.

Reynolds, David. 1999. The living wage movement sweeps the nation: Coalitions created by living wage campaigns are building a broader base for a progressive social movement. *Working USA* 3, no. 3 (October): 61–80.

Ritzer, George. 1996. *The McDonaldization of Society.* Thousand Oaks, CA: Pine Forge Press.

Ritzer, George. 2004. *The Globalization of Nothing.* Thousand Oaks, CA: Pine Forge Press.

Robertson, Roland. 1994. Globalisation or glocalization. *Journal of International Communication* 1:33–52.

Robinson, William, and Jerry Harris. 2000. Toward a global ruling class? Globalization and the transnational capitalist class. *Science & Society* 64, no. 1 (Spring): 11–54.

Ross, Andrew. 2004. *Low Pay High Profile.* New York: New Press.

Rothkoph, David. 1997. In praise of cultural imperialism? *Foreign Policy* 107 (Summer): 38–53.

Ruane, Janet M., and Karen A. Cerulo. 2004. *Second Thoughts*, 3rd ed. Thousand Oaks, CA: Pine Forge Press.

Rubin, Beth A. 1996. *Shifts in the Social Contract.* Thousand Oaks, CA: Pine Forge Press.

Rubin, Lillian. 1995. *Families on the Fault Line.* New York: Harper Perennial.

Ryan, John C., and Alen Thein Durning. 1998. The story of a shoe. *World Watch Institute* (March/April). http://www.worldwatch.org/node/451.

Saenz, Rogelio. 2004. *Latinos and the Changing Face of America.* New York: Russell Sage Foundation and the Population Reference Bureau. http://www.prb.org.

Safa, Helen I. 1990. Women and industrialization in the Caribbean. In *Women, Employment and the Family in the International Division of Labour*, ed. Sharon Stichter and Jane L. Parpart, 72–97. Philadelphia: Temple University Press.

Safa, Helen I. 1995. *The Myth of the Male Breadwinner: Women and Industrialization in the Caribbean*. Boulder, CO: Westview Press.

Samuelson, Paul. 1960. Interview. *US News and World Report* (December 26).

Santos de Morais, Clodomir. 2000. The large group capacitation method and social participation: Theoretical considerations. In *A Future for the Excluded*, ed. Raff Carmen and Miguel Sobrado, 26–38. London: Zed Press.

Sassen, Saskia. 1990. Finance and business services in New York City: International linkages and domestic effects. *International Social Science Journal* 42:287–306.

Sassen, Saskia. 1998. *Globalization and its Discontents: Essays on the New Mobility of People and Money*. New York: New Press.

Sassen, Saskia, and Robert C. Smith. 1992. Post-industrial growth and economic reorganization: Their impact on immigrant employment. In *U.S.–Mexico Relations, Labor Market Interdependence*, ed. Jorge Bustamante, Clark Reynolds, and Raul Hinojosa, 372–393. Stanford, CA: Stanford University Press.

Schenk, Sonja J. 2003. *Population Trends and Population Growth in West Tennessee Counties 1970 to 2020*. University of Memphis, Regional Economic Development Center (Spring). http://planning.memphis.edu/originalREDC.htm.

Scholte, Jan Aart. 2000a. Global civil society. In *The Political Economy of Globalization*, ed. Ngaire Woods, 173–201. London: Macmillan.

Scholte, Jan Aart. 2000b. *Globalization: A Critical Introduction*. New York: Palgrave.

Schumpeter, Joseph. [1942] 1975. *Capitalism, Socialism and Democracy*. New York: Harper Press.

Scott, Allen J. 1996. The manufacturing economy: Ethnic and gender divisions of labor. In *Ethnic Los Angeles*, ed. Roger Waldinger and Mehdi Bozorgmehr, 215–244. New York: Russell Sage Foundation.

Selvin, Molly. 2006. Firms want the grads, but do the grads want them? *Los Angeles Times*, May 13. A:1.

Sen, Amartya. 2000. Will there be any hope for the poor? *Time Europe* May 29, vol. 155, no. 21. http://www.time.com/time/europe/magazine/2000/0529/v121poor.html.

Sen, Amartya. 2002. How to judge globalization. Special Issue *American Prospect* (Winter): A2–A6.

Sen, Gita, and Caren Grown. 1987. *Development, Crises and Alternative Visions: Third World Women's Perspectives*. New York: Monthly Review Press.

Sernau, Scott. 2001. *Worlds Apart: Social Inequalities in a New Century*. Thousand Oaks, CA: Pine Forge Press.

Shulman, Beth. 2003. *The Betrayal of Work*. New York: New Press.

Silvestri, George T. 1997. Employment outlook: 1996–2006. Occupational Employment Projections to 2006. *Monthly Labor Review* 120, no. 11 (November): 58–83.

Simon, Stephanie. 2005. Labor and religion reunite. *Los Angeles Times*, July 17. A:1.

Sinclair, Upton. [1906] 2002. *The Jungle*. New York: WW Norton and Company.

Singer, P. W. 2003. *Corporate Warriors: The Rise of the Privatized Military Industry*. Ithaca, NY: Cornell University Press.

Sklair, Leslie. 1999. Competing conceptualizations of globalization. *Journal of World-Systems Research* 5, no. 2:143–162.

Sklair, Leslie. 2000. The transnational capitalist class and the discourse of globalization. http://www.lse.ac.uk/collections/globalDimensions.

Smith, Anthony D. [1990] 2003. Towards a global culture? In *The Global Transformations Reader*, ed. David Held and Andrew McGrew, 278–286. Cambridge: Polity Press.

Sobrado, Miguel, and Juan Rojas. 2004. *América Latina: Crisis del estado clientelista y la construcción de republicas ciudadanas*. México, City: Talleres Gráficos del Cámara de Diputados.

Soenthrith, Saing, and Ian Neubauer. 2004. Sex workers abducted in raid on NGO. *Cambodian Daily* (December 9).

Srivastava, Snigdha, and Nik Theodore. 2004. *America's High Tech Bust*. Chicago: Center for Urban Economic Development, University of Illinois at Chicago.

Steans, Jill. 1998. *Gender and International Relations*. Cambridge: Polity Press.

Steger, Manfred B. 2003. *Globalization: A Very Short Introduction*. Oxford: Oxford University Press.

Stiglitz, Joseph. 2002. *Globalization and Its Discontents*. New York: Norton.

Strange, Susan. 1997. The erosion of the state. *Current History* 96 (November): 365–369.

Stull, Donald, Michael J. Broadway, and Ken Erickson. 1992. The price of a good steak: Beef packing and its consequences for Garden City, Kansar. In *Structuring Diversity: Ethnographic Perspectives on the New Immigration*, ed. L. Lamphere, 35–64. Chicago: University of Chicago Press.

Stull, Donald, Michael J. Broadway, and David Griffith. 1995. *Any Way You Cut It: Meat Processing and Small-Town America*. Lawrence: University Press of Kansas.

Sturgeon, Timothy, and Richard Florida. 2004. Globalization, deverticalization, and employment in the motor vehicle industry. In *Locating Global Advantage: Industry Dynamics in the International Economy*, ed. Martin Kenney and Richard Florida, 52–81. Stanford, CA: Stanford University Press.

Sum, Andrew, Neeta Fogg, and Paul Harrington. 2002. *Immigrant Workers and the Great American Job Machine: The Contributions of New Foreign Immigration to National and Regional Labor Force Growth in the 1990s*. Boston: Northeastern University, Center for Labor Market Studies.

Suro, Roberto. 2003. *Latino remittances swell despite U.S. economic slump*. PEW Hispanic Center. Migration Policy Institute. Migration Information Source (February 1). http://www.migrationinformation.org/USfocus/display.cfm?ID=89.

Tabb, William K. 2001. *The Amoral Elephant*. New York: Monthly Review Press.

Tabb, William K. 2002. *Unequal Exchange*. New York: New Press.

Thompson, Grahame. 1996. Economic globalization? In *A Globalizing World? Culture, Economics, Politics*, ed. David Held, 85–126. London: Open University Press.

Thompson, William E., and Joseph V. Hickey. 2005. *Society in Focus*, 5th ed. Boston: Allyn and Bacon.

Thurow, Lester. 1987. A surge in inequality. *Scientific American* 256:31–37.

Thurow, Lester. 1996. *The Future of Capitalism: How Today's Economic Forces Shape Tomorrow's World*. New York: William Morrow.

Tichell, Adam, and Jamie Peck. 1995. Social regulation *after* fordism: Regulation theory, neo-liberalism, and the global–local nexus. *Economy and Society* 24, no. 3:357–386.

Tiempos del Mundo. 2004. Privatización en América Latina. (agosto). A:1.

Torres, Vicki. 1995. Bold fashion statement. *Los Angeles Times*, March 12. D:1.

Uchitelle, Louis. 2003. A missing statistic: U.S. jobs that went overseas. *New York Times*, October 5. 1:24.

UNCTAD (United Nations Conference on Trade and Development). 2005. Trade and development report. http://www.unctad.org/en/docs/tdr2005_en.pdf.

UNDP (United Nations Development Program). 1998. *Consumption for Human Development*. New York: Oxford University Press.

UNDP (United Nations Development Program). 1999. *Globalization with a Human Face*. New York: Oxford University Press.

UNDP (United Nations Development Program). 2002. *Deepening Democracy in a Fragmented World*. New York: Oxford University Press.

UNDP (United Nations Development Program). 2004. *Cultural Liberty in Today's Diverse World*. New York: Oxford University Press.

UNDP (United Nations Development Program). 2005. *International Cooperation at the Crossroads*. New York: Oxford University Press.

UNDP (United Nations Development Program). 2006. *Beyond Scarcity: Power, Poverty, and the Global Water Crisis*. New York: Oxford University Press.

Unger, Roberto Mangabeira. 1998. *Democracy Realised: The Progressive Alternative*. London: Verso Press.

Unitarian Universalistic Service Committee. 2005. Living wage campaigns. A Human Rights Web Log. http://www.uusc.org/blog/2005/07/waging-living-wage-campaigns.html.

United for a Fair Economy. n.d. Income inequality. http://www.faireconomy.org/research/income_charts.html.

United for a Fair Economy. 2001. *Executive Excess Report: Layoffs, Tax Rebates, the Gender Gap*. Washington, D.C.: Institute for Policy Studies and United for a Fair Economy.

United for a Fair Economy. 2006. *New data: The wealth divide widens*. http://www.faireconomy.org/press/2006/wealth_divide_widens.html.

Urry, John. 1999. Citizenship and society. *Journal of World-Systems Research* 5, no. 2:311–324. http://jwsr.ucr.edu/archive/vol5/number2/html/urry/index.html.

U.S. Bureau of the Census. 2000–2005. http://www.census.gov.

U.S. Bureau of the Census. 2000. Poverty thresholds 2000.

U.S. Bureau of the Census. 2002. *Statistical Abstract of the United States: 2002*. http://www.census.gov/compendia/statab.

U.S. Bureau of the Census. 2004. Poverty thresholds 2004. Same as above-citation. http://www.census.gov/hhes/www/poverty/threshold/thresoo.html.

U.S. Bureau of the Census. 2004. Labor force, employment, and earnings. Section 12 in *Statistical Abstract of the United States*. Washington, D.C.: GPO.

U.S. Bureau of the Census. 2004/2005a. Labor force, employment, and earnings. Section 12 in *Statistical Abstract of the United States*. Washington, D.C.: GPO.

U.S. Bureau of the Census. 2004/2005b. Income, expenditures, and wealth. Section 13 in *Statistical Abstract of the United States*. Washington, D.C.: GPO.

U.S. Bureau of the Census. 2005c. People in poverty by nativity: 1993 to 2005. http://www.census.gov/hhes/www/poverty/histpov/histpov23.html.

U.S. Bureau of the Census. 2006. *Poverty*. http://www.census.gov/hhes/www/poverty/histpov/histpovtb.html.

U.S. Bureau of Citizenship and Immigration Services. 2003. *Estimates of the Unauthorized Immigrant Population Residing in the U.S.: 1990 to 2000*. Washington, D.C.: Office of Policy and Planning.

U.S. Bureau of Economic Analysis. 2004. *Personal Income and Outlays* (January). Washington, D.C.: GPO.

U.S. Bureau of Labor Statistics. 2002. *Current Population Survey* (March Suppl.). Washington, D.C.: GPO.

U.S. Bureau of Labor Statistics. 2004. *A Profile of Working Poor*. Report 976 (September). Washington, D.C.: GPO.

U.S. Bureau of Labor Statistics. 2005. *Women in the Labor Force: A Data Book*. Washington, D.C.: GPO. http://www.bls.gov/cps/wlf-databook2005.htm.

U.S. Bureau of Labor Statistics. 2006. Apparel trade and footwear employment figures. *Current Employment Statistics*. http://www.bls.gov/ces/home.htm.

U.S. Department of Labor. 2002–2004. Occupational employment statistics. http://www.bls.gov/oes/home.htm.

U.S. Department of Labor. 2004. *Highlights of Women's Earnings in 2003*. Report 978. Washington, D.C.: GPO.

U.S. GAO (General Accounting Office). 2000. *Unemployment Insurance: Role as Safety Net for Low-Wage Workers Is Limited*. Report to Congressional Requestors, GAO (December), GAO-01-181. Washington, D.C.: GPO.

Vazquez, Mario F. 1981. Immigrant workers and the apparel manufacturing industry in southern California. In *Mexican Immigrant Workers in the U.S.*, ed. Antonio Rios Bustamante, 85–96. Los Angeles: UCLA Chicano Studies Research Center.

Vernez, Georges. 1999. *Immigrant Women in the U.S. Workforce: Who Struggles? Who Succeeds?* Lanham, MD: Lexington Books.

Vilas, Carlos. 2002. Globalization as imperialism. *Latin American Perspectives* 29, no. 6:70–79.

Wallach, Lori, and Michelle Sforza. 1999. *The WTO: Five Years of Reasons to Resist Corporate Globalization*. New York: Seven Stories Press.

Wallach, Lori, Patrick Woodall, and Ralph Nader. 2004. *Whose Trade Organization: The Comprehensive Guide to the WTO*. New York: New Press.

Waltz, Kenneth. 1979. *Theory of International Politics*. New York: Addison-Wesley.

Warren, Elizabeth, and Amelia Warren Tyagi. 2003. *The Two-Income Trap*. New York: Basic Books.

Waters, Malcom. 1995. *Globalization*. New York: Routledge.

Weber, Max. 1978. *Economy and Society*, 2 vols., ed. Guenther Roth and Claus Wittich. Berkeley: University of California Press.

Wenger, Jeffrey. 2003. Share of workers in "nonstandard" jobs declines. *Economic Policy Institute*. Briefing Paper 137. http://epinet.org.

Wilkinson, Tracy. 2006. The new foreign aid: Kenya. Los Angeles Times, April 22. A.1

Williams, Carole J. 2006. The new foreign aid: Haiti. Los Angles Times, April 18. A.1

Williams, Joan. 2000. *Unbending Gender: Why Family and Work Conflict and What to Do About It*. Oxford: Oxford University Press.

Williamson, Lewis. 2002. Globalisation: World-changing or word-changing? *Guardian*, October 31. http://www.guardian.co.uk/globalisation/story/0,7369,823296,00.html.

Wilson, William J. 1996. *When Work Disappears: The World of the New Urban Poor*. New York: Knopf.

Winpisinger, William. 1989. *Reclaiming Our Future: An Agenda for American Labor*. San Francisco: Westview Press.

Wolf, Diane. 1988. Father knows best about all in the family: A feminist critique of household strategies. Paper presented at the annual meeting of the American Sociological Association, Atlanta, GA.

Wolff, Edward N. 2000. *Recent Trends in Wealth Ownership, 1983–1998*. Working paper no. 300. The Levy Institute (April). http://www.levy.org/default.asp?view =publications_view&pubIO=f7a204517.

Wolff, Edward N., and Ajit Zacharias. 2006. Household wealth and the measurement of economic well-being in the United States. Working Paper 447. Levy Economics Institute (May). http://www.levy.org/default.asp?view=publications_ view&pubID=10b5deb89de.

World Bank. 1991–2006. *World Development Report*. New York: Oxford University Press.

WTO (World Trade Organization). 2005. International trade statistics 2004. http://www.wto.org/english/res_e/statis_e/its2004_e/its04_toc_e.htm.

Yates, Michael, D. 2003. *Naming the System: Inequality and Work in the Global Economy*. New York: Monthly Review Press.

Yi, Daniel. 2006. U.S. employers look offshore for healthcare. Los Angeles Times July 30.

Young, Brigitte. 2000. The mistress and the maid in the globalised economy. In *Socialist Register 2000: Working Classes, Global Realities*, ed. Leo Panitch and Colin Leys, 315–328. London: Merlin Press.

Zeitlin, Maurice. 1984. *Civil Wars in Chile*. Princeton: University of Princeton Press.

Zentgraf, Kristine M. 2001. Through economic restructuring, recession and rebound: The continuing importance of Latina immigrant labor in the Los Angeles economy. In *Asian and Latino Immigrants in a Restructuring Economy: The Metamorphosis of Southern California*, ed. Marta Lopez-Garza and David R. Diaz, 46–74. Stanford, CA: Stanford University Press.

Zlotnik, Hania. 2003. The global dimensions of female migration. Migration Information Source. *Data Insight* (March 1). http://www.migrationinformation.org/ Feature/display.cfm?ID=109.

INDEX